COLONIAL PLANTATIONS AND ECONOMY IN FLORIDA

Colonial Plantations and Economy in Florida

edited by Jane G. Landers

University Press of Florida

Gainesville · Tallahassee · Tampa · Boca Raton
Pensacola · Orlando · Miami · Jacksonville · Ft. Myers

05 04 03 02 01 00   6 5 4 3 2 1

Library of Congress Cataloging-in-Publication Data
Colonial plantations and economy in Florida / edited by Jane G. Landers.
p. cm.
Includes bibliographical references and index.
ISBN 0-8130-1772-6 (c: alk. paper)
1. Florida—History—To 1821. 2. Florida—Economic conditions—18th
century. 3. Florida—Economic conditions—19th century. 4. Plantations—
Florida—History—18th century. 5. Plantations—Florida—History—19th
century. I. Landers, Jane G.
F314.C696 2000
975.9—dc21   99-046086

The University Press of Florida is the scholarly publishing agency for the
State University System of Florida, comprising Florida A&M University,
Florida Atlantic University, Florida Gulf Coast University, Florida
International University, Florida State University, University of Central
Florida, University of Florida, University of North Florida, University of
South Florida, and University of West Florida.

University Press of Florida
15 Northwest 15th Street
Gainesville, FL 32611–2079
http://www.upf.com

Contents

Illustrations and Maps

Illustrations

Maps

Tables

Acknowledgments

This volume has been a long time in the making. That it actually has become reality is due in large part to the old friendships and collegiality among its authors. While pursuing independent career paths, we still have managed to collaborate on a number of projects over the years, sharing ideas, sources, and a deep commitment to Florida history—which all of us believe has unappreciated national and international significance.

During a conversation between sessions at a St. Augustine conference on Native American history, Susan R. Parker and I remarked to Walda Metcalf, then editor-in-chief of the University Press of Florida, that most people would be surprised to know that, in Florida's British and Spanish colonial periods, prosperous and large-scale plantations dotted the landscape. Walda immediately saw the potential and encouraged us to submit a proposal. Within a few minutes, we had recruited other enthusiastic conferees, including our dear friend John Griffin, whose unfortunate demise deprived us of his planned contribution to this volume. Although Walda and director George Bedell moved on, the University Press of Florida's new director, Ken Scott, and new editor-in-chief, Meredith Morris-Babb, adopted the project and gave it their full support. Although Susan Parker also had to move on to other more pressing obligations, I would like to acknowledge her important role in the initial conception of this volume and thank her for all the thoughtful feedback she gave me at various points in its development. The commitment of the contributors kept me going, too, and at long last, the collection is actually finished.

On behalf of my colleagues, I would like to acknowledge our collective debts to the historians and archaeologists of colonial Florida, on whose work we have all built, especially Amy Turner Bushnell, Kathleen A. Deagan, Michael Gannon, John H. Hann, Eugene Lyon, Bonnie G. McEwan, Paul Hoffman, Samuel Proctor, John J. TePaske, and J. Leitch Wright, Jr. Other colleagues also offered enthusiasm and encouragement for the project, and we would like to thank Bertram Wyatt-Brown, Peter H. Wood, and Jack Greene in particular. We are deeply indebted also for the help we received from the fine staffs of several archives, including Elizabeth Alexander and Bruce Chappell of the P. K. Yonge Library of Florida History; David Coles of the Florida Department of Archives and History; Joe Knetsch of the Florida Department of Survey and Mapping; and Page Edwards, Taryn Rodríguez-Boette, Dorothy Lyon, Charles Tingley, and Eddie Joyce Geyer of the St. Augustine Historical Society. We lament the loss of Page Edwards, whose dedication to Florida history and support of Florida scholars advanced the field in so many ways over the years. Finally, I would like to express my gratitude to Ms. Brenda Hummel, administrative assistant in the Department of History at Vanderbilt University, whose unfailing good nature and efficiency helped me produce this book.

Jane G. Landers

Chronology

Introduction

JANE G. LANDERS

Despite Florida's many linkages to Anglo-American and Caribbean settlements and to the numerous Indian nations of the interior, scholars of the Atlantic world have paid the colony little attention. Important new works on the political, agricultural, and economic development of the colonial South demonstrate the need to understand regional precedents for later developments, but they, too, address Florida only in passing and usually refer only to the twenty-year span (1763–84) when Britain controlled the colony.[1] The neglect of Florida in the Second Spanish Period (1784–1821) may be attributed in part to language barriers and in part to the fact that Florida has traditionally been portrayed as little more than a hard-luck military post and a stagnant backwater of Spain's empire, almost entirely dependent on government subsidies for survival.[2] There is little doubt that a contributing factor has also been the Anglophilic perspective of most colonial histories.

Scholars, including those represented in this volume, are now mining Florida's rich archival materials and unearthing its material culture through archaeological investigations. They are discovering that Florida's colonial economy was much more diversified and integrated into the wider Atlantic commerce than previously has been understood. Were it not for the repeated violence that wreaked havoc in the colony in the eighteenth and early nineteenth centuries, Florida might have achieved the prosperity its boosters once predicted.

Despite older perceptions, the work of Amy Turner Bushnell on the vast Menéndez Márquez estates of La Chua and of John H. Hann on the cattle and wheat ranches of Governor Benito Ruiz de Salazar Vallecilla in Asile shows that, by the seventeenth century, Florida was already more than a dependent military settlement.[3] Bonnie G. McEwan's archaeological investigations of the Mission San Luis also demonstrate that the entre-

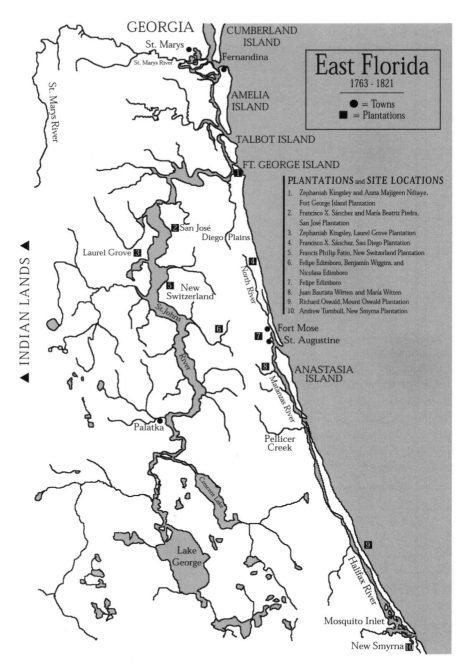

GEORGIA

St. Marys

St. Marys River

CUMBERLAND
ISLAND

Fernandina

AMELIA
ISLAND

TALBOT ISLAND

FT. GEORGE ISLAND

St. Marys River

▲ INDIAN LANDS ▲

San José

Diego Plains

Laurel Grove 3

New
Switzerland

St. Johns River

North River

Fort Mose
St. Augustine

ANASTASIA
ISLAND

Matanzas River

Palatka

Pellicer
Creek

Crescent Lake

Lake
George

Halifax River

Mosquito Inlet

New Smyrna 10

East Florida

1763 - 1821

● = Towns
■ = Plantations

PLANTATIONS and SITE LOCATIONS

1. Zephaniah Kingsley and Anna Majigeen Ndiaye,
   Fort George Island Plantation
2. Francisco X. Sánchez and María Beatriz Piedra,
   San José Plantation
3. Zephaniah Kingsley, Laurel Grove Plantation
4. Francisco X. Sánchez, San Diego Plantation
5. Francis Philip Fatio, New Switzerland Plantation
6. Felipe Edimboro, Benjamín Wiggins, and
   Nicolasa Edimboro
7. Felipe Edimboro
8. Juan Bautista Witten and María Witten
9. Richard Oswald, Mount Oswald Plantation
10. Andrew Turnbull, New Smyrna Plantation

Map 1. Locations mentioned in the text. Map by Jim Landers.

preneurial Florencia family and other settlers in Apalachee province carried on a vibrant, if illicit, economic exchange with Havana. This incipient economic development of Florida was destroyed by attacks by the British and their Indian allies at the beginning of the eighteenth century. The destruction of the Spanish mission system and the death and enslavement of several thousands of Florida's Christian Indians in Apalachee and near St. Augustine not only ruined Florida but enriched the new plantation economy of Carolina.[4]

Challenging Spain's claim to sovereignty over the whole Atlantic coastline, Barbadian planters settled Charles Town in 1670 and began carving out new plantations, developing export crops, and establishing an Atlantic trade. For almost a century, the Carolina planters and their counterparts in Georgia would compete with Spanish Floridians for control of southeastern Atlantic terrain, populations, and commerce. Repeated English attacks against the Spaniards and their few remaining Indian allies forced them to concentrate around St. Augustine and made it dangerous, if not impossible, to work the hinterlands. Finally, Gen. James Oglethorpe attempted in 1740 the total destruction of the Spanish colony with an invasion force of an estimated 1,620 Carolinians, Georgians, and Indians. Supporting Oglethorpe were seven warships of the Royal Navy, which bombarded St. Augustine for a month. Although Oglethorpe failed to expel the Spaniards from Florida, the job was accomplished soon thereafter by international diplomacy.[5] In 1763 Spain gave up Florida to ransom Cuba and the Philippines from the British; Spaniards, Indians, and free blacks loyal to the Spanish government staged a massive evacuation of the province. Over 3,000 persons departed for Cuba, taking with them all the infrastructure and movable property they could load on a flotilla of ships.[6]

Even prior to the exodus of Florida's indigenous nations, Lower Creek groups who would become the Seminoles had begun moving into the interior savannahs, where they established flourishing villages.[7] In the 1770s, the Pennsylvania naturalist William Bartram visited Cuscowilla, the capital of the La Chua Seminoles, and described a prosperous settlement based on agriculture, "innumerable droves of cattle," and "squadrons of the beautiful fleet Seminole horse."[8] Using historical and archaeological sources, Brent Weisman traces how Seminole prosperity also suffered from the continual political disruption of Florida, and how the Seminoles and their economy adapted to constant change.

When Britain acquired Florida in 1763, the incoming governor, James Grant, initiated a campaign to develop what J. Leitch Wright, Jr., called "Britannia's New Eden."[9] Grant encouraged colonization by offering political offices and generous land grants to prominent Carolina planters. Wildly enthusiastic promotional literature on Florida also may have spurred investors to take a chance on the new colony. Soon, as Daniel L. Schafer's essay shows, veteran planters were transferring skilled "country-born" slaves from South Carolina and Georgia and importing hundreds of African slaves to break in their extensive new estates in Florida.[10] Richard Oswald transported hundreds of slaves from his factory on Bance Island, in the middle of the Sierra Leone River, to work his parliamentary grant of twenty thousand acres in the Mosquito district south of St. Augustine.[11] Large slave forces toiled in the brutal Florida heat to clear and fence land, plant crops, erect buildings, build dams and drains, and transform vast stretches of inhospitable swamp and hammocks into profitable fields. By the sweat and blood of Africans, British Florida planters established impressive plantations along the St. Marys and St. Johns Rivers and along the Mosquito coast, producing rice, cotton, indigo, oranges, and sugarcane. British planters also exported and profited from Florida's timber and naval stores.

While official policy called for white Protestant settlement, Governor Grant encouraged slave imports for strenuous work, stating that "Africans are the only people to do the work in warm climates." Grant noted that white laborers were unsatisfactory because "[u]pon their landing they are immediately seized with the pride which every man is possessed of who wears a white face in America, and they say they won't be slaves and so they make their escape."[12] Patricia Griffin's essay shows that beleaguered indentured servants from Minorca and other Mediterranean locales did just that when they could no longer stand the intolerable conditions and killing work regime at Andrew Turnbull's twenty-thousand-acre indigo plantation south of St. Augustine. Despite the rich grade of indigo produced at New Smyrna, hoped-for profits were consumed by bad planning and rebellion. The hard-working Minorcans finally fled New Smyrna and remade their lives in St. Augustine, where they became small farmers and petty merchants and contributed to the urban economy of both British and Second Spanish Period Florida.

As the American Revolution wound to a close, Loyalists fled Charleston and Savannah for East Florida, accompanied by more than eight thousand slaves. Their intent was to transplant their plantations to Florida, but the ongoing turmoil of the war made operations almost impossible. Georgian marauders attacked plantations and stole slaves, other slaves escaped to the interior Seminole villages, and planters were forced to allocate some of their remaining slaves to militias formed to fight the multiple enemies.

Some planters moved to safer locations, requiring their slaves to start anew the back-breaking process of plantation-building. Finally, on hearing that Florida was to be retroceded to Spain in 1784, major British planters, like James Grant, John Moultrie, and Richard Oswald, shipped their slaves back across the northern border to South Carolina or Georgia, or southward to the Bahamas, Dominica, and other Caribbean sites where they might still own slave property.[13]

Once again a major colonial transfer disrupted economic progress, and this time it was distraught Loyalists who packed up belongings, families, and slaves, and calculated their losses as they sailed away from their Florida estates. When the Spanish officials returned from Cuba, they complained of the remnant disorder and general disrepair of the colony.[14]

Only two plantations were still said to be functioning, and one was the New Switzerland (*Nueva Suiza*), belonging to Francis Philip Fatio. Susan R. Parker describes the life of baronial splendor Fatio created on this ten-thousand-acre plantation which stretched along two miles of the eastern bank of the St. Johns River. At New Switzerland, Fatio's large slave work force herded and slaughtered cattle, pigs, and sheep, and tended groves of sweet and sour oranges, citrons, and lemons, and fields of cotton, corn, and other crops. They also harvested lumber and made tar, resin, and turpentine for export to circum-Caribbean and Atlantic ports on Fatio's own ships.[15]

The other estate that still provided sustenance for the incoming Spaniards belonged to Francisco Xavier Sánchez. Sánchez "rose from a state of obscure poverty to a degree of wealth seldom attained," amassing vast land holdings as the meat and firewood contractor for three successive regimes in Florida (First Spanish, British, and Second Spanish).[16] In 1784 his main estate, the San Diego, encompassed more than one thousand acres, on which Sánchez kept a herd of eight hundred to nine hundred cattle, thirty to forty horses, and thirty-four slaves.[17] Jane G. Landers tracks Sánchez's career as he acquired other plantations, and finds his economic success was built on the family's early acquisition of choice land, diversification, and government patronage.

Despite these examples of early success, Florida's Second Spanish Period economy was slow in recovering from the damage of the American revolutionary war years, the uncertainty of the change in regimes, and "banditti" violence. Moreover, incoming Spanish homesteaders brought few slaves with them, and Florida suffered a chronic labor shortage.[18] Development was also stifled by Spain's mercantile policies, which required all cargo to be carried on Spanish ships with Spanish crews and prohibited the introduction of foreign goods.[19] However, the network of waterways lacing Florida and the shortage of government personnel made strict enforcement of mercantile regulations impractical. Moreover, when approved supplies failed to arrive from Cuba or proved to be of poor quality, Spanish governors took the initiative to purchase flour and other foodstuffs in Philadelphia and New York, or cattle from Georgia, banking on post-facto royal dispensation based on the colonists' dire need. Many U.S. merchants and traders were eager to supply Florida the goods Spain could not, and they often extended credit and offered cheaper prices than their Cuban counterparts.[20]

After repeated pleas from Florida's governors, Spain enacted a series of policies designed to encourage settlement and development of the colony, including royal subsidies of such critical industries as shipbuilding; exemption of the required *diezmos* tithe; provision of free tools from the royal factories in Vizcaya; and cattle paid for by the royal accounts. The Crown also granted Florida the unlimited introduction of slaves. In 1790 Spain also began to offer new settlers (*nuevos pobladores*) generous land grants based on a British headright system, and a virtual land and population boom followed.[21]

Attracted by the prosperity came one of the most fascinating and successful of the new settlers, the Quaker planter, coffee and slave trader, and advocate of moderate race relations Zephaniah Kingsley. Daniel L. Schafer illustrates how Kingsley's international mercantile experience and connections combined with African slaving networks and paternal management of slaves all contributed to the economic success of his Laurel Grove Plantation. The Patriot Rebellion of 1812, discussed in several of the essays in this volume, ruined Laurel Grove and forced Kingsley's relocation to Fort George Island, where he bought John McQueen's old plantation from the failed rebel John Houston McIntosh. Kingsley soon made the Fort George Island estate profitable as well.

Kingsley was not the only Floridian undone by the Patriot invasion. As he later testified for the U.S. Congress, the province had been flourishing only five years earlier, but now "[e]verything was thrown into disorder, the houses all burned . . . fields ravished; the cattle stolen or driven away . . . [the country] was left by the patriots a perfect desert."[22] Recognizing its culpability because it covertly supported the rebellion, the United States later settled many of the claims made against it by the ruined Floridians.

Although the repeated instances of political upheaval destabilized the frontier and caused much damage to Florida's economic progress, they also contributed, paradoxically, to the development of a free black homesteading class. Jane G. Landers shows that Spanish law and custom required that all free citizens be provided sufficient land to provide for their families, and free blacks who petitioned Spanish governors for land received it. Other free blacks bought or inherited property and yet another important group, members of the free black militias, received land as a reward for their military service. While they never acquired the impressive estates of a Fatio or a Sánchez, free blacks worked hard and built up substantial farms and herds during the rare interludes of peace.

Although planters and black farmers largely concentrated on agricultural production and timbering, Susan R. Parker demonstrates that much of Florida's wealth also derived from cattle. She shows how the cattle trade linked disparate groups in the economy of Spanish Florida. Large planters like Fatio and Sánchez, small planters, free blacks, Seminole Indians, and the Spanish government all participated in this essential frontier commerce.

Florida's natural wealth was generated primarily in the hinterlands—vast herds of cattle, impressive stands of valuable hardwoods, and export crops such as indigo, rice, and cotton. However, James G. Cusick's essay shows how the hinterland production and the colony's economic life centered on the polyglot Spanish capital of St. Augustine, a small but vital Atlantic port city. Using Spanish shipping records and travel accounts, Cusick shows that St. Augustine's culturally and racially diverse population enjoyed widespread family and trade networks connecting to major ports on both sides of the Atlantic and throughout the Caribbean.

The essays in this volume challenge the often stereotypical image of a "typical" or antebellum plantation. Colonial Florida produced a wide variety of plantation types. Some, like those belonging to Francis Philip Fatio and Francisco Xavier Sánchez, were virtual baronies of thousands of acres, self-sufficient and diversified and able to endure the political vagaries and military conflicts that racked Florida. The work forces of "smaller" plantations, like those of Zephaniah Kingsley, were equally important and interesting, and the size of their acreage and of their slave forces would qualify them as "large" just across the northern border. But such large estates did not preclude the development of smaller holdings belonging to less-powerful Floridians, including women, persons of African and Mediterranean descent, and Seminoles. Thus, the dynamism and cultural heterogeneity of Florida's colonial past allow the authors to address issues of race, class, and gender through their plantation studies.

Although these essays make a start, much yet remains to be done to explore fully the social and economic history of early Florida. The appendixes that accompany this volume were selected to demonstrate the range of documentary evidence available for such work. They include private correspondence, inventories, wills, government reports, legal records, and newspapers. The East Florida Papers, on which many of the essays are based, are held in the Library of Congress and are available in microfilm copies in many research libraries in the United States. These are the complete archive of the Second Spanish Period government, and they not only detail Spanish Florida's history but include important material on Georgia, South Carolina, the Indian nations, and the greater Caribbean. Language and paleographic training are always helpful, but many of these rich records are already in English, either because they were generated in that language or because conscientious Spanish administrators translated them. We hope a new generation of Florida scholars will follow us and track our leads as we tracked those left for us by earlier scholars. We also hope that these essays will encourage other colonial historians of the wider Atlantic world to consider how Florida connected to their areas of study, because it almost certainly did.

Notes

1. Although she does not focus primarily on British East Florida, Joyce Chaplin notes the early enthusiasm many Scots had for that land and its prospects; see *An Anxious Pursuit: Agricultural Innovation and Modernity in the Lower South, 1730–1815* (Chapel Hill: University of North Carolina Press, 1993). David Hancock is one of the first non-Florida scholars to incorporate the colony into the larger British Atlantic history in *Citizens of the World: London Merchants and the Integration of the British Atlantic Community, 1735–1785* (Cambridge: Cambridge University Press, 1995). Daniel L. Schafer challenges Bernard Bailyn's view of British East Florida as an exotic failure; see "'Yellow Silk Ferret Tied round Their Wrists': African Americans in British East Florida, 1763–1784," in *The African American Heritage of Florida,* ed. David R. Colburn and Jane Landers (Gainesville: University Press of Florida, 1995). For other recent works that point to the economic potential of the region, see Alan Gallay, *The Formation of a Planter Elite: Jonathan Bryan and the Southern Colonial Frontier* (Athens: University of Georgia Press, 1989), and Daniel H. Usner, Jr., *Indians, Settlers, and Slaves in a Frontier Exchange Economy: The Lower Mississippi before 1783* (Chapel Hill: University of North Carolina Press, 1992). Peter H. Wood tackled an estimate of comparative white, Indian, and black demography in the colonial Southeast and included Florida in his study "The Changing Population of the Colonial South: An Overview by Race and Region, 1685–1790," in *Powhatan's Mantle: Indians in the Colonial Southeast,* ed. Peter H. Wood, Gregory A. Waselkov, and M. Thomas Hatley (Lincoln: University of Nebraska Press, 1989). Timothy Silver's work ex-

cises Florida from the region and its study; *A New Face on the Countryside: Indians, Colonists and Slaves in South Atlantic Forests, 1500–1800* (Cambridge: Cambridge University Press, 1990).

2. The powerful images of impoverishment were more accurate for the First Spanish Period, as shown in John Jay TePaske's valuable study *The Governorship of Spanish Florida, 1700–1763* (Durham, N.C.: Duke University Press, 1964). The newer work of Eugene Lyon in testamentary records and property inventories shows that even in earlier periods, however, the repeated official references to shortages and poverty did not reflect the real economic conditions in Florida. See his "Richer Than We Thought: The Material Culture of Sixteenth-Century St. Augustine," *El Escribano* 29 (1992).

3. Amy Bushnell, "The Menéndez Márquez Cattle Barony at La Chua and the Determinants of Economic Expansionism in Seventeenth-Century Florida," *Florida Historical Quarterly* 56 (April 1978): 407–31; "Documents Pertaining to the Asile Farm," manuscript translated and annotated by John H. Hann, on file at the San Luis Archaeological and Historic Site, Tallahassee, Florida.

4. Moore claimed to have captured four thousand Indians, although based on estimates of village populations John H. Hann believes that figure to be exaggerated. See John H. Hann and Bonnie G. McEwan, *The Apalachee Indians and Mission San Luis* (Gainesville: University Press of Florida, 1998), 104–7, and Bonnie G. McEwan, "Hispanic Life on the Seventeenth-Century Florida Frontier," in *The Spanish Missions of La Florida,* ed. Bonnie G. McEwan (Gainesville: University Press of Florida, 1993), 295–321.

5. Verner W. Crane, *The Southern Frontier, 1670–1732* (New York: W. W. Norton & Co., 1981); Peter H. Wood, *Black Majority: Negroes in Colonial South Carolina from 1670 through the Stono Rebellion* (New York: W. W. Norton, 1974); TePaske, *Governorship of Spanish Florida,* 141–46; Chaplin, *An Anxious Pursuit;* Gallay, *Formation of a Planter Elite.*

6. Robert L. Gold, *Borderlands Empires in Transition: The Triple-Nation Transfer of Florida* (Carbondale: University of Southern Illinois Press, 1969). Peter H. Wood's estimated demographic figures for Florida in 1760 show a population that included 2,700 whites, 700 Indians, and 500 blacks (*Powhatan's Mantle,* ed. Wood, Waselkov, and Hatley, 35–103).

7. John K. Mahon and Brent R. Weisman, "Florida's Seminole and Miccosukee Peoples," in *The New History of Florida,* ed. Michael Gannon (Gainesville: University Press of Florida, 1996), 183–206; Brent R. Weisman, *Like Beads on a String: A Culture History of the Seminole Indians in North Peninsular Florida* (Tuscaloosa: University of Alabama Press, 1989).

8. Mark Van Doren, ed., *Travels of William Bartram* (New York: Dover Publications, 1928), 164–65; Gregory A. Waselkov and Kathryn E. Holland Braund, eds., *William Bartram on the Southeastern Indians* (Lincoln: University of Nebraska Press, 1995).

9. J. Leitch Wright, Jr., *Florida in the American Revolution* (Gainesville: University Press of Florida, 1975), chap. 1.

10. John Moultrie transferred 180 slaves from South Carolina to Florida to build the Bella Vista estate on the Matanzas River, and Robert Bissett and his son Alexander brought in more than 100 slaves to build Mount Plenty (Schafer, "'Yellow Silk Ferret'"). The Bissetts' main plantation comprised 9,500 acres and held a "Negro Town of good houses for seventy Negroes"; see Wilbur Henry Siebert, ed., *Loyalists in East Florida, 1783–1785 : The Most Important Documents Pertaining Thereto, Edited with an Accompanying Narrative,* 2 vols. (DeLand, Fla.: Florida State Historical Society, 1929), 2:92–99, 250–56).

11. Schafer, "'Yellow Silk Ferret,'" 71–103. David Hancock describes the international nature of Oswald's contacts and diverse enterprises and how they enabled him to "integrate backward" into agriculture in Florida (*Citizens of the World,* chaps. 5 and 6, 203–4).

12. Daniel L. Schafer, "'Settling a Colony over a Bottle of Claret': Early Plantation Development in British East Florida," *El Escribano* 19 (1982): 47–50; Schafer, "'Yellow Silk Ferret,'" 10.

13. Schafer, "'Yellow Silk Ferret,'" 93–97; Wright, *Florida in the American Revolution.*

14. Jane G. Landers, *Black Society in Spanish Florida* (Urbana: University of Illinois Press, 1999), chap. 3.

15. See also Susan R. Parker, "'I Am Neither Your Subject nor Subordinate'," *El Escribano* (1988): 44–60; Claims of F. J. Fatio and Francis P. Fatio, Historical Records Survey, *Spanish Land Grants in Florida* (Tallahassee: Works Project Administration, 1941), 3:67–71.

16. Patrick Tonyn to Vicente Manuel de Zéspedes, July 5, 1784, in *East Florida, 1783–1785: A File of Documents Assembled and Many of Them Translated,* ed. Joseph Byrne Lockey (Berkeley: University of California Press, 1949), 215.

17. 1786 Census of Father Hassett, Census Returns, 1784–1814, East Florida Papers (hereafter cited as EFP), P. K. Yonge Library of Florida History, University of Florida, Gainesville (hereafter cited as PKY).

18. Susan R. Parker, "Men without God or King: Rural Planters of East Florida, 1784–1790," *Florida Historical Quarterly* 69 (October 1990): 135–55; Jane Landers, "Slave Resistance on the Southern Frontier: Fugitives, Maroons, and Banditti in the Age of Revolutions," *El Escribano* 32 (1995): 12–24.

19. Ramón Romero-Cabot, "La defensa de Florida en el segundo período Español," thesis, University of Seville, 1982, PKY, 39–44.

20. Landers, *Black Society,* 74–75.

21. Ibid.; Schafer, "'Yellow Silk Ferret'," 71–103.

22. Testimony of Zephaniah Kingsley, Senate Miscellaneous Document, no. 55, 36th Cong., 1st sess., 24, cited in Rufus Kay Wyllys, "The East Florida Revolution of 1812–1814," *Hispanic American Historical Review* 9 (1929): 415–55, 444.

1

"A Swamp of an Investment"?

Richard Oswald's British East Florida Plantation Experiment

DANIEL L. SCHAFER

Over the past half-century, historians who have studied East Florida during its two-decade experience as a British colony have given it failing marks. Charles Loch Mowat was tentative in a 1943 assessment, calling it "a small and insignificant colony whose growth was slow and whose return to Spain after twenty years was a confession of failure." Mowat's conclusion also recognized the colony's unfulfilled potential and the uncontrollable circumstances that contributed to its failure: "[T]wenty years is no long time by which to judge a country. For East Florida, at least, the span was too short to produce a firm and reliant society, too short for the roots to take much hold of the soil."[1] In the last decade, judgments have been harsher. Paul David Nelson said of the colony's first governor: Despite "all his labors to repopulate East Florida . . . James Grant detected very little concrete accomplishment."[2] Bernard Bailyn pinned the label "Failure in Xanadu" on the British East Florida experience.[3]

The most recent assessment of East Florida is the harshest to date. In 1995, David Hancock judged Richard Oswald's 20,000-acre plantation south of St. Augustine "a bog, useless for anything but 'indifferent' indigo or rice; and East Florida . . . for Oswald and most planters, a swamp of an investment."[4] The experience was "one loss after another," and, after 1769, "little was exported but the produce of one or two plantations."[5] Hancock attributes Oswald's misfortune to "poor soil and climate, the lack of infrastructure, and the pervasive use of slaves," along with an inability to "stick with a single crop long enough to make it pay." Hancock calls the Amelia Island estate of the Earl of Egmont the "most dramatic" failure, but says "Egmont's loss was mirrored by that of many other Florida grantees."[6]

After five decades of increasingly negative commentary on British planting efforts in East Florida, reconsideration is needed. This chapter focuses on Richard Oswald's endeavors, and suggests that David Hancock was mistaken in judging Mount Oswald a "swamp of an investment," and that Bernard Bailyn's characterization of East Florida as "Failure in Xanadu" was also off the mark. Both authors considered the impediments imposed by the environment and the nonexistent infrastructure inherited by the British in 1763; neither, however, gave sufficient attention to the traumatic disruptions of trade and planting caused by the American Revolution. Nor did they consider the evacuations in 1783 and 1784 of thousands of residents who had rebuilt their lives and estates in the months after the fighting ended, only to see the colony ceded to Spain. At Mount Oswald and other locations south of St. Augustine, and along the St. Johns, St. Marys, Trout, and Nassau Rivers, successful plantations were established before the destabilizing events of the American Revolution intervened. The enslaved Africans who established the plantation, far from being a hindrance to development, were a crucial advantage. International political crises and the disruption, violence, and warfare that accompanied the American Revolution became insurmountable problems.

In previous publications, I have argued that James Grant arrived at St. Augustine in August 1764 with a preconceived plan to transform East Florida into a plantation province through the labor of African slaves. The new governor's model was South Carolina, the only British mainland colony with a black population majority; there the English planters discovered early that enslaved Africans possessed skills as cattle drovers and rice farmers, as well as a degree of immunity to malaria and yellow fever that white laborers lacked. By 1735 a Charles Town resident expressed what had already become a common belief: "[Rice] can't (in any great quantity's) be produced by white people. Because the Work is too laborious, the heat very intent, and the Whites can't work in the wett at that Season of the year."[7]

From the Chesapeake through the Carolinas and West Indies, planters tried white indentured laborers but eventually replaced them with enslaved Africans in tobacco, rice, and cane fields. When expenses for white artisans increased, planters trained their slaves to be carpenters and coopers, especially the Creole slaves born in America. James Grant had observed the Caribbean and South Carolina colonies before he was appointed governor of East Florida. He had also received, in April and May of 1764, detailed instructions for the development of an East Florida plantation from his intended co-partner in a planting scheme, the wealthy London merchant Richard Oswald, a fellow Scot who owned estates in Virginia, South Carolina, Georgia, and Jamaica. As co-owner of Bance Island, an important British-owned factory for the assembly and export of slaves located at the mouth of the Sierra Leone River, Oswald was able to purchase African laborers at reasonable prices and transport them to East Florida aboard his own ships.[8]

The conditions Grant found when he reached East Florida confirmed his plan to rely on slave labor. St. Augustine was an empty town with a garrison force of fewer than 200 men. Outside the town walls the governor discovered only "a State of Nature . . . not an acre of land planted in the Country and nobody to work or at work."[9] Three thousand residents had evacuated with Spanish forces in January 1764, leaving behind only three families. Grant repeatedly characterized the province as a "New World . . . [in] a State of Nature."[10]

He enticed planters from South Carolina with offers of free land and political office, John Moultrie being the best example. The Carolina planters brought with them large numbers of enslaved men and women who were already familiar with the slash-and-burn techniques necessary to clear virgin lands and turn them into rice, indigo, and corn fields. Successful plantations, the governor thought, would encourage dozens of British absentee landlords whom Parliament had given 10,000- and 20,000-acre tracts of prime Florida land to invest in their property rather than speculate on an increase in land values. Idle land would spell doom and also beckon to the intrepid southern frontiersmen to whom Grant contemptuously referred as "straggling woodsmen" or "crackers."[11]

From the outset, the governor considered Parliament's requirement that grantees must settle their lands with Protestant white families (one person per hundred acres within ten years) to be unworkable. His silent partner, Richard Oswald, commented similarly in 1767: "[T]he obligation of introducing such a number of White people is a great discouragement and to most people an absolute bar to settlement."[12] He urged King George III to substitute enslaved blacks for white Protestants: "Without that the province can never be settled by British proprietors and must remain as it is until there is an overswarm of Crackers to take up the premises."[13]

To the grantees, the governor delivered a consistent message: White indentures, whether common laborers or tradesmen, became either lazy or debilitated by the heat in Florida and abandoned the rural settlements for the colonial towns. Even German immigrants, so prized in the northern colonies, "won't do here," Grant wrote in 1766. They were "industrious" when self-employed, but when contracted to work for others they routinely absconded: "Upon their landing they are immediately seized with the pride which every man is possessed of who wears a white face in America and they say they won't be slaves and so they make their escape."[14] He wrote to the Earl of Cassillis that "no produce will answer the expense of white labor [in Florida],"[15] and to the Earl of Egmont: "Settlements in this warm climate must be formed by Negroes."[16] Only after plantations were established and profitable could white laborers and small planters be introduced, "but such a plan . . . is not to be thought of till this new world has in some means been created . . . [and] this country can only be brought to that rich and plentiful state by the labor of slaves."

Grant counseled each proprietor to invest heavily at the outset and to expect development to proceed slowly. "Five years are necessary to establish a new plantation," he told the Earl of Hillsborough.[17] Investing in enslaved Africans, however, would minimize the initial investment and also produce a continuing labor force. With common laborers from England demanding a minimum of four shillings for a daily wage in St. Augustine, and artisans at least six, the annual outlay for a transient white worker could approximate or even exceed the purchase price of a healthy male African slave. There are numerous records of slaves selling in East Florida for prices ranging from 22 Sterling to 105, the costs depending on age, sex, country of birth, and skills. The governor purchased eight "Carolina born" workers at an average cost of £62, and later bought five "Angola boys" for £30 each. James Penman paid £101 for a black manager and his wife. Black workers, Grant advised Lord Moira, require only a "trifle" thirty shillings a year for food, clothing, and tools, and they provide a natural increase in numbers and value. Based on his own experience, he told the Earl of Egmont: "My Negroes, about forty working hands, live in Palmetto huts for the time in the course of winter without putting me to any expense but the first cost of the boards and a few nails. The Negroes after doing their tasks will find scantling and clapboards and will build their houses themselves without any assistance."[18]

In *Voyagers to the West,* Bernard Bailyn castigates East Florida for its "inability to mobilize a population of British settlers" to create small family-owned farms worked by whites. Because East Florida's development was based instead on a system of "plantations, large and small, worked by gangs of black slaves and nurturing a distinctive culture," Bailyn concluded, the colony was a failure. An informed contemporary like Governor Grant had different judgments. Grant was aware of New England's successful family farms, but he believed the path to profitable development in Florida would be first trod by "country born" Negroes— Creoles born in New World colonies—followed by "seasoned" Africans resident in the colony long enough to have gained familiarity with the crops and language, and "New Negroes" direct from the coast of Africa.[19]

Grant turned plans into practice at Mount Oswald, a 20,000-acre estate at the confluence of the Tomoka and Halifax Rivers, which he helped establish for Richard Oswald. In 1765 and 1766 he and Oswald were silent partners in a planting venture. Grant pledged to select 20,000 acres of the best land in the province and to conduct periodic on-site supervision; Oswald was to provide the finances and the laborers. The plan called for purchase of thirty "country-born" slaves to begin clearing and fencing land and constructing houses in the start-up year. This initial work force would plant provisions crops and build houses for thirty additional Carolina-born slaves, scheduled to arrive in the second year. During the third year, sixty "new" Africans would arrive from Bance Island. The partners envisioned self-sufficiency in foodstuffs during the first year; separate indigo, cotton, and sugar plantations by the end of the third; and a rice plantation later. Oswald wanted cotton to be the first export crop at Tomoka, and he was willing to purchase older and experienced slaves from either Antigua or St. Christophers to guide the early planting efforts. He initially opposed planting rice, but Grant convinced him that rice would provide inexpensive food for the laborers and livestock and would become a profitable export crop.[20]

By February 1765 Grant had chosen a site called Nocoroco by the Native Americans who had partially cleared it decades earlier. The 20,000-acre tract was "covered with cabbage trees" when Grant and engineer James Moncrief examined it. They found the tract low-lying but not swampy, and capable of producing indigo, the commodity the governor predicted would become the colony's leading export. He recommended immediate planting of indigo seeds even before the cabbage trees were cleared from the site.[21]

While Grant was selecting the land, merchant Henry Laurens advertised in the *South Carolina Gazette* for "two Negro Carpenters, two Coopers, three pair of Sawyers, forty Field Negroes, young men and women, some acquainted with indigo making, and all with the ordinary course of

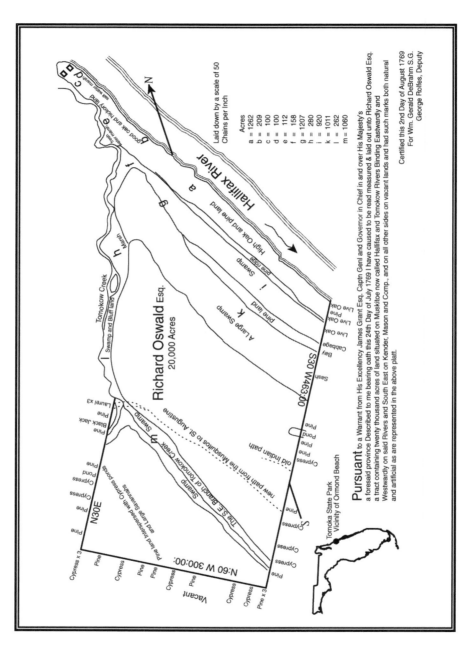

Map 2. Plat map of Mount Oswald Plantation. Computer generated by Teresa St. John, based on PRO T77 13 150.

Plantation work in this country."[22] Laurens, the leading supplier of slaves to East Florida planters and a longtime business associate of Oswald, purchased twenty-four men, seven women, and three children and shipped them to St. Augustine in April 1765. Nine of the men were "new" Africans, billed at an average price of £29. Of the seven women, four were described as capable of a variety of domestic skills as well as field work. Several of the males were skilled sawyers, coopers, and carpenters, and could tend to horses, butchering, and driving carts. Laurens found it difficult to fill Grant's order for the second round of Carolina-born laborers, and suggested instead "fine young Gambians or Gold Coast [Africans] fit to work immediately and the next year will be as good hands as any and less inclined to wander."[23] When the first slaves arrived in St. Augustine, Grant found them healthy and well-behaved and put them to work at his own farm just beyond the northern gate of St. Augustine, clearing brush, planting corn, and ditching.[24]

During these early months, Grant repeatedly complained to Oswald about the unwillingness of the wealthy absentee landlords to invest adequately in their Florida properties. He was also piqued by Oswald's plan to bring five other investors into their Florida partnership, sarcastically suggesting the extent of their involvement would be to discuss "American plantations perhaps once in a Winter, over a Bottle of Claret, but I am upon the Spott," and unwilling to "go slow."[25] Grant's entreaties convinced Oswald to increase spending for development and to drop his other partners from involvement in the Mount Oswald venture. He assured Grant in February 1766 that as soon as the initial work at Tomoka was completed, "my assistance will not be wanting."[26]

Grant delayed the start up work at Mount Oswald pending the arrival of Marmaduke Bell, an overseer from South Carolina who had worked for Francis Kinloch, one of the principal rice planters in North America. When Bell opted instead to settle his own estate on the St. Johns River, Grant informed Oswald he was reluctant to send the "Negroes alone into the Wilderness." Oswald was unfazed. In June, he authorized payment for thirty more "seasoned" laborers to be sent from Charleston and arranged shipment of grape vines to Grant's farm near St. Augustine for eventual transplantation at Tomoka and other plantations. Of greater consequence was his promise to ship as many Africans as Grant requested from Bance Island in summer 1767.[27]

An overseer, Samuel Hewie, finally arrived in June 1766, whereupon the governor "immediately" ordered him to Tomoka with twelve male slaves.[28] Laurens had heard that Hewie was a capable manager, yet he was concerned that the combination of isolated conditions at Mount Oswald and "the arbitrary power of an Overseer" might prompt the slaves "to knock him in the head & file off in a Body."[29] His fears were heightened by reports of Hewie's quarrels with the governor and difficulties controlling the laborers. The governor objected to Hewie's drunken episodes and to his excessive and abusive labor demands, unreasonably severe punishments, and ensuing incidents of slave runaways; nonetheless, he was able to report at the end of November that work had progressed as expected and that none of the laborers had died.[30]

Before the year ended, however, Hewie and two of the workers drowned in what was either a tragic accident or a rebellion. Laurens was moved to lament: "The catastrophe of the wretched [Hewie] & the poor Negroes is affecting. He might have been, according to his credentials a good Servant, but I see clearly that he was unfit for the sole management of a Plantation. His successor the Indian Johnson must behave above the rank of common Carolinian Fugitives, to save his Scalp a whole year. He must be discreet & carry a steady command otherwise the Blacks will drown him too, for of all Overseers they love those of their own colour least."[31]

Oswald was "greatly disappointed" that Laurens "couldn't easily find me a good overseer" and blamed him for the plantation being "retarded as a result," but the death of Hewie did not diminish Oswald's enthusiasm for Florida.[32] His replacement, the "Indian Johnson," impressed the governor and supervisors of neighboring estates by restoring order and producing a surplus of provisions crops in the first six months of 1767. Laurens implied that Johnson was a black man, or of mixed-race ancestry; historians have concluded he was Native American. His background, however, mattered less than his capable management of Mount Oswald. Johnson disappeared mysteriously in June 1767 and was replaced by a man known only as Mr. Parry.[33]

Oswald received encouraging reports in March 1767 from Dr. Andrew Turnbull, who as Patricia Griffin describes in this volume, was about to launch a massive planting venture at New Smyrna with 1,400 indentured servants from several Mediterranean countries.[34] During a London visit, Turnbull described the bountiful cornfields he had seen along Tomoka River, prompting Oswald to accelerate development by sending three or four white overseers to enhance security and direct daily activities. "I propose to send out a few trusty persons, successively, upon wages for the term of three years after their arrival, and after their time is out, if they behave well, to lend them money to buy two, three or four Negros and settle them on their own land."[35] He had also convinced several wealthy grantees to make substantial investments in plantations near Mount Oswald; these included Thomas Thoroton, Peter Taylor, William Elliot, and Sir John Delavel. Oswald planned to hire an agent to supervise several of these new estates.

In May 1767 Oswald informed Grant that the *St. Augustine Packet* would anchor off St. Augustine in September with a cargo of Africans, seventy of whom were intended for Mount Oswald. Worried that "it might be of bad consequence if the men slaves now on the Plantation remained longer unprovided with wives," Oswald "ordered 30 young women to be shipped and 30 more lads and large girls of such age as they may be fit for field labor in about two years."[36] His agents in Africa were directed "to send a few full grown men, not exceeding ten in number . . . [who were] used to the Trades of their country believing they will become soon useful and handy in a new plantation."

To obtain Africans of "the best quality," Oswald was willing to pay £22 per person, a price he implied was high for the time. Clothing for the workers already at Tomoka was packed aboard the vessel, along with complete "Sutes of cloathing" for those aboard, which Captain Savery was to "deliver out to them when he draws nigh the Coast of America." There would also be iron pots and copper cooking kettles aboard, and a ship carpenter named Phillip Herries hired "for the service of the Plantation . . . a good sober man who had been a sergeant in the army." Herries was expected to train Oswald's slaves to do carpentry work, and, if all went well, Oswald planned to add a "Smith and Smith's Shop at Timoka— a Wheeler or two, a Cooper or two & a few other white people, who shall be obliged to teach the Negros."[37]

The seventy Africans arrived early in 1768, but only twenty were old enough to be considered working hands. The other fifty were boys and girls too young for field work. Oswald worried about the stores of provisions on hand and advised Grant to consider selling the "smallest [children] for good bills or cash" if the supply was inadequate to feed them properly. However, he predicted that eventually they would be "worth two imported at full age" if they were raised at Mount Oswald.[38] How they were reared, whether in barracks under adult supervision or in households of male and female couples, whether they were permitted to experience a period of childhood or were thrown into agricultural field work while still children, is not mentioned in the extant record. It is a disturbing image of the slavery system that underlay the prosperity of East Florida plantations: fifty boys and girls torn from families somewhere in the interior of Sierra Leone or Guinea, packed into the hold of a slave ship owned by one of London's most respected and affluent merchants, and delivered to a remote wilderness plantation.[39]

Lt. John Fairlamb served as Oswald's plantation agent in East Florida from 1768 until June 1772. Fairlamb, a former artillery officer, alternated between the estates of Thomas Thoroton and Oswald in the capacity of a "general superintendency . . . by giving the necessary orders to the various overseers."[40] In 1770, two of Oswald's employees in England and Germany, Frederick Robertson and Donald McLean, lived at Mount Oswald and managed on a daily basis the establishment of indigo, sugar, and cotton fields and successfully integrated another 100 Africans into the Mount Oswald labor force.

The Mount Oswald slaves planted fields of sugarcane, which Oswald rejoiced that the winter cold did not kill. Aware, though, that the cane stalks needed time to mature before he could expect profitable returns from sugar production, Oswald was temporarily "contented with indigo," samples of which he judged worth seven or eight shillings a pound in 1770. He advised Fairlamb to sell the indigo crop "in country" as soon as it cured, even if it meant sacrificing one or two shillings a pound, rather than risk the delays of shipping it to London, where the larger "St. Domingo" produce would drive prices down. Fairlamb's supervision drew repeated praise from Oswald, including the unqualified: "I never was acquainted with a man of more genuine worth."[41] Fairlamb resigned in anger in June 1772 when falsely informed that Oswald had replaced him as senior agent, but he stayed in East Florida until the British evacuation, acquiring two estates near Mount Oswald and three north of St. Augustine.[42]

Frederick Robertson succeeded Fairlamb as principal overseer at Mount Oswald between 1772 and 1779, during which time many of the leading citizens of the colony visited and left eyewitness accounts of the plantation's operations. John Moultrie, Frederick George Mulcaster, and the Reverend John Forbes all thought Mount Oswald the finest plantation and labor force combination in the entire province. Mulcaster credited overseer Donald McLean for directing the thirty laborers who processed

3,000 pounds of indigo in 1772. He also commented that Robertson was developing the sugar fields with seventy workers.[43]

Tension between Robertson and McLean prompted the latter to leave Oswald's employ in June 1773, an event Mulcaster called "the worst thing ever [to] befall Mount Oswald."[44] He visited in May 1774 and found fields "in a horrid state," yet production of indigo increased from 3,000 pounds in 1773 to 4,000 pounds in 1774. David Yeats, Governor Grant's agent and secretary of the province, thought Robertson was a "good but sickly" manager and thought "the Negroes not properly looked after and the fields rather dirty," although the sugarcane "looks very good and he is building a sugar works."[45]

Robertson's supervisory tasks were undoubtedly tested severely during 1774, a year when he adjusted to the loss of McLean and managed a doubling of the labor force following Oswald's decision to ship "one hundred . . . Grametas or island slaves" from Bance Island to East Florida. The "grumetes," or "grumettas," had been purchased in the normal fashion of the African trade for work at Bance and the adjacent mainland rather than for sale to European slave ships. The historian George Brooks writes that grumetes generally were "selected for their skills as boatmen, carpenters, blacksmiths, requisite for maintaining a trading place by doing construction, ship building and repair."[46] Fearing "the Neighbouring King & his people would immediately Seize & Sell them to the next Trading Vessel" if they were freed and left in Africa, Oswald decided to send the "Island Slaves" to East Florida. Henry Laurens reported, "Mr. Oswald is desirous of keeping them all together or in plantations near each other & objects to hiring any of them out."[47]

At the end of 1774, a tumultuous year at Mount Oswald and yet one of solid accomplishment developmentally, John Moultrie wrote: "At Oswald's the man [James] Brown that he sent out has been making a mill to grind cane for 2 years past, tis just finished since the cane was destroyed [by an early frost]. McLean I think a loss to Oswald plantation. The present man [is] honest, diligent, anxious to do well, but not as well acquainted with Negroes, their work and the method of agriculture in these regions as the Highlander. Oswald's tract in my opinion is certainly the best in the province."[48]

Mulcaster, an engineer with a fine eye for plantation affairs, commented on the estate after a 1775 visit: "Oswald's wheel which was contrived by the mad ship carpenter is good for nothing. Robertson is the principal overseer at the Mount, is attentive this spring to indigo. His field I hear is in good order, but the drought prevents the indigo from coming up and kills what is up. We have had no rain these many many months, a dryer winter we have never seen anywhere. The sugar plantation at the Mount goes on also."[49]

Within weeks after Mulcaster's visit, spring rains led to bumper crops throughout the province. "Almost every planter has made his provisions, many a great deal to share," Moultrie observed. "I have above 800 bushel of corn to share of the Bella Vista crop, a fine crop of rice at the Musquetos already reaped and in the barn, a second cutting of the same rice almost ripe."[50] Three weeks later, at rice fields across the Tomoka River and directly north of Mount Oswald, Moultrie's workers were reaping a second cutting "very little inferior to the first."[51] If Moultrie's success was mirrored south of the Tomoka River, Mount Oswald would have experienced successful harvests of provisions, indigo and rice for four consecutive years, 1772 through 1775.

While Fairlamb, Robertson, and McLean supervised the labor at Mount Oswald, their employer provided generous financial support and encouragement for experimentation and innovation. This was especially true of sugar cultivation at what became known as the Swamp Settlement, where cane seedlings grown in Oswald's hothouse in Scotland were planted under the supervision of a specialist imported from Jamaica. As early as May 1764, Oswald also contemplated sending specially bred jackasses from Italy to East Florida because of reports of the abundant pastures in the province. By breeding the jackasses with mares from Georgia, he anticipated profits from sales of the offspring in the sugar islands. Three years later, after Mount Oswald was in operation, he announced plans to send Spanish jackasses to breed with local mares. His estate in Scotland had between thirty and forty jackasses, which he thought could be used to supply the entire West Indies market. Oswald also ordered cattle and horses from Savannah to be driven overland to the Tomoka River. Like many other British investors who had estates in the British Caribbean and North American colonies, Oswald tested samples of soil from his Florida estate and sought out information on the proper soil mixtures for building lasting rice dams. He investigated improvements in agricultural technology and sent a new and improved rice-pounding machine to Tomoka. He hired specialists from Jamaica to supervise harvests of the cane and to build an elaborate factory for processing it into sugar. He also authorized

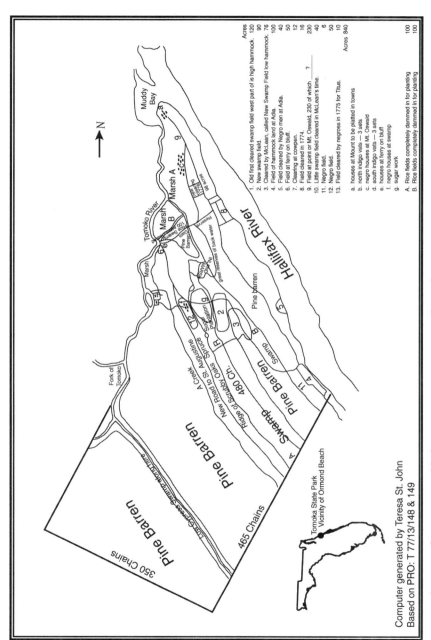

Map 3. Plat map of Mount Oswald Plantation, ca. 1780, mapmaker unknown.

funds for a grinding mill, cooking kettles, and a rum distillery. Anticipating his varied exports to be significant in the future, Oswald commissioned construction of a warehouse and dock facility at the proposed town of Hillsborough (today's Fernandina) on the St. Marys River.[52]

John Anderson, Oswald's nephew and a London business associate, estimated the total investment at Mount Oswald at approximately £18,000. With this level of investment, it is clear that Oswald was not an aristocratic dilettante reluctant to invest in his Florida property. His involvement was innovative and entrepreneurial, and must have exceeded the expectations of as demanding a critic as Governor Grant. Oswald's enthusiastic experimentation and generous investment are reminiscent of the activities of entrepreneurs chronicled in Joyce Chaplin's *An Anxious Pursuit,* one of the few studies to consider East Florida as part of the general pattern of agricultural development in the southeastern colonies.[53]

Despite Oswald's involvement and the evidence of the elaborate infrastructure established by the enslaved Africans prior to 1776, the historians who have looked back at Mount Oswald and the East Florida colony have seen "very little concrete accomplishment." Basing their conclusions on the scant records of production, income, and expenses that have survived to the present, the historians have seen only "Failure in Xanadu" and "a swamp of an investment."

On the contrary, Mount Oswald prior to 1776 should be seen as a major accomplishment. In seven years, with steady financial support from Oswald and the skill and strength of an enslaved African labor force, five separate settlements were carved from the wilderness pine barrens and wetlands at Tomoka and Halifax Rivers. On a 20,000-acre tract that John Moultrie described as "perfectly uncultivated" in 1766, a major agricultural complex with diverse crops and processing equipment was created in less than a decade. The main housing complex, the Mount Oswald Settlement, at the northeastern point of the tract where Tomoko Creek and Halifax River joined, featured 300 acres cleared and fenced for provisions and indigo fields and works for processing the cut weed into blocks of dye. It also included a functioning rice field with labor-intensive dams, canals, and a freshwater pond which Africans had transformed from an adjacent freshwater marsh. One witness said the buildings included quarters for the enslaved Africans and "a very good Dwelling House . . . 40 feet by 20 framed and weather boarded Shingled & Glazed, a large framed Barn about 60 feet by 30, floored Weather boarded and shingled. A shell framed Overseers House, Kitchen and Negroe Houses."[54]

Further inland and four miles to the south was the Ferry Settlement, also used for provisions-cultivation and indigo. Ferry Settlement was located at the point where the Kings Road, the main north-south artery in the colony, crossed the Tomoka River. In the marshes near the ferry crossing was another 100-acre rice field. The Adia Settlement, further south, was cleared for corn and indigo cultivation. The Cowpens was an upland pine barren dedicated to grazing and livestock breeding. At the Swamp Settlement, slaves had planted 300 acres in sugarcane and built a sugar works, distillery, and warehouses. Ruins of the sugar works and distillery can still be visited at the site, a testimony to the skill of the brick mason imported from Jamaica and the African apprentices who constructed them.[55]

Each of the settlements had houses for overseers and workers, barns and stables, corn cribs, storage buildings, and shops for coopers, blacksmiths, and other artisans. These are concrete accomplishments, paid for at heavy financial cost by Oswald but at a much greater sacrifice in human suffering by the Africans who did the clearing, ditching, planting, and building.

Planters like Moultrie, Henry Strachey, Jermyn Wright, and Samuel Potts were jubilant about the future of plantations in East Florida in 1775. Their estates and several others were established successes. What the Florida planters were not anticipating were the shockwaves that soon would be generated by the American Revolution and which would bring a sudden end to the British East Florida colony. During 1776 and 1777, invaders from Georgia looted and destroyed plantations north and west of the St. Johns River. Increasingly, shipping and market networks for East Florida exports were disrupted, and enslaved laborers were drafted away from agricultural fields to build defense installations throughout the province. Until the fighting on land and sea was ended, the East Florida estates stagnated.

In 1776 fears that rebellious activity would spill as far south as Tomoka River prompted Oswald to send his nephew, James Anderson, to supervise Mount Oswald. The young man proved to be a capable manager under adverse conditions. In 1780, after Anderson had been four years at the task, John Moultrie wrote: "Oswald plantation is now in a way of doing well . . . His nephew who is an Attorney is active. A large body of marsh taken in for rice, and a capital reserve [pond] covering 5 or 600 acres finished. Water for the rice never can fail, tis a beautiful lake."[56]

Moultrie acknowledged that the plantations south of St. Augustine faced grave danger after Spain joined its old ally, France, in the war against Great Britain in June 1779. By September, Bernardo de Gálvez, the newly appointed governor of Spanish Louisiana, had captured Manchac, Baton Rouge, and Natchez from British troops and turned his attentions toward the Gulf Coast. By March 1780 Mobile was in Spanish possession and Gálvez was planning an attack on Pensacola. With Spanish Cuba menacingly close to the British plantations spread along the Atlantic coast, East Florida residents were deeply worried. In March 1780 Moultrie lamented that a raid by Cuban privateers on estates in the vicinity of New Smyrna were a "Spanish plunder [which] broke up all the plantations except Oswalds and my own, [which now] stand fast to plant rice & corn."[57] Relieved that the British government had stationed an armed ship on patrol and was "building a blockhouse at the [Mosquito] inlet," Moultrie believed his estates were sufficiently protected.

Richard Oswald disagreed. He directed his nephew to dismantle Mount Oswald and move the laborers to a vacant estate near Savannah, Georgia. The successes of British arms in the southern colonies in 1779 and 1780, including the capture of Savannah and Charleston, may have convinced Oswald that his workers would be safer at Savannah than at Tomoka River. Acreage near Savannah had special appeal after October 1779, when Gen. Augustine Prevost successfully defended that port city from an attack by a powerful French fleet. In St. Augustine, however, David Yeats was shocked to learn of Oswald's order "to sell off everything and move instantly into Georgia with the whole of his Negroes," calling it an impetuous act resulting in the loss of "a year of planting . . . his provision crop is already planted."[58]

After dismantling and packing, loading provisions, farm animals, tools and other movable property onto transports, more than 240 enslaved men and women departed Mount Oswald. Their troubles increased en route. During the voyage, the ship was attacked by American privateers, who abducted seventy of the passengers. Those who survived the attack debarked at a plantation owned by John Graham, a leading Savannah merchant and long-time business associate of Oswald. Graham was the lieutenant governor of Georgia, a member of the provincial council, and the owner of extensive acreage idled by wartime disturbances. Oswald's workers cleared and replanted abandoned fields, unaware that dramatic events in Europe were about to disrupt their lives once more. Ironically, Oswald would play a major role in negotiating the decisions that determined the fate of his enslaved Africans.

The British campaign in the South which offered so much promise in 1780 had turned sour by late summer 1781, when Gen. George Washington marched his army south from New York to Chesapeake Bay to meet a French fleet sailing from the Caribbean. The maneuver trapped Lord Charles Cornwallis and his army at Yorktown between a larger American land force and the French fleet, and forced Cornwallis's surrender on October 19, 1781. The spectacular American victory prompted the British government to negotiate for peace. Richard Oswald, an advocate of generous terms for the Americans, was a leading member of the British delegation that bargained with Americans Benjamin Franklin, John Jay, and John Adams. It was at Oswald's hotel rooms in Paris that the preliminary peace treaty was signed on November 30, 1782, which recognized the independence of the thirteen rebellious colonies.[59]

Even before the peace terms were agreed to, however, colonists loyal to England had started the painful process of evacuating their homes. Thousands of disheartened refugees began moving by land and sea to East and West Florida and Canada, where the Union Jack still flew. British military garrisons were withdrawn in New York, Charleston, and Savannah, and transports were arranged to assist in the exodus of Loyalist refugees. Savannah was evacuated in July 1782, Charleston a few months later. In all, more than 13,000 Loyalist refugees resettled temporarily in East Florida before the province was itself ceded back to Spain.[60]

David Yeats was at St. Augustine harbor to witness the arrival of "thousands of Refugees and Negroes . . . from Georgia upon the evacuation of that Province." One exhausted and dispirited group drew his special attention, the enslaved laborers of Richard Oswald. Yeats wrote that John Graham had chartered five transports in Savannah in July 1782 to carry "300 to 400 Negroes [to Florida], including those of Richard Oswald who are back at Mount Oswald, greatly reduced in number."[61]

Oswald's nephew, James Anderson, did not return to East Florida. Instead he moved to South Carolina and became an American rice planter. For the next two years, John Graham's agent, Lt. Col. John Douglas, supervised activities at Mount Oswald from St. Augustine. Finally, in 1784, following Britain's decision to return East Florida to Spain, Oswald arranged to close down his Tomoka River estate and ship his slaves to

South Carolina. In March the much-traveled Africans departed Mount Oswald for the final time, arriving at Charleston in April. Henry Laurens informed Oswald that "the poor Negroes were safe in harbour."[62] En route to Santee River rice plantations, 170 survivors of a tragic trans-Atlantic migratory odyssey—a cultural mixture of "country born" and, by 1784, "well seasoned" Africans, who had carved an important plantation from the new world wilderness of British East Florida—were temporarily "safe in harbour."

Mount Oswald, its empty buildings intact and its indigo, corn, sugar, cotton, and rice fields soon to be engulfed by brush and weeds, was abandoned for the second time. No doubt squatters or beleaguered travelers sought temporary shelter in the decaying edifices in subsequent years, but the estate would be without a proprietor for decades. Richard Oswald's massive investments had come to naught. Loyalist planters pressed claims to Parliament for losses suffered as a result of the cession of East Florida to Spain, but compensation fell short of the massive investments.[63]

Before Spanish planters finally restored the fields at Mount Oswald, death would overtake the two adventurers who had financed and directed its initial development. Richard Oswald died on November 6, 1784, at the age of eighty. James Grant died on April 13, 1806, at age eighty-two. Much has been written about their lives. An equally interesting story remains to be told, but the work of telling it will be a formidable challenge. Somewhere in the archives of colonial Britain and the records of South Carolina rice plantations are the strings that tie together the lives of the enslaved black men and women who endured the travails of plantation-building at Tomoka and Halifax Rivers. These involuntary immigrants to British North America, chattel property until the American Civil War, created families and histories in addition to wealth for their owners. Their life histories await a biographer.

Historians who have been critical of the efforts at Tomoka as well as the overall British East Florida experience, have misread the dynamics of the attempt to create in two decades a profitable plantation colony from the "State of Nature" that James Grant discovered in August 1764. At Tomoka River, the enslaved labor force overcame enormous environmental obstacles through arduous land and swamp clearance to establish provisions and cane fields. By ditching, draining, and constructing dikes and dams, they created two functioning rice plantations with the requisite freshwater reserve ponds. By 1775 they had established the infrastructure for a major agricultural complex and had experienced successful harvests for four consecutive years.[64] When the aborted efforts of 1766 and 1767 are discounted (one overseer perished and the other disappeared; the labor force was very limited in number), Mount Oswald was established in less than a decade. It was then positioned to repay Oswald's investment many times over. Had the turbulence and chaos that attended the American Revolution not occurred, there is little doubt that Mount Oswald would have become a continuing economic success. The demise of Mount Oswald did not result from "gangs of black slaves . . . nurturing a distinctive culture" or from "poor soil and climate"; instead, blame lies with the international political crisis that accompanied a revolutionary war and forced the retrocession of East Florida to Spain. The violence and economic disruptions of the American Revolution ended a brief but promising experiment in plantation-building based on African labor.

At places other than Mount Oswald there were tragic disappointments in the British East Florida experience, especially two colossal failures: Charlottia, or Rolles Town, on the St. Johns River and New Smyrna on Halifax River. Denys Rolle's huge estate was indeed conceived and operated foolishly, but the blame for the enormous losses resides with him, not with the province. Despite his setbacks, however, Rolle was still enthusiastic about the future of East Florida as late as 1780, when he purchased several established plantations.[65] As Patricia C. Griffin's essay in this volume details, Andrew Turnbull initiated New Smyrna on a massive scale with over 1,400 indentured laborers from several Mediterranean nations, for whom few preparations had been made prior to their arrival in August 1768. Sick and exhausted after the Atlantic crossing, soon to suffer high mortality rates in an inhospitable environment, the New Smyrna workers nevertheless cleared brush and planted fields of provisions and indigo along seven miles fronting the Halifax River. Joyce Chaplin credits Turnbull with innovation in indigo processing and for exporting high-quality dye worth £13,500 in 1772, and for "an astonishing 42,283 pounds [weight] between 1772 and 1777," worth at least £15,000 when sold in London.[66] Turnbull claimed 350 indigo vats installed by 1770, with another 150 planned, prompting Chaplin to call New Smyrna "more factory than agricultural estate." Turnbull and his financial backers claim that income from New Smyrna was immediately reinvested and that income paled when compared to an initial investment of more than £30,000 in the first two years alone.[67]

Both Rolles Town and New Smyrna are extreme examples of failure. More typical were the successful estates created west and north of the St. Johns River for Governor Tonyn (the governor of East Florida who succeeded James Grant), for Henry Ferguson, for the heirs of Lord Egmont, and for Jermyn Wright (the brother of Sir James Wright, the governor of Georgia), all of which were destroyed by invaders from Georgia in 1776–80. The rich lands between the St. Johns River and the Florida-Georgia border at the St. Marys River became a "no man's land" subject to repeated raids which led to abandonment and destruction of numerous estates.[68]

John Moultrie's several plantations south of St. Augustine escaped the post-1776 raids which devastated the plantations north of the St. Johns River. As early as 1771, Moultrie was so convinced he would "grow rich" in Florida that he sold his South Carolina plantations and made plans to "immediately bring all my Negroes" to St. Augustine.[69] The extent to which Moultrie succeeded can be gauged by his remarks to James Grant in 1783 after learning that the province had been ceded to Spain: "No recompense that will be made for turning me adrift can be so agreeable to me as to have been left in possession of my property. I live in real plenty, ease and some elegance, more so than ever I did in my life."[70]

As lieutenant governor, Moultrie traveled throughout the province for nearly two decades, paying close attention to the status of the developing farms and plantations. He made dozens of visits to the profitable indigo estate six miles north of St. Augustine initiated by Governor Grant's laborers in November 1768. He advised Grant's agent and slaves as they created a rice plantation twenty miles north of the capital only two years before the final British evacuation. Grant's indigo estate—with its extensive processing works, buildings, tools, farm animals, and fifty enslaved laborers—produced a 15 percent return on investment with its second crop. The produce of the 1773 crop repaid the entire investment; for the next eleven years, Grant received handsome annual returns.[71]

Also familiar to Moultrie was the 1,000-acre Beauclerc Bluff Plantation, owned by Henry Strachey and located at Goodby's Creek and the St. Johns River. Strachey's income figures show annual net profits for fifteen years. Near Beauclerc Bluff, Joshua Yallowley's 350-acre estate, known as Orange Bluff, produced annual orange juice exports of 600 gallons a year from 1773 to 1785.[72] Moultrie also visited settlements of refugees who had supported King George III and fled to safety in East Florida late in the Revolutionary War. In 1783 he said of the refugees: "Thousands of poor

Loyalists with what they could save of their Negroes and other property have settled here and were just made comfortable, and quite happy, astonished at the crops in the ground. They have really built already a surprising town at Hester Bluff on St. John's of good houses, had this province not been ceded in the course of this year every part would have been full of industrious people, the only thing wanted to make it great and flourishing."[73]

Contemporary opinion—whether expressed by Loyalist refugees from the rebel colonies who had made new lives for themselves in East Florida, or by elite planters like John Moultrie—was that East Florida by the 1780s had become a valuable British province which should not be bargained away in the peace negotiations. In June 1782, after hearing rumors of plans to cede the colony to Spain, David Yeats was thrown into the "utmost consternation." He wrote to his friend James Grant: "I am totally ruined and see nothing but want and misery before me."[74] One year later, John Moultrie lamented that he was about "to be turned adrift, and again seek a resting place."[75] He contemplated freeing his slaves and burning his houses, hoping that "England . . . will bring me up. My feelings, principles, everything prevents me having any idea of remaining in America."

Revisionist historians might reconsider the experiences of Yeats, Grant, Moultrie, and other planters who transformed East Florida from a "State of Nature" into a prosperous plantation colony through the labor of African slaves. The balanced views of Charles Mowat, published more than fifty years ago, still have relevance. "Twenty years is no long time by which to judge a country," Mowat concluded. "For East Florida, at least, the span was too short to produce a firm and reliant society, too short for the roots to take much hold of the soil."[76] The evidence suggests that the roots did take hold briefly, but that the tendrils were torn from the soil by the turbulence of the American Revolution and by the subsequent cession of the province to Spain.

Author's note

I thank Joan Moore, my wife, for the love and support that makes this and my other work possible. Her editing along with the careful attention of my friend and excellent copyeditor Jean Parker Waterbury greatly improved the writing in this chapter. I also thank Jane Landers for her perceptive comments.

Notes

1. Charles Loch Mowat, *East Florida as a British Province, 1763–1784* (Berkeley: University of California Press, 1943; reprint, Gainesville: University Press of Florida, 1964), 149.

2. Paul David Nelson, *General James Grant: Scottish Soldier and Royal Governor of East Florida* (Gainesville: University Press of Florida, 1993), 65.

3. Bernard Bailyn, *Voyagers to the West: A Passage in the Peopling of America on the Eve of the Revolution* (New York: Alfred A. Knopf, 1986), chap. 12.

4. David Hancock, *Citizens of the World: London Merchants and the Integration of the British Atlantic Community, 1735–1785* (Cambridge: Cambridge University Press: 1995), 159.

5. Ibid.

6. Ibid., 160, 163. My interpretation of the success of Egmont and his heirs differs dramatically. See "Plantation Development in British East Florida: A Case Study of the Earl of Egmont," *Florida Historical Quarterly* 63 (October 1984): 172–83.

7. Samuel Eveleigh, quoted in Peter H. Wood, *Black Majority: Negroes in Colonial South Carolina, from 1670 through the Stono Rebellion* (New York: Alfred A. Knopf, 1974), 84. Daniel L. Schafer, "'Yellow Silk Ferret Tied Round Their Wrists': African Americans in British East Florida, 1763–1784," in *The African American Heritage of Florida*, ed. David R. Colburn and Jane L. Landers (Gainesville: University Press of Florida, 1995), 71–103. For seventeenth-century responses of English colonists to heat in the tropical colonies, see Karen Ordahl Kupperman, "Fear of Hot Climates in the Anglo-American Colonial Experience," *The William and Mary Quarterly*, 3d ser. 61 (April 1984): 213–40. For resistance to fevers, see Philip D. Curtin, "Epidemiology and the Slave Trade," *Political Science Quarterly* 83 (1968): 198–99; Kenneth F. Kiple and Virginia H. Kiple, "Black Yellow Fever Immunities, Innate and Acquired, as Revealed in the American South," *Social Science History* 1 (1977): 420–22; Wood, *Black Majority,* 85–91.

8. Oswald to Grant, "Sketch of a Plan," May 3, 5, 1764, in The Papers of James Grant, Ballindalloch Castle Muniments, bundles 517 and 470, hereafter BCM followed by the bundle number. The Grant Papers are in possession of Sir Ewan Macpherson-Grant, Bart. Access permission must come from The Secretary, National Register of Archives (Scotland), P.O. Box 36, Edinburgh. For transition from white indentures to enslaved Africans, see three books by David W. Galenson: *White Servitude in Colonial America; An Economic Analysis* (Cambridge: Cambridge University Press, 1981), 153–68, 177–78; *Markets in History: Economic Studies of the Past* (Cambridge: Cambridge University Press, 1989), 52–96; and *Traders, Planters, and Slaves: Market Behavior in Early English America* (Cambridge: Cambridge University Press, 1986).

9. Grant to Egmont, June 16, 1768, in the governor's letterbook, a series of bound ledgers identified as BCM 659.

10. Grant to Oswald, September 20, 1764, BCM 659. For evacuation see the chapters by Jean Parker Waterbury and Daniel L. Schafer in *The Oldest City: St. Augustine, Saga of Survival,* ed. Jean Parker Waterbury (St. Augustine: St. Augustine Historical Society, 1983), and Maj. Francis Ogilvie to Board of Trade, St. Augustine, January 26, 1764, Great Britain, Public Record Office, Colonial Office, ser. 5, vol. 540 (hereafter CO 5/540). Eugene Lyon, Amy Turner Bushnell, John H. Hann, and Charles A. Arnade, in their chapters in *The New History of Florida*, ed. Michael Gannon (Gainesville: University Press of Florida, 1996), discuss Spanish East Florida prior to 1763.

11. Grant to Oswald, September 20, 1764, BCM 659.

12. Oswald to Grant, June 19, 1767, BCM, bundle 295.

13. Oswald to Grant, February 10, 1768, BCM 295.

14. Grant to Oswald, August 31, 1766, BCM 659.

15. February 9, 1768, BCM 659.

16. Grant to Egmont, June 16, 1768, BCM 659.

17. December 25, 1767, BCM 659.

18. Grant to Egmont, September 11, 1769, BCM 369. See Schafer, "'Yellow Silk Ferret'" regarding slave sales and prices. Grant's advice to Moira is June 20, 1768, BCM 659. See also Grant to Egmont, February 9, 1768, BCM 369. Around 1800, Spanish pesos and U.S. dollars were of equal value: U.S.$1.00 traded for £4.4 British Sterling. Based on my examination of commodity prices in Northeast Florida probate records over several decades, I estimate that U.S.$1.00 in 1800 would be worth approximately $30 today, excluding land and slave values, probably closer to $35 (slave and land prices are not meant to be included in this correlation). Scot Derks, ed., *The Value of a Dollar: Prices and Incomes in the United States, 1860–1989* (Detroit: A Manly, 1994), rates U.S.$1.00 in 1860 at $30.83 in 1989. See "Composite Commodity Price Index," p. 2.

19. Michael Mullin, *Africa in America: Slave Acculturation and Resistance in the American South and the British Caribbean, 1736–1831* (Urbana: University of Illinois Press, 1992), 22–33, discusses naming patterns and labels affixed to enslaved workers.

20. The best discussion of Oswald and Bance Island is to be found in Hancock, *Citizens of the World,* chap. 6. See also A. P. Kup, *A History of Sierra Leone, 1400–1787* (Cambridge: Cambridge University Press, 1961), 190–91, and *Public Ledger,* Edinburgh, September 11, 1784, advertising the sale of Bance Island (copy in National Library of Scotland, Edinburgh). Partnership arrangements and instructions for crops and planting are in Oswald to Grant, May 3, 1764, BCM 470; July 25, 1764, BCM 295; November 21, 1764, BCM 659.

21. Grant to Oswald, February 12, 1765. Nocoroco, the southernmost Timucuan village on the Atlantic coast, was the site of the Mount Oswald settlement,

at today's Tomoka State Park, near Ormond Beach. See John H. Hann, *A History of the Timucua Indians and Missions* (Gainesville: University Press of Florida, 1996), 169–73.

22. Laurens to Grant, February 23, 1765. See Rogers, *The Papers of Henry Laurens*, vol. 4, *September 1, 1763–August 31, 1765,* ed. George E. Rogers, assistant editor David R. Chesnutt (Columbia: University of South Carolina Press, 1974), 585.

23. April 20, 1765, BCM 359.

24. Grant to Oswald, October 12, 1765, BCM 659.

25. Ibid.

26. Oswald to Grant, February 12, 1766, BCM 295. See February 24 concerning his partners and for approval of plans for planting indigo and cotton at Mount Oswald.

27. Oswald to Grant, June 9 & 14, 1766, BCM 295. Oswald complained that the price for Africans was then high at £22 Sterling each. On April 28, 1766, he wrote that Bell was a good choice "to take charge of our settlement" and approved the purchase of thirty additional experienced laborers.

28. Grant to Oswald, August 31, 1766, BCM 659. After Hewie began work, Grant promised to nurture Oswald's investments but withdrew from their partnership.

29. Laurens to Oswald, August 12, 1766, Rogers, *Papers of Henry Laurens*, 5:156.

30. Grant to Shelburne, November 27, 1766, CO 5/548.

31. Laurens to Grant, January 30, 1767, in Rogers, *Papers of Henry Laurens*, 5:227. For Hewie and his successor, see Thomas W. Taylor, "'Settling a Colony over a Bottle of Claret': Richard Oswald and the British Settlement of Florida" (Master's thesis, University of North Carolina at Greensboro, 1984), 34–36. Hancock says of Hewie: "While fishing one day . . . he drowned while plantation slaves looked on. His death was barely lamented; the loss of the two slaves who went down in the same boat was greater" (*Citizens of the World,* 167). Until 1763 runaway slaves from Carolina could claim religious sanctuary and win freedom in Spanish Florida; Laurens's references to "Carolinian Fugitives" and overseers "of their own colour" suggest that the Indian Johnson may have had at least some African ancestry. See Jane Landers, "Gracia Real de Santa Teresa de Mose: A Free Black Town in Colonial Florida," *American Historical Review* 95 (February 1990): 9–30.

32. Oswald to Grant, February 19, 1768, BCM 295.

33. See Taylor, "'Settling a Colony'," 34–36, and Hancock, *Citizens of the World,* 168, regarding Johnson.

34. Oswald to Grant, March 15, 1767, BCM 295. Turnbull reported a promising 150-acre cornfield at Mount Oswald with cabbage palms amid the corn.

35. Oswald to Grant, March 15, 1767, February 19, 1768, BCM 295. Oswald first believed that it would be possible to divide part of the estate into fifty lots of

100 acres each and give each white family that settled there one lot along with tools, livestock, and other necessaries to begin planting. The land would serve as security for repayment of the loan. When small farmers did not move to East Florida, however, he decided to send laborers from Britain to Mount Oswald to work under indenture contracts. See Oswald to Grant, July 25, 1764, BCM 295.

36. Oswald to Grant, May 20, 29, 1767, ibid.

37. Ibid.

38. Oswald to Grant, February 19, 1768; Grant to Hillsborough, March, 1768, CO 5/5439; Grant to Oswald, February 9, 1769, BCM 659.

39. For one of the few studies of enslaved children, see Wilma King, *Stolen Childhood: Slave Youth in Nineteenth-century America* (Bloomington: Indiana University Press, 1995).

40. Oswald to Grant, July 6, 1767, BCM 295. He may have begun in late 1767, but it is more likely that his agency started in 1768.

41. Oswald to Grant, February 19, 1768, BCM 295. Comments on cane and indigo are in April 6, June 8, November 7, 1770, BCM 295.

42. Oswald to Grant, February 1, 1769, BCM 295. Francis Levett apparently spread the false rumor that he had supervisory powers. Mulcaster to Grant, St. Augustine, June 19, 1772, and January 15, 1773, BCM 260. I can find no records of an agent replacing Fairlamb until James Anderson arrived in 1776. Claim of Frederick Robertson, Documents of the East Florida Loyalist Claims Commission, 1784–86, Treasury 77, box 15, file 10, Public Records of Great Britain, Public Record Office, Kew England (hereafter T 77, 15/10), says Robertson left to supervise a plantation owned by James Moncrief. He owned four tracts of land at evacuation prior to settling in Jamaica. See also Claim of John Fairlamb, T 77 6/1.

43. Mulcaster to Grant, January 15, 1773, BCM 260. Mulcaster judged McLean to be the better manager and thought that Robertson divided workers into small inefficient gangs. Grant returned to England in May 1771, intending to mend his health problems and return to Florida to resume his governorship. Lieutenant Governor John Moultrie governed during the interim. When Grant resigned instead, he was replaced in March 1774 by Lt. Col. Patrick Tonyn. Grant's departure generated a large and valuable correspondence between him and East Florida officials and planters.

44. Mulcaster to Grant, May 14, 1774; also February 6, August 9, 1774, and June 13, 1773, all in BCM 369. McLean began planting on his own at an estate north of Tomoka River previously owned by William Drayton and located near Moultrie's rice plantation.

45. Yeats to Grant, May 24, 1774, BCM 369.

46. I thank George Brooks for this information from personal correspondence of August 1, 1998.

47. Laurens to Gervais, Westminster, April 9, 13, 1774, in Rogers, *The Papers of Henry Laurens,* 9:395–98, 445–47.

48. Moultrie to Grant, December 23, 1774, BCM 521. See also September 11, 1773, BCM 370.

49. Mulcaster to Grant, March 25, 1775, BCM 308, referring to Phillip Herries, who came to East Florida aboard the *St. Augustine Packet* in early 1768. David Hancock found evidence that the mill was a disaster, producing "only a small amount of sugar each day, and, when used, broke the slaves' legs" (*Citizens of the World,* 163).

50. Moultrie to Grant, October 4, 1775, BCM 242.

51. Moultrie to Grant, October 28, 1775, ibid. Moultrie and Oswald were the only planters in the province raising rice in freshwater marshes.

52. Oswald to Grant, July 25, 1764; January 12, June 14, 1766; March 15, May 25, 1767; February 19, September 18, 1768; May 15, 1769; April 6, June 8, 1770, in BCM 295.

53. "The Memorial of Mary Oswald, No. 29, Loyalist Claims," in Wilbur H. Siebert, ed., *Loyalists in East Florida, 1774 to 1785* (DeLand, Fla.: Florida State Historical Society, 1929), 2:54–61; Joyce Chaplin, *An Anxious Pursuit: Agricultural Innovation and Modernity in the Lower South, 1730–1815* (Chapel Hill: University of North Carolina Press, 1993).

54. "Testimony of John Douglas," in Siebert, *Loyalists in East Florida,* 2:57–61. Moultrie's recollections of Mount Oswald are probably the most accurate accounts that have survived.

55. Taylor, "'Settling a Colony'," passim. Archaeologist Ted Payne conducted excavations in 1996 at the site of the main settlement, now part of Tomoka State Park. He kindly showed me remains of the distillery and sugar works at the former "Swamp Settlement."

56. Moultrie to Grant, March 12, 1780, BCM 242.

57. Ibid. Andrew Turnbull described the raid in a letter to Lord Shelburne on March 14, 1780. See J. Leitch Wright, Jr., *Florida in the American Revolution* (Gainesville: University of Florida Press, 1975), 162n.37; Gálvez is discussed on 72–83. See also David J. Weber, *The Spanish Frontier in North America* (New Haven: Yale University Press, 1992), 265–70.

58. Yeats to Grant, March 20, 1781, BCM 250. Yeats noted that the workers had just cleared "200 acres of fine marsh . . . for rice" and feared that the Spanish capture of West Florida would lead to raids on East Florida. The slaves at Grant's Villa narrowly escaped raiders from Georgia (see September 14, 1781, BCM 628, and Wright, *Florida in the American Revolution,* 81–83). Yeats reported on March 9, 1782, that the workers were placed at a vacant Georgia estate owned by Lieutenant Governor John Graham, a wealthy planter and Savannah merchant.

59. For a comprehensive discussion of the peace negotiation, particularly concerning the role of Oswald, see Richard B. Morris, *The Peacemakers: The Great Powers and American Independence* (New York: Harper & Row, 1965), passim.

60. Mowat, *East Florida as a British Province,* 135–38.

61. Yeats to Grant, September 15, 1784, BCM 628. A biographical portrait of Graham is in Siebert, *Loyalists in East Florida,* 2:226–27, as is testimony of John Anderson, a nephew of Oswald, that "in July 1782, upon the evacuation of Georgia, from 170 to 176 [slaves] were brought back again to East Florida and continued upon the plantation till the cession" (2:55).

62. Laurens to Oswald, April 22, 1784, from unpublished letters at the University of South Carolina used by Taylor in "'Settling a Colony'." Laurens, John Gervais, and John Owen agreed to supervise the sale of the Mount Oswald slaves.

63. See Yeats to Grant, September 14, 1784, BCM 250; Claim of Richard Oswald, T 77 13/8 (the total claim for losses at Mount Oswald and an undeveloped 20,000-acre tract at Ramsay Bay was less than £10,000). See "Memorial of Mary Oswald," in Siebert, *Loyalists,* 2:54–61.

64. According to one Oswald employee, total income from agricultural exports was only £3,037, but this figure is doubtful. Production records are scanty, but reports of cured indigo yields of 3,000 and 4,000 pounds net weight in 1772, 1773, and 1774 would have sold for at least £4,000. Considering that provisions, rice, and sugar would have provided either return, it seems that income must have been greater ("Testimony of John Anderson," Siebert, *Loyalists,* 2:54–61).

65. Claim of Denys Rolle, T 77 15/13. Rolle claimed to have transported 200 white indentureds to East Florida between 1764 and 1779 and to have invested over £23,000 Sterling. Rolles Town consisted of 76,000 acres. In November 1780 Rolle bought Jericho Plantation from James Penman for £4,600. It consisted of more than 1,000 acres on the St. Johns River near Cowford Ferry and 51 slaves, 24 horses, buildings, tools, and rice and provisions fields. See also Claim of James Penman, T 77 14/6. Michael Craton, in "Hobbesian or Panglossian? Two Extremes of Slave Conditions in the British Caribbean, 1783 to 1784," *William and Mary Quarterly, A Magazine of Early American History*, 3d ser. 35, no. 2 (April 1978): 324–56, traces the fate of the Rolle slaves after they were evacuated to Great Exuma, Bahamas.

66. Chaplin, *Anxious Pursuit,* 204–5. High-quality East Florida indigo sold for seven to nine shillings per pound. At seven shillings, the export value would have been nearly £15,000. For the indigo vats, Chaplin cites Turnbull to Grant, October 22, 1770, BCM 253.

67. For New Smyrna, see Claim of Andrew Turnbull, T 77 17/15, and the claim of his partners, Lords Duncan, Grenville, and Temple (T 77 7/3), who together held deeds to 101,400 acres of East Florida Land. See also Patricia C. Griffin, *Mullet on the Beach: The Minorcans of Florida, 1768–1788* (Jacksonville: University of North Florida Press, 1991); and E. P. Panagopoulos, *New Smyrna: An Eighteenth-Century Greek Odyssey* (Gainesville: University of Florida Press, 1966). High-quality East Florida indigo sold for between seven and nine shillings per pound.

68. The Claim of Henry Ferguson, T 77 6/4; Col. Patrick Tonyn, T 77 17/10; employees and heirs of Lord Egmont: Stephan Egan, T 77 5/4; Spencer Perceval, T

77 14/7–8–9–10. The leading secondary work is Martha Condray Searcy, *The Georgia-Florida Contest in the American Revolution, 1776–1778* (Tuscaloosa: University of Alabama Press, 1985).

69. Moultrie to Lord Hillsborough, June 27, 1771, CO 5/552.

70. Moultrie to Grant, June 17, 1783, BCM 261.

71. See Grant to Michael Herries, October 1, 1770; Grant to John Gordon, October 4, December 12, 1770, BCM 659; David Yeats to Grant, November 20, 1773, February 8, 1774, BCM 370.

72. T 77/16/21, Claim of Henry Strachey, and T 77/18/26, Claim of Elizabeth Yallowley.

73. Moultrie to Grant, June 17, 1783, BCM 261. Moultrie's insights are supported by Carole Watterson Troxler, "Loyalist Refugees and the British Evacuation of East Florida, 1783–1785," *Florida Historical Quarterly* 60 (July 1981): 1–28; and "Refugee, Resistance, and Reward: The Southern Loyalists' Claim on East Florida," *Journal of Southern History* 55 (November 1989): 563–96.

74. Yeats to Grant, June 18, 1782, BCM 628.

75. Moultrie to Grant, June 17, 1783, BCM 261.

76. Mowat, *East Florida,* 149.

2

Blue Gold

Andrew Turnbull's New Smyrna Plantation

PATRICIA C. GRIFFIN

Planters in British East Florida hoped to produce indigo of such quality that when one of the finished blocks was cracked open, a glint of gold would show against the much-prized deep blue color of the dye. Pleasure in this gold sparkle lay not so much in its visual charm as in its guarantee of monetary gold in English pound sterling. Some of the best indigo grown in North America was produced in East Florida, and some of the best of that best was produced at the New Smyrna Plantation on the central Atlantic coast of Florida. Some scholars describe the plantation, which operated from 1768 to 1777, as a failed experiment. But for a brief time, it was full of golden promise.

When England added Florida to its colonial chain in 1763, it planned to tame and people the "wilderness" to promote economic success and to ensure continued political dominion of the eastern seaboard of North America. England designed a plantation economy similar to the one in South Carolina for the newly gained possession. The British parliament promulgated a plan offering large grants for agricultural development to suitable individuals, those of stature and means in the mother country. Grantees were to settle their grants with white Protestants, who would in time work out their indentures and become loyal citizens of towns on the granted lands, thus effectively populating the colony.

England divided Florida into the provinces of East and West Florida. East Florida covered the peninsula and stretched west to the Apalachicola River. James Grant, the first governor of East Florida, followed the policy of encouraging large grants—usually 10,000 to 20,000 acres—but was convinced that slaves were the only labor adapted to farm in the warm, humid climate. He recruited slaves for his own plantations, and other grantees followed his lead. As it turned out, only two plantations in British

East Florida were settled with white workers. Several hundred homeless individuals and those who had fallen afoul of the law in England, as well as a sprinkling of more-promising immigrants, were settled on the St. Johns River by Denys Rolle in what became Rolles Town. Likewise, in accordance with the parliamentary mandate, colonists recruited for the plantation at New Smyrna, the subject of this essay, were white Mediterranean farmers and craftsmen and their families.[1]

Dr. Andrew Turnbull, a Scottish physician but practicing in London at the time, had a scheme for peopling a Florida plantation with white workers from Greece, who were—unlike their counterparts in the north of Europe—inured to working in extreme heat. Having served as a British consul in Greece for a few years, and incidentally having married a woman from Smyrna, he found ample opportunity for observation of the indigenous peoples there. However, Turnbull doubtless also saw the pamphlet by a fellow Scotsman, Archibald Menzies, recommending recruitment to the southern colonies of these hardy Mediterraneans saying, "The people I mean are the Greeks of the Levant, accustomed to the hot climate and bred to the culture of the vine, olive, cotton, tobacco, madder, etc., as also to the raising of silk." Menzies believed the people to be "in general, sober and industrious; and being reduced by their severe masters [the Turks], to the greatest misery, would be easily persuaded to fly from slavery."[2]

Turnbull was part of a group of prominent individuals known as the East Florida Society who met regularly in London to discuss opportunities in the new colony. Many of their exchanges focused on the conflicting reports about the unknown land. Was it a dismal sandbank of a place or a tropical paradise ripe for agricultural development? Turnbull wanted to believe the rosier stories. Caught up in "Florida fever," he joined with William Duncan, a baronet, to secure land grants in Florida. Later, as their plans became more grandiose, they were joined by George Grenville, then prime minister, acting through an agent, Sir Richard Temple. The partners eventually secured 101,400 acres of granted land, 40,000 acres of which, lying on the coast at Mosquito Inlet seventy miles south of St. Augustine, was planned as the main plantation. The government surveyor, William Gerard DeBrahm, commissioned by Governor Grant to survey the area in preparation for this large development, identified this land as some of the best in East Florida in terms of soil and climate. Since Turnbull was to be the on-site manager, he found it prudent to buy a 300-acre private cotton plantation for himself on a neck of land adjoining the main plantation to the north. The whole venture had the aspect of a proprietorship, perhaps the last one of its kind in North America.[3]

Fig. 2.1. Dr. Andrew Turnbull, proprietor of the New Smyrna Plantation. Courtesy of the St. Augustine Historical Society, St. Augustine, Florida.

Turnbull established his family in a house in St. Augustine and began preparing for 500 Greek colonists. Through his agent in Charleston, Henry Laurens, he ordered supplies, slaves, and cattle to be sent to the plantation, and he began construction on three houses on his own land: the manor house for the Turnbull family; a house for the head carpenter, William Watson; and a third dwelling for a Mr. Davis, who appears to have been one of Turnbull's agents and a man knowledgeable about local cultivation due to his prior residence in the Mosquitoes area.

Recruiting the Colonists

Once his own plantation was underway, Andrew Turnbull mounted an expedition to the Mediterranean to recruit colonists. In slightly less than a year, he had enlisted 1,403 individuals to sail to the New World with him. Although recruitment of Greeks was difficult because of Turkish interference, Turnbull's agents found about fifty Greeks on Corsica who were willing to join the expedition. Turnbull himself was able to secure additional Greek families from the mountainous areas of the Peloponnesos. Smaller numbers came from the Greek islands and probably from the Greek colony on the island of Minorca.[4] Turnbull also recruited 110 young single men from Leghorn on the Italian peninsula, but by far the largest number, perhaps as many as 1,000, came from the island of Minorca in the Balearic Islands off the coast of Spain. England acquired Minorca in the same treaty as the Floridas, so Turnbull used Mahon—famed as of the best deep water ports in the world—as his staging area.

At that time, the Minorcan *isleños* were suffering from crop failure and resulting starvation. Unpredictable weather for several years, including a severe unseasonable freeze in 1766, destroyed the crops. Pleas to the British governor for importation of wheat and barley brought poor results, as other areas in the Mediterranean likewise had suffered from the disastrous weather. In 1767, the year before the colonial expedition departed, the death rate on Minorca increased dramatically—as much as two to three times the normal number in several towns. With relatives and friends dying around them, it was easy to attract immigrants to the New World. According to oral tradition, Mercadal became a ghost town after so many people left. To keep his flock company and to ensure their spiritual well-being, the Catholic priest from Mercadal, Fr. Pedro Camps, sailed with his parishioners, having obtained a promise from Andrew Turnbull of 300 pesos a year in compensation. Fr. Bartolemeo Casasnovas, an Augustinian monk from the farming town of Alayor, also joined the expedition.[5]

Recruits were indentured, although later claims and counterclaims make it difficult to determine for how long. The only contract that has been found to date was published more than 100 years later in a book on the history of Minorca and is signed only by Andrew Turnbull, with no signatures from other parties to the contract. The document calls for the "peasants" to work on equal shares with the proprietor(s) for ten years, at which time they would receive 100 shares of land for each head-of-family and an additional fifty shares for each family member. In addition to the ordinary farmers, skilled craftsmen were signed on for fewer years to work at a salary. For example, Louis Margau, evidently a Frenchman, was contracted to work for Turnbull as a blacksmith for five years. He must have been a skilled worker, because, at the request of Margau's wife, Rafela Triay, a Minorcan, he was released from jail in order to go. He was to receive fifty French crowns the first year, with ten crowns added each year thereafter plus better food rations than the ordinary workers. Then, at the end of his contract period, he was to receive the land promised to him. Given the scant documentation on the contracts, it seems very likely that they were actually all verbal agreements, and the one written by Turnbull was left behind for bureaucratic purposes. Removal of 1,000 people from a constituency with a population of 27,000 required documentation.[6]

The ocean trip was not easy, and several of the eight ships were blown off course. However, only approximately 148 died on the crossing—mostly old people and children, according to Turnbull's report. This fatality rate of 10.5 percent was within the range of 10–20 percent expected for transatlantic passage of emigrants or detachments of soldiers in the late eighteenth century. Worse was to come when the settlers reached Florida.

Initially, Governor Grant wrote ecstatically to the Count of Shelbourne, "This, my Lord, I believe is the largest importation of White inhabitants that ever was brought into America at a time." Two years later his enthusiasm was considerably tempered as he made a plea to the British authorities for monetary relief, "to repair the first fault [of Turnbull's] of exceeding the number of people to be imported." Looking at the record, it seems doubtful that adequate preparations were made for the expected 500 people, certainly not for the 1,255 who actually landed.[7]

The size of the enterprise created problems from the very beginning. Turnbull's original seven-year plan, based on half of the plantation—the 20,000 acres that were at that time in his name—called for the importation of 75 white families during the first year, each family to comprise a man, a woman, and two children. He also planned to purchase 20 black slaves. By the fourth year, the number of slaves was to be increased to 60; by the fifth year, 43 more white families were to be imported, bringing the number to 110 families (440 individuals). An orderly plan likewise was developed for employing overseers and constructing necessary buildings. Turnbull recorded an expected outlay and income for the project including shares for the settlers and profits for the partners. Multiplied by two, and including Duncan's 20,000-acre grant, we see that he planned for no more than 600 persons to arrive in the first year, and instead more than twice that number landed. Had Turnbull followed his original tight plan, the plantation's outcome would have been quite different.[8]

Instead, the large number of people actually brought to the plantation necessitated a huge outlay of funds. Some began to question whether an undertaking of this scale should be in private hands. The English partners were dismayed as the bills mounted, yet they felt compelled to continue to support the plantation or else suffer the loss of monies already sunk in the endeavor. At the instigation of Governor Grant, the government offered some relief in the form of supplies and a bounty on the indigo exported, but it was not enough. Turnbull's two partners settled the matter in 1769, agreeing to pay £24,000 toward the latest bills in exchange for reducing Turnbull's share in the company. His interest was decreased from one-third to one-fifth, with each of the others retaining two-fifths interest. In addition, subsequent grants obtained by Turnbull were to be allocated in the same fashion. With this chastisement and consequent damage to his reputation, it is not surprising that Andrew Turnbull was frantic to turn a profit.[9]

Rebellion and Death

In early August of 1768, ships carrying a large contingent of the Italian and Greek recruits arrived at the plantation to find appalling living conditions. Lacking sufficient housing, many of the earlier arrivals had built themselves rude, palm-thatched huts (*casas de guano*)—dirt floored, leaky in the rain, and rife with insects. The food was inadequate and the work of clearing the land onerous. People were dying at an alarming rate. This was not the expected land of promise. Less than two months after the first ships anchored at St. Augustine, the laborers' discontent turned to rebellion. One day after Turnbull conducted a distinguished party from the Carolinas on a tour of his enterprise and accompanied them to the Mount Oswald plantation to the north, most of the Italians and some of the Greeks mounted a full-scale attempt to escape to Havana. The insurgents plundered the warehouses, commandeered a ship, and threatened death to any of the Minorcan islanders who informed Turnbull of their actions. They cut off the ears and some of the fingers of the chief overseer, Mr. Cutter, who eventually died of his wounds, and also mortally wounded Dr. William Stork, one of the visitors, who had remained in the settlement and was walking about armed only with an umbrella. The 300 rebels made the mistake of spending three days loading the escape vessel, meanwhile enjoying the stolen rations, especially the rum. During that time, Turnbull who had been informed, sent a message to the governor in St. Augustine. As the overloaded rebel vessel attempted to leave the harbor, the *East Florida* arrived with troops aboard, and the revolt ended abruptly. Authorities tried the ring leaders and sentenced three men. Elia Medici, convicted for stealing a cow, was allowed to go free after he performed the execution of Carlo Forni, the leader of the revolt, and of Guisippi Massadoli, who killed Dr. Stork. Turnbull and the other planters in the area asked for a detachment of soldiers to guard the settlement. Governor Grant complied with this request, but a planned fort was never built. For the rest of the plantation's existence, however, it was an armed camp.[10]

About a year after this large-scale rebellion, several other indentured laborers tried to escape from New Smyrna. In depositions given at St. Augustine, they reported continuing abuses at the plantation. Antonio Stephanopoli testified that he had seen ten or more, sometimes as many as fifteen, Minorcans dying in a day. When he was recaptured he received 110 lashes; for sixteen months, he wore a fifteen-pound chain, even when at work. His food allotment was cut, and he believed that he would have starved to death if some of the Minorcans had not given him some corn and peas. Giosefa Marcatto, another deponent, told a similar story of "being so ill used, and almost starved to death, he agreed with some other men to run away, but was catched and brought back and confined in Goal, with his legs ironed." These and other atrocities continued for some time.[11]

Both British sources and the depositions by laborers reported that a population crash of major proportions occurred in the plantation's first two years. By the end of 1769, about half of the colonists, more than 600 individuals, were dead, with multiple deaths often occurring in one day. As the death rate rose, the birth rate correspondingly fell, with only five babies born and living long enough to be baptized in 1769.[12] Baptisms were the sole records kept by the priests during the plantation years, so only the sketchy comments in the official records and in the reports of Father Camps sent to the bishop in Havana suggest the causes of the dramatic population collapse. The principal causes given for deaths were scurvy, starvation, bad water, "dropsy," fevers, pleurisy, gangrene, and particularly, malaria. The area was aptly named *Los Mosquitos* in Spanish times.[13]

If the testimony in the depositions is accurate, a number of New Smyrna workers also died as a result of severe punishment or from starvation when their food allotment was cut. Whether these were outright murders or whether it was a matter of one more assault on already weakened bodies is often difficult to tell.

While never easy to document, demoralization probably also played a part in the death rates. These indentured servants were undergoing what was then called "seasoning" when applied to slaves adjusting to the New World environment—an adjustment involving interrelated physical and emotional elements. As in the case of the Africans, most of the colonists experienced catastrophic times on both sides of the Atlantic and survived the deaths of many friends and relatives. The priests found themselves more frequently conducting burial masses than celebrating marriages or baptisms.

The Plantation Landscape

The land on the large tracts that made up the New Smyrna Plantation was far from uniform. Along the river to the east ran a relatively high coastal ridge composed of an underlying vein of coquina rock (donax shell aggregate) capped, at least part of the way, by shell kitchen-middens created by aboriginal inhabitants.[14]

Behind the ridge stretched miles of intermixed and banded areas of pinelands, both saltwater and freshwater marshes, savannahs, and wet hammocks (hardwood forest zones). The westernmost section, excellent land for growing certain crops, stretched for miles parallel to the coast. This section became known as Turnbull's Back Swamp, a designation continued on maps for 200 years. However, even the best soils of the hardwood hammock and freshwater swamp areas were described by the English as "grey sand." To improve the poor soils, marsh mud or green manure (decaying plant matter) became the preferred fertilizers. Although DeBrahm voiced the general opinion when he advised that "Dung increases the Heat more, than is necessary, besides infecting the ground with worms and New seeds," the farmers of Minorca used animal dung to enrich their crops; it is reasonable to assume that they did the same in their kitchen gardens in New Smyrna, since they kept chickens and occasionally cows.[15]

The deficiencies of the soil at New Smyrna were offset by a long growing season, including twenty-five more growing days than St. Augustine enjoyed; adequate and usually well-distributed rainfall; and a good transportation lane. The river, called the *Río Surruque* by the Spanish and renamed the Hillsborough River by the English, was actually a marine estuary on the other side of one of the buffer islands that lie like sections of a dotted line along the south Atlantic seaboard. The New Smyrna Plantation was purposely situated in the immediate vicinity of Mosquito Inlet, the first navigable inlet south of St. Augustine. It drew nine feet at high tide and was relatively easy for mid-sized craft to negotiate. In addition to these natural advantages, Governor Grant commissioned the King's Road to be extended to the Mosquitoes area. William Bartram, the naturalist who accompanied DeBrahm during his survey of the area, "observed then, where New Smyrna now stands, a spacious Indian mount and avenue, which stood near the banks of the river; the avenue ran on a straight line back, through the groves, across the ridge, and terminated at the verge of natural savannas and ponds." The Indian trails, built on by the Spanish and later used by the English, most likely were based originally on the paths made by the larger wildlife.[16]

Fig. 2.2. Minorcan worker of the mid-eighteenth century, with short-handled hoe. Courtesy of the St. Augustine Historical Society, St. Augustine, Florida.

The plantation grants were modified parallelograms slanting back from the waterway, giving, by their shape, maximum waterfront property per acreage. Within these confines, the fields and buildings were laid out somewhat in conformity with the natural landscape and partly along the lines of some of the patterns common at the time in the Carolinas and Georgia.[17] South of the proprietor's complex on Turnbull's own plantation, the worker plots were stretched out every 210 feet along the shell bluff fronting the waterway for eight miles. About two-thirds of the way down this string of habitations, Turnbull placed a central complex containing craft shops, three dormitories for the young single men, warehouses, "stores for provisions," an indigo house, and barracks for the military detachment. This complex was served by a stone wharf, the remains of which are still visible today at low tide. The Church of San Pedro and its *convento* were in this complex or nearby. The impressive coquina ruin still standing on the bayfront north of where the central "town" existed may have been the foundations of the church, although it has been identified variously as a fort, Turnbull's mansion, or a warehouse. In an urbane frame of mind, Andrew Turnbull wrote to Lord Shelbourne, describing the plantation:

"The nearness of the Hutts to one another gives the whole a resemblance to an Eastern or Chinese plantation."[18]

It is doubtful that the colonists shared Turnbull's quaint enthusiasm. If importing too many people was his first mistake, his second mistake was settling the families in violation of their own cultural patterns. Like indigenous peoples all over southern Europe, these Mediterraneans were accustomed to living in densely populated villages, going out by day to cultivate their farm plots, and returning at night to the company of their families and friends. Living more than one-third of a mile from one's close kin was *muy lejos* (very far). Turnbull, in contrast, was more familiar with the crossroads-hinterland tradition, in which habitations were scattered around the countryside on individual plots of land. Once the plantation broke up and the Minorcans moved to St. Augustine, the village pattern was reaffirmed, giving mute evidence of their own cultural preference.[19]

The Plantation Production

When William Bartram traversed the New Smyrna landscape, he observed no cleared fields or habitations but did comment on the Indian mounds (one of them quite large) and numerous orange trees planted casually by Spanish horsemen. The Spanish had also engaged in cattle ranching, but whether Joaquín de Florencia, whose grant, Santa Ana de Afafa, later became the New Smyrna plantation, used his land for that purpose has not been determined. In the British Period and immediately prior to the founding of the plantation, "liveoakers" worked the area felling trees to use in ship-building.[20]

Before Turnbull first began to set up the plantation, he contracted for cattle that were "bred to the salts," thus able to subsist on marsh grass, a fallback forage in lean pasture times. A slave named "Grey Eyes" drove the cattle down from Georgia using the newly constructed road from St. Augustine. Once Turnbull had his cattle range established, he broke in the main crop-growing area, where he experimented with several crops, exporting some rice in the early days of the plantation. He also planted olive and mulberry trees for silkworm culture, but neither did well. Turnbull even imported cochineal insects in the belief that the red dye extracted from the females could be a cash crop. Like all Florida planters, he grew corn and *menestras* (mixed dried vegetables) for occasional export, but indigo became and remained by far Turnbull's principal production.[21]

In the days of manufactured chemical dyes, it is difficult to appreciate how highly natural indigo was prized for its blue brilliance and subtle rosy undertones, but in the late eighteenth century, England was paying dearly

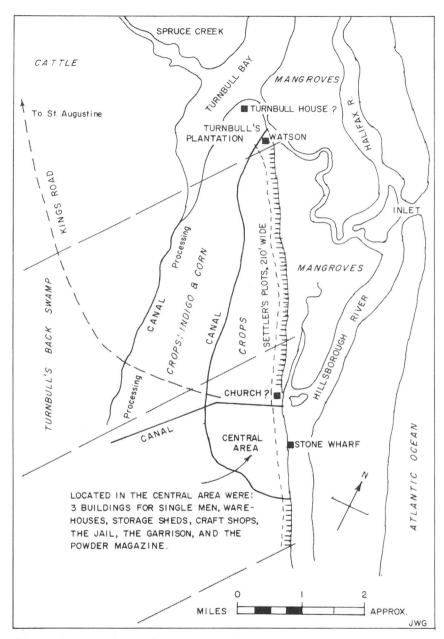

SPRUCE CREEK

CATTLE

TURNBULL BAY

MANGROVES

HALIFAX R.

↑
To St. Augustine

■ TURNBULL HOUSE ?

TURNBULL'S
PLANTATION

■ WATSON

KINGS ROAD

INLET

Processing

CANAL

CROPS: INDIGO & CORN

CANAL

CROPS

SETTLER'S PLOTS, 210' WIDE

MANGROVES

HILLSBOROUGH RIVER

TURNBULL'S BACK SWAMP

Processing

CANAL

CHURCH ? ■

CANAL

CENTRAL
AREA

■ STONE WHARF

ATLANTIC OCEAN

N
↗

LOCATED IN THE CENTRAL AREA WERE:
3 BUILDINGS FOR SINGLE MEN, WARE-
HOUSES, STORAGE SHEDS, CRAFT SHOPS,
THE JAIL, THE GARRISON, AND THE
POWDER MAGAZINE.

0   1   2

MILES   APPROX.

JWG

Map 4. Conjectural map of New Smyrna Plantation. De Brahm map of 1769 used as a base. From *Mullet on the Beach: The Minorcans of Florida, 1768–1788*, by Patricia C. Griffin (Gainesville: University Press of Florida, 1991).

in the world market for it. Indigo is a warm-climate crop, and although England had Caribbean colonies, they were largely devoted to get-rich-quick sugar-cropping. Carolinians had been growing indigo for several decades, but their crop was of an inferior quality, perhaps because of the shorter growing season, inept processing, or, in some cases, purposeful adulteration with clay and other materials. Carolina indigo brought only one-third the price of the later Florida product on the British market. DeBrahm boasted, "the Indigo has really been brought to Perfection, equal to that made at Quatamala [Guatemala] in New Spain which is estimated the best manufactured in the World."[22]

An easily grown legume, indigo was optimally planted on high hammock ground or in drained swamp locations, when the danger of frost was past. Growers sometimes drove cattle into the fields to tamp down the shallowly planted seeds and to weed the indigo, which the livestock rarely ate. In cooler climates indigo needed full sun to come to maturity. However, in the hot Florida climate, the plant also flourished in partial shade, and thus in New Smyrna it could be sown before the land was completely cleared. Another advantage in the mid-Florida coastal climate was a yield of four to five cuttings a year, in contrast to two to three cuttings in the cooler climates of South Carolina and Georgia. The plant is a perennial, although quality falls in two to five years and reseeding is necessary.[23] DeBrahm described how Floridians ingeniously controlled the crop's main pest by digging three-foot-wide trenches around the indigo fields. Caterpillars trying to cross the barren ditch died for lack of moisture. Some of the smaller ditches located at New Smyrna may have been used for caterpillar control rather than for irrigation.[24]

Workers harvested the long slender, stalks of the indigo, with their branching leaves, early in the morning from June through November and even in December in good years. They took great care not to bruise the leaves or destroy the "blush" on the fresh harvest. In well-controlled operations, each cutting was accomplished just as the pink and yellow flowers began to come into bloom. The leaves contained the most indigo, so the careful overseer made sure that the number of stalks included in the difficult processing was minimal.

Growers processed the indigo in two or three vats, graduated in size from large to small. Later observers saw the ruins of coquina-stone vats, but carpenter William Watson also built "22 Double [wooden] setts of Indigo Vatts at £50 Each." A set of vats was required for each seven or eight acres of indigo grown, and Turnbull installed more than 300 sets of indigo vats in the early years of the plantation.[25] Workers placed the newly harvested plants in the first and largest vat, covered them with water, and allowed them to ferment for up to twenty-four hours, depending on the air temperature. Using contrivances that resembled bottomless barrels or wooden-paddle beaters, they beat the liquid continually until a yellowish fluid developed. That they drew off into the second vat, where oxidation and precipitation took place. After the indigo particles sank to the bottom of the vat, workers drained off the water and left the remaining mess to dehydrate either in the same vat or in a third vat. Eventually, they hung the sludge to dry in cloth sleeves, then rolled it into long sheets, and finally cut it into bricks. The bricks were placed onto shelves in an open shed to dry further before shipment. In the early days North American indigo manufacturers used stale urine to hasten the processing; however, by the time indigo was being processed in New Smyrna, growers used other reagents in the beating vat. The documents mention lime water (slaked lime or calcium hydroxide), which was easily made by calcinating shells. However, Turnbull also made barilla (sodium carbonate) by burning the marsh plant salt wort, and he may have been using that product to process his indigo.

Certainly it is known that Turnbull experimented to perfect the quality of his indigo. After his first crop had an undesirable purplish hue, which he likened to an "Episcopal colour," he consulted with a Mr. Skinner (probably Alexander Skinner) to improve his crop. He also consulted with John Ross, a nearby plantation owner, and with a poor white named Jemmey Wallace who had a knack with the processing of the dyestuff. Known as an "Indigo Cracker" Wallace carried bits of indigo around in his pocket, absentmindedly sniffing it from time to time. Turnbull combined local advice with knowledge of chemical reactions gained through his medical practice, and experimented with the length of vat time and the amount and timing of the use of lime water. As a result, he enjoyed a fair degree of success: His innovations were widely known in the province and many followed his lead in careful production of the finished product.[26]

While the proprietor was basking in his success—11,558 pounds produced in the first successful harvest of 1771—the colonists not only had to grow the difficult crop but also had to clear land and establish kitchen gardens to ward off starvation. Once the indigo was ready to be harvested, they worked to exhaustion in what amounted to a twenty-four-hour operation. Next followed the processing, which was so hazardous that the Spanish Crown prohibited the Indians in Guatemala from engaging in the work. Poisonous vapors rising from the rotting vegetation were chemically equivalent to that of rotting carrion and feces, with attendant health problems. The indole produced led to headaches, nausea, respiratory or other infections, and sometimes pneumonia, as the workers at times came in contact with the infectious solid matter as well as breathing the almost intolerable fumes. The noxious mess attracted so many flies that even cattle had to be kept at a safe distance. Those toiling at the vats were not as lucky as the livestock. Although the first two vats were somewhat noxious, the last or third vat was called the "devil's vat" because the effluvia emanating from the last part of the processing was especially bad.

Plantation Work Groups and Regime

Although the work force suffered extremely during the nine years of New Smyrna's existence and eventually won sanctuary in St. Augustine, Turnbull attempted a scientific and efficient plantation management. For his overseers he recruited knowledgeable white men, whom he directed personally; below the overseers he placed drivers, known as "corporals," who were usually single Greeks and Italians rather than Minorcans enmeshed in family networks. A few of the drivers, such as Simon, mentioned prominently in the depositions, may have been experienced black men from Carolina. Turnbull also used blacks to whip the workers who failed to live up to expectations.

The role of the black slaves at New Smyrna remains an enigma. Turnbull's own cotton plantation, it seems, was largely manned by black slaves, but because no eighteenth-century map of this plantation has yet been found, there is no evidence of where they were housed. Although only scattered documentary evidence of individual black workers exists, it is clear that the plantation work force included gangs of slaves. We know this because when the Greek colonist Anthonio Stephanopoli twice attempted to escape from the plantation, Turnbull threatened to "make him work in the field among the Negroes untill [*sic*] he died."[27]

Craftsmen enjoyed the most-favored position at New Smyrna, being outside the usual line of authority but apparently directly under Turnbull's or the head overseer's supervision. If craftsmen created any difficulties, however, they were demoted to the field or worse. Turnbull punished the blacksmith Louis Margau because he asked to be released from his indenture at the end of the allotted time. Margau reported that "the said Dr. Turnbull asked this deponent to follow him, which happened to be to the Goal, and ordered him fifty lashes, which he received from a Negro and then put this deponent in irons and confined him to Goal without any Subsistence except a little Indian corn and water." Turnbull ordered Margau's wife to work in the fields, although she was still nursing her six-

Fig. 2.3. Bayfront ruins in New Smyrna Beach. Photo by Patricia C. Griffin.

month-old baby. At this point, the desperate blacksmith signed a paper agreeing to work four more years as a common laborer. Some fifteen months later, when things were not going well at the blacksmith shop, Turnbull reinstated Margau in his position but still held him to the increased contract time.[28]

Turnbull organized tasks and work groups by age and sex and excluded almost no one from the difficult labor. Men dug the irrigation canals while women carried the dirt in baskets to add to the spoil pile. Even children worked hard. One poignant deposition described how a driver, Louis Ponchintena, beat and forced the ten-year-old Guillermo Vens into the fields although he was sick. When the young boy could not work, the driver ordered the other boys to stone him, and he consequently died in the field.[29] Turnbull even required pregnant women to work in the field. Giosefa Lurance testified that his sister-in-law, Paola Lurance, "being in the field at work" was propositioned by the driver Simon. When the woman refused his advances, the driver beat her despite her entreaties, and three days later she was delivered of a dead child.[30]

Turnbull's work organization violated the pattern common in the Mediterranean, where investment of physical energy was at the worker's discretion and family groups worked together with a diffuse leadership pattern. The tools Turnbull furnished his workers were also of a design foreign to the Minorcans. In Minorca and throughout the Mediterranean, short-handled implements were traditional, but Turnbull provided them with Crowleys Broad Hoes and other husky, long-handled implements, necessitating a muscular realignment for the workers.[31]

Turnbull also fell afoul of the work/leisure patterns of his workers. In the Mediterranean, where winter crops like wheat and barley were grown, the harvest was finished by St. John's Day (June 24) and the rest of the summer was devoted to social festivities, with a brief interruption for the late summer grape harvest. In Florida, however, colonists had to process indigo from June through November, their customary holiday time. In Minorca, holidays occupied about one-fourth of the people's time, but Turnbull seems to have agreed with one eighteenth-century Englishman who concluded that in Minorca "the multitude of feasts that are maintained by the people in voluptuous indolence, set a dangerous example to the inhabitants of any country." He contrasted this way of life, saying, "on the other hand the trade and manufactures of a Protestant country are carried on with briskness and alacrity. The people have but few holy days and are not very strict in their observation of them."[32] A Greek man, Pietro Cozisacy, testified that "he hath served Dr. Turnbull Sundays, Holidays and all times whatsoever but that he hath always been badly used by the said Dr. Turnbull." Several other men told a similar story. For example, Giosefa Marcato complained of "working days and nights, not even Sunday excepted without any rest." Rafel Hernandez likewise told of being beaten for refusing to work on a Holy day.[33]

Plantation Subsistence

In the plantation's earliest days, Governor Grant took a paternal interest in the enterprise and helped Turnbull provide the settlers with corn gruel and small portions of salt pork on which to survive. Turnbull also encouraged the people to grow kitchen gardens. Because the plantation was settled in the middle of the summer, however, the colonists had missed the optimal winter and best spring plantings. The subsistence repertoire of the Mediterraneans was extensive and related to long experience with the climate, plants, and animals in their homelands; eventually, they learned to adapt to their new environment. For example, in Minorca they relied on dandelion roots and figs in lean years, whereas they learned in New

Smyrna to make flour by processing the roots of the wild coontie (*zamia*) and accustomed themselves to broth made with acorns from the numerous live oak trees.[34] Once the workers could grow a few of the common vegetables in New Smyrna, they were able to return to the vegetable stews and soups of their former diets. They learned to use clams and other seafood to enhance the taste, and they made a remarkable discovery that the meat of the gopher tortoise, common in coastal Florida, was delicious when added to a vegetable stew. To season both gopher stew and clam chowder, they added the very spicy datil peppers growing in the region.[35]

The Minorcan islanders were accustomed to supplementing their diets by fishing, snaring birds, and hunting small game, such as rabbits, but in New Smyrna such activities clashed with the plantation routine; workers alleged they were forced to eat snakes and other unpleasant vermin when Turnbull confiscated their clams and fish. Turnbull denied this, saying, "every encouragement and assistance was given to them for fishing, in which they became so dexterous and successful that many families had for the most part great quantities of dried fish in their houses; fish being so plenty in the river, on the lands of which their houses were built, that one man could generally catch as much in one hour, as would serve his family in twenty-four, almost all having small canoes for that purpose."[36] Probably the truth lies in between these two contradictory accounts. Mullet and other fish ran in late summer and early fall, the very time that the indigo needed attention. It seems likely that Turnbull and his overseers discouraged fishing during those months. But with habitations right on the water side of the plantation, it was not difficult to slip off to go fishing in their homemade canoes. Then, and for a hundred years afterward, the estuary of Mosquitoes area was described as teaming with fish, so numerous that they jumped into the canoes at times. In fact, this section of the coast was so well known as a good fishing ground that fishermen from Cuba came up to work the locale as they had during Spanish times.[37]

Turnbull prohibited his workers from hunting, and they charged that he actually picked through some of their meals searching for meat or fish. In the British Isles, hunting and fishing were the preserve of the gentry, and poaching incurred severe punishment for the common people. During the British domination of their homeland, the Minorcans were "disarmed all over the island" with the exception of the "Spanish cavaliers" and a few designated hunters. Meanwhile, "the gentlemen [including English officers were] permitted to wear swords, and firearms, as well as for the security of their houses, as for their diversion in the field."[38] Mart Stewart, writing of the Georgia experience, makes the point that gentlemen owning large grants had control of all uses of their land, and that maintaining certain traditional customs was part of setting the social order in proper balance. Turnbull kept an African hunter, London, to supply game for his own table in accordance with the ancient custom, as did Denys Rolle at Rolles Town on the St. Johns River. The workers charged that when Turnbull discovered that his hunter had sold or given them meat, the angry proprietor had London whipped so severely that he later died. Turnbull denied that charge, averring that London died two years later while on the plantation of Mr. [William] Ross.[39]

A Time of Promise

In spite of start-up problems and the hardships suffered by the settlers, the middle years of the plantation's existence lulled the proprietor and colonists alike into a sense of optimism. By the time of the first indigo export from the plantation in 1772, the workers had cleared a total of 1,600 acres of land, approximately 180 acres of which was devoted to the colonists' habitations and gardens, and for the central town complex. The remaining 1,420 acres were devoted to plantation cropping proper. If approximately 100 acres were used for corn and other crops, approximately 1,320 acres remained available for indigo cultivation.[40]

Turnbull was beginning to turn a profit for himself and his partners, and he had joined the East Florida plantocracy. Resident plantation owners, including the governor, controlled the court system and the governing council, of which Turnbull was secretary, and together they made decisions favoring their own economic ventures.

Although life was still difficult for the colonists, they were enduring the hardships in expectation of the end of their indentures and the subsequent receipt of the promised farm plots. By 1772 the tragic time of starvation was over, and the 100 houses built offered workers much better protection from the elements. Demographically the population was in good balance, the death rate having decreased by 1771, and births exceeded deaths by a good margin. Father Camps, writing to the bishop in Havana in 1772, reported that "in the first year many people died because of the defects of the air, and scanty room, for lack of homes. But now things are better, and in the past year nine children and eleven adults died, and there were born twenty-nine." The priest counted 600 in his parish and noted that the Italians and Corsican Greeks (who were Roman Catholic) were by that time married to Minorcan women. As these peoples from various parts of the Mediterranean coalesced into a closely interacting community, the whole group gradually became known as the Minorcans because of their predominance in number. Only the Greeks from the Peloponnesos, being of the Greek Orthodox religion, remained somewhat separate. Father Camps described the church in which he preached every Sunday and at Lent and the "high respect" with which he believed the English viewed his flock. He added that the "Lady of the Lord of the plantation is a Catholic, and very devout, frequenting the church and in general giving good example."[41]

Indian Contacts

The Mediterranean settlers at New Smyrna experienced an unexpected scare when in May of 1771 the Seminole leader Cowkeeper camped his band on the edge of the settlement.[42] New Smyrna lay in a disputed zone, and it was unclear where English lands ended and Indian lands began. Nonetheless, the Seminoles considered the colonists as interlopers. Furthermore, Cowkeeper had long been allied with the English against the Spanish and considered the colonists to be very like the Spanish in language and complexion. Within a month of the settlers' arrival, the same group, decorated with black war paint, visited Governor Grant in St. Augustine, demanding to know how these "Spaniards" had come to settle in the Mosquitoes. Governor Grant, a man skilled in Indian negotiations, reassured them that the Minorcans were not "White people" but nevertheless were loyal British subjects who had come to the New World to help their "brothers," the English, to cultivate the new lands.[43] This explanation temporarily satisfied the Seminoles. However, three years later they were back in the settlement itself in search of a group of Spaniards and Yamasee Indians, also their enemies, whom they heard were at the Mosquitoes. On this occasion, Turnbull placated Cowkeeper's band by wining and dining them and allowing them to tour his estates. At a final feast, some of the Seminoles imbibed too much and ran through the settlement terrorizing the settlers, stealing provisions, and threatening to kill a calf belonging to a Minorcan family. Cowkeeper flogged the perpetrators, and Turnbull presented the Indians with a calf from his own herd. Mollified, the Seminoles finally left.

The End of the Plantation

Indians were not the undoing of New Smyrna, however. The explanation for its failure lies in a complex interaction of international rivalries and economic factors, in human relations, and in the vagaries of the natural world. Governor Grant departed Florida for London in 1772, and the subsequent inept administration by Lt. Gov. Moultrie left the province a shambles. In March of 1774, Lt. Col. Patrick Tonyn arrived in St. Augustine to assume the governorship of Florida. Floridians had awaited the new governor's arrival with optimism, but they were soon and sadly disappointed. Whereas Grant had been an able administrator, Tonyn was not; whereas Grant was skilled in Indian relations, Tonyn was not; whereas Grant was a part of the gentry, Tonyn was not; whereas Grant was the leader of the social life in the province, Tonyn dined at home alone with his wife and drank water, not choice Madeira. Tonyn's administrative and social skills were sorely lacking, so political harmony was not restored; in fact, matters deteriorated.[44]

Patrick Tonyn and Andrew Turnbull took an instant dislike to each other. Tonyn was well aware that some of the remaining gentry in town had promoted Turnbull to be named governor, and Turnbull's high-placed friends in England had worked for his appointment as well. Tonyn considered himself the superior patriot and tried to prove that Turnbull's sympathies lay with the rebelling colonists to the north. In turn, Turnbull systematically snubbed the new governor socially. He did not allow Mrs. Turnbull to return Mrs. Tonyn's original social call, because it was thought at the time that the Tonyns were not actually married. Operating under colonial social assumptions (the larger the plantation, the higher the planter stood in the colonial plantocracy), Turnbull also demeaned the new governor as the owner of an insignificant plantation, which he compared negatively to his premier plantation at New Smyrna. As a result, Governor Tonyn did everything to undermine the plantation and nothing to encourage its survival.

Then nature also intervened. The deforested hammock soils had deteriorated, and the drained swamps suffered the same fate. John Bartram, William Bartram's father, recorded the effect on indigo in his 1775–76 diary: "I observed ye adjacent higher ground which was nothing but sand . . . there was indigo planted, but it was thin and poor . . . when the ground is more mellow & ye roots rotten it may do better but I believe it soon wears out." Francis Fatio reported in 1785, "In 1771 some of the inhabitants tried the planting of indigo. The quality was good (or nearly so) as that of Guatemala; but the light soil did not yield the same quantity as in the neighboring provinces."[45] Adding to the problem of depleted soils was the severe drought that set in in 1773 and continued into 1775.

To cope with the shortage of rainfall, Turnbull constructed an irrigation system so extensive that a good part of the elaborate network is still

Fig. 2.4. Canal on the New Smyrna Plantation. By permission of Gary Luther.

visible near the town of New Smyrna Beach. Some canals and ditches were already in place for drainage and to provide water needed for processing the indigo. Now Turnbull's workers dug canals that were deep and wide, with smaller feeder canals and with headgates to control the flow. The largest canals also allowed water transport. Turnbull likened the hydrologic pattern he established to the Egyptian system he had observed in his former travels. He declared that "this is new to American planters and is talked of as Chimeral; but as I have seen the utility of such modes of culture. . . . I go on, being certain of succeeding."[46]

Large mounds of dirt left from that project were still visible on the plantation's location more than a century later. A. E. Douglass, an amateur archaeologist, believing them to be Indian mounds, was greatly puzzled to find no traces of aboriginal inhabitants when he excavated them in 1882. He reported, "we found not a thing, no pottery, no burial, no relics." The largest mound in what came to be known as Rock House Hammock was 18 feet high and 110 feet in diameter. Douglass reported it as "peculiarly constructed," since 2 or 3 feet from the top he unearthed a solid coquina platform. This may have been a large spoil heap used as an observation platform or even to anchor the windmill that the carpenter William Watson reported building.[47]

In terms of cost/benefit, the installation of this elaborate irrigation system probably was not worth the amount of labor effort expended, compared with increased profits for the owners. The indigo exports fell from 10,262 pounds in 1773 to 1,633 pounds in 1774. The modest increase to 1,948 pounds exported in 1775 likely resulted from some rains late in the summer, rather than from the irrigation system alone. When nature again smiled, 6,390 pounds were exported in 1776—the last year of a substantial crop on the plantation.[48]

The drought affected the kitchen gardens as well as the cash crops, and again the Minorcans faced starvation. The death rate began to show a steady rise, continuing in an upward trend until the breakup of the plantation. The birth rate correspondingly took a plunge. Demoralization set in, exacerbated by Turnbull's failure to honor contracts with the craftsmen. So far as is known, neither common workers nor craftsmen ever received the promised profit shares.

Worker discontent mounted after Father Casasnovas was deported from the province in 1774. The Minorcans recounted that Casasnovas petitioned Turnbull on their behalf about mistreatment and contracts, but the proprietor failed to respond. When the priest took their case to the authorities in St. Augustine, Turnbull convinced the governor that Casasnovas was part of a Spanish intrigue involving Cuban fishermen putting into the inlet.

Seminole scouts were also keeping track of the Cuban fishermen and of New Smyrna. As Brent Weisman discusses in chapter 7, the Seminoles were dependent on their cattle herds and on corn for sustenance. The drought of 1773–75 had hit them as well, and when green forage failed in the interior, it was their custom to drive their cattle to the coast to subsist on marsh grass. The Seminoles also adapted to necessity by raiding, and at New Smyrna they stole cattle and raided houses for supplies. Some of them found women's clothes, dressed themselves, and danced about the settlement. This time the colonists took their complaints directly to the governor. Governor Tonyn responded by threatening to execute any Indians caught in similar crimes, but this warning failed to keep the Seminoles from camping on the edge of the settlement next to Turnbull's cowpen for the rest of the following fall.

In the meantime, the course of the American Revolution eventually led to an open rupture between the governor and Turnbull. Florida was a loyalist colony, and the governor mustered as many men as he could to create the East Florida Rangers. Still needing additional recruits, he enlisted Creek Indians and considered enlisting enslaved Africans as well. Tonyn also wrote to Turnbull requesting a report on the potential military contribution of the young men at New Smyrna. Turnbull, in a stilted but polite reply, indicated that there were 200 men of fighting age, but, after avowing their loyalty to his Majesty, concluded, "I think that it is a duty incumbent on me to beg Your Excellency would grant such a Protection for these industrious Foreigners, as may prevent their being disturbed from Agriculture, without which they, with their Families must starve."[49]

In actuality, the loyalty of the colonists was suspect, because it was known that Spain hoped to profit from the American Revolution by regaining the Floridas. Nearby plantation owners became alarmed, and Capt. Robert Bissett advised Governor Tonyn that the Minorcans were not to be trusted with firearms. He suggested that the authorities take the most "turbulent" among the Minorcans into custody to prevent them from joining the rebels in case of an invasion. From another quarter, it was rumored that the Georgia rebels had offered to come to the relief and deliverance of the Minorcans if they would join the cause for independence.[50]

Angered by Turnbull's refusal to let his plantation workers join loyalist forces, Tonyn accused both William Drayton and Andrew Turnbull of being implicated in the "Bryan affair"—an attempt to secure Indian lands on the St. Johns River, which the governor thought illegal. The governor planned to strip Drayton of his position as chief justice and Turnbull of his position of clerk of the council. Fearing that they would also be imprisoned, the two men escaped on a ship bound for England in March 1776 with the avowed intention of seeing Patrick Tonyn removed from the governorship.

Turnbull left his twenty-year old nephew, also named Andrew Turnbull, in charge at New Smyrna; although the younger Turnbull made a valiant effort, his age and inexperience militated against him. Not daring to approach the angry governor directly, he wrote his friend Arthur Gordon to beg that he and Mr. Penman petition the governor for more troops to guard the settlement, noting that among the "white people . . . there is a good number of them at present a little discontented." He believed that if more troops were not assigned to keep them in "awe," he could "see plainly that they [would] grow very insolent and unruly."[51]

Soon thereafter a disturbing rumor caused great consternation among the colonists. Variously ascribed to either Governor Tonyn or his wife, it alleged that the Minorcans would never receive lands in New Smyrna, because they were Roman Catholic. In 1776 and continuing into 1777, some of the colonists made clandestine trips to St. Augustine to request sanctuary there. At first, the governor ordered the petitioners to go home and attend to their crops, but eventually the matter fell to the court to decide. After a review of twenty-one depositions (filed by seventeen individuals), the court finally released the colonists from their indentures and permitted them to move to St. Augustine. In a mass exodus in the summer of 1777, they walked the dreary seventy-five miles down the King's road to St. Augustine, taking with them only what they could carry.[52]

Meanwhile, after failing to have Governor Tonyn removed, Turnbull returned from England to find the plantation a shambles. Learning that many of his workers had died in St. Augustine, he wrote to Lord Germain in protest. In the aftermath of the American Revolution, however, nothing came of his demands, and Turnbull eventually moved to Charleston, where he resumed a successful medical career. Turnbull and the heirs of Duncan and Grenville dissolved their partnership and, like other ruined Loyalists, filed land claims for their losses but received only minimal compensation.

Conclusion

Although acknowledging the New Smyrna plantation as the largest single pre-Revolutionary settlement in England's North American colonies, Bernard Bailyn, in his Pulitzer Prize-winning book *Voyagers to the West,* calls it the "most wasteful of human and material resources." He also argues that Andrew Turnbull was the worst of entrepreneurs, that the colonists were a "bizarre collection," and that the settlement was a "death camp." Bailyn's assessment mirrors that of Bernard Romans, who in 1775 described New Smyrna as a "Bashawship from the Levant," and Turnbull as a cruel and unprincipled man.[53]

Was Andrew Turnbull the cruel and evil taskmaster that he was made out to be? And was the plantation truly a failure? While the plantation ultimately failed, its significance was greater than Bailyn suggests. At New Smyrna, Turnbull laid down an English template that transformed the

Florida terrain. New Smyrna's departed workers left behind 3,107 cleared and cultivated acres, canals that crisscrossed the land, and an extensive built environment. Subsequent plantation owners on the same land built upon this altered landscape. Although the sole remnants of New Smyrna's extensive infrastructure are the large ruin on the waterfront, remains of the wharf, and some building foundations currently being unearthed by archaeologists, other evidence of the plantation's impact can be traced on the landscape. Indigo grows in wild profusion in places near New Smyrna, and in dry years remote descendants of the cochineal insects imported by Turnbull are found in cottony masses on the cactus plants.[54] Moreover, Turnbull's private cotton plantation served as a crucible for cotton-growing in the southern United States. One of Turnbull's overseers was John Earle, an early innovator in cotton-growing and processing. When Earle left the province, he gave Turnbull extensive notes and other materials, later used by Turnbull's eldest son Nichol on his large cotton plantation on Skidaway Island, Georgia. The cotton that Nichol Turnbull sent to England in 1787 is credited with being the first sizable export from the United States.

Notes

1. Although it generally has been assumed that Rolle's colonists were all beggars, vagrants, prostitutes, and other unsavory individuals, Robert Legg shows in *Pioneer in Xanadu, Denys Rolle: 1725–1797* (Hampshire: Blasinstoke Press, 1997) that some of those recruited were substantial persons who paid their own way to East Florida.

2. Archibald Menzies, "Proposal for Peopling His Majesty's Southern Colonies on the Continent of North America" (Megerly Castle, Pethshire, 1763) photostatic copy, St. Augustine Historical Research Library (hereafter SAHS).

3. George C. Rogers, Jr., "The East Florida Society of London, 1766–1767," *Florida Historical Quarterly* 54 (1976): 479–96; *DeBrahm's Report of the General Survey of the Southern District of North America*, ed. Louis De Vorsey, Jr. (Columbia: University of South Carolina Press, 1971).

4. E. P. Panagopoulos, *An Eighteenth-century Greek Odyssey* (Gainesville: University Press of Florida, 1966); Patricia C. Griffin, *Mullet on the Beach: The Minorcans of Florida, 1768–1788* (Gainesville: University Press of Florida, 1991).

5. After more than 200 years, the Catholic Church in Florida was again under proprietary aegis (Peticions de la Universidad 152, 1763–73, Archivo Historico Provincial, Mahon, Menorca [hereafter cited as AHP]; Parochial Cuitadela, Menorca, Archivo Diocesano de Menorca [hereafter cited as ADM]; Alior Defunctiones, 1748–91, ADM; Mercadal Defunctiones, 1738–1807, ADM). Oral accounts have come down in both Minorca and Florida regarding the mass exodus

of families from Mercadal to join the colonial expedition. *Menorca* is the Spanish/ Catalan spelling, whereas *Minorca* is the English spelling.

6. The contract was published in Pedro Riudavets y Tudury, *Historia de la Isla de Menorca* (Mahon: Fabregues, 1887), 2:1381–83. The deposition of Margau is in the Colonial Office Papers (hereafter cited as C.O.) 5/557:441–42. These depositions are reprinted in their entirety in Philip D. Rasico, *The Minorcans of Florida: Their History, Language and Culture* (New Smyrna Beach: Luthers, 1990), 147–57.

7. C.O. 5/549:253; C.O. 5/545:33–34.

8. This plan is published in full in Jane Quinn, *Minorcans in Florida: Their History and Heritage* (St. Augustine, Fla.: Mission Press, 1975), 20–23.

9. Landsdowne Mss. Vol 48:393; Treasury 77/7.

10. C.O. 5/549:282–83.

11. C.O. 5/557:429–32; 435–36.

12. For an analysis of the conflicting statistics, see Griffin, *Mullet on the Beach*, 36–37.

13. Turnbull noted that many of the Greek colonists died. Modern research has determined that the Greeks from the mountainous area of the Peloponnesos did not carry the gene for Beta Thalassemia (Mediterranean anemia), which, when inherited in its minor form, is, like the sickle cell trait, a protection against malaria. The protective aspect of this trait for the Minorcan Island settlers is evidenced by facts that: (1) the descendent Minorcan population in Florida continued to carry this genetic anomaly into the twentieth century, and (2) they constituted 80 percent of the group later in Spanish St. Augustine, although they were originally no more than 55–60 percent of the recruits (Patricia C. Griffin, "Thalassemia: A Case Study of the Minorcans of Florida," Unpublished manuscript, copy at SAHS, 1976). For a recent article on the continuing prevalence of the Beta Thalassemia trait in Menorca, see "Campanya per a la Deteccio de la B Talassemia Minor I, Prevencio de la Major a l'Illa de Menorca: Experiencia de Cinc Anys (1)" in *Revista de Menorca* 1–2 (1992): 141–60. Census figures of 1784, 1786, 1787, and Parish records are collated in Griffin, *Mullet on the Beach* and presented in table 2.1, p. 13. During the plantation years, Fr. Pedro Camps recorded only baptisms in *The Golden Book of the Minorcans: 1768–1784* (Parish Records, Diocese of St. Augustine, microfilm at SAHS).

14. The Surruque Indians, who had occupied most of the Mosquitoes area, and their Timucuan neighbors to the north practiced some agriculture. On the early Floridians, see Eugene L. Lyon, "More Light on the Indians of the Ays Coast," unpublished paper, copy in possession of the author, St. Augustine, Florida; John R. Swanton, *The Indian Tribes of North America* (Washington D.C.: Smithsonian Institution, Bureau of American Ethnology, Bulletin 145), 121–22, 131, 133; Irving Rouse, *Survey of Indian River Archaeology* (Yale University Publications in Anthropology, no. 44), 270–71.

15. De Vorsey, *DeBrahm's Report,* 222; John Armstrong, *The History of the Island of Minorca* (London: Printers to the Royal Society, 1756), 178.

16. Mark Van Doren, ed., *The Travels of William Bartram* (New York: Dover Publications, 1928), 134n.

17. These British plantations on the southeastern seaboard were, in turn, often modeled after the plantations in Ireland in the seventeenth century that were worked by Irish laborers, who, in effect, were quasi-slaves (Nick Brannon, "Archaeology of the 17th Century Plantation in Ulster," unpublished paper presented at the Society for Historical Archaeology, Kingston, Jamaica, January 1992).

18. Turnbull to Shelbourne, New Smyrna, September 24, 1769, Landsdowne Mss. 88:155. Aside from the paucity of documentation, the reason that latter-day archaeologists have been unable to establish the purpose of the extensive ruins on the bayfront in New Smyrna must be laid to the door of the 1930s W.P.A. excavations in which the artifacts disappeared. Besides the Catholic church, a small Protestant church also existed on the plantation, served for a time by an Anglican minister.

19. See Griffin, *Mullet on the Beach.*

20. *Travels of William Bartram,* 91–92.

21. Grant to Hillsborough, July 21, 1769, C.O. 5/554:205.

22. Joyce E. Chaplin, *An Anxious Pursuit: Agricultural Innovation and Modernity in the Lower South, 1730–1815* (Chapel Hill: University of North Carolina Press, 1993), 205; DeVorsey, *DeBrahm's Report,* 214.

23. The sources on the growing and processing of indigo are numerous. A sampling of those used here include, Anonymous, "Indigo in America," (Parsipany, N.J.: BSF Wyandotte, 1976); William Crookes, "A Practical Handbook of Dying and Calico" (London: Longstrum Colles, 1874); Murdo J. McLeod, *Spanish Central America: A Socioeconomic History* (Berkeley: University of California Press, 1973); Manual Rubio Sánchez, *Historia de Añil* (San Salvador: Ministerio de Educación, 1976), tomo 1; Johann David Schoepf, *Travels in the Confederation, 1783–1784,* trans. and ed. Alfred J. Morrison (Philadelphia: William J. Campbell, 1911); Joseph François Charpentier de Cossigny, "Memoir, containing an unabridged treatise on the Cultivation of Indigo . . . ," trans. Manuel Cantopher (1789); reprint from poor original by Landmarks of Science, Readex Microprint, 148–49 (courtesy of the New York Public Library); Florence H. Pettit, "America's Indigo Blues," (New York: Hastings House, 1974).

24. In a flight of fancy, DeBrahm reasoned that the dead caterpillars could be dried and powdered and processed into the blue dye (De Vorsey, *DeBrahm's Report,* 215).

25. Treasury 77/7.

26. Potash (potassium carbonate) was used elsewhere in the South and also may have been employed in indigo production at New Smyrna (Chaplin, *Anxious Pursuit,* 204).

27. Deposition of Anthony Stephanopoli, C.O. 5/557:429–32.

28. C.O. 5/557:441–42. It is necessary to note that we have only one side of the story in this Frenchman's deposition. Considering that this blacksmith was released from jail to join the colonial enterprise, it is possible that he was a contentious character.

29. Deposition of Michael Alamaon. C.O. 5/557:445–47.

30. C.O. 5/557:454–55.

31. Descendants of the Minorcan workers still seine for mullet on the Florida beaches using a consensus model, and it is difficult to determine who leads the work force since different individuals direct at different points in the endeavor. Boys take part in these modern work groups in an apprenticeship pattern, not in the age-graded system evidently used on the plantation.

32. See John Armstrong, *The History of the Island of Minorca,* 4th ed. (London: Printers to the Royal Society, 1756). See also George Cleghorn, M.D., *Observations on the Epidemical Diseases in Minorca, from the Year 1744–1749 to which is Prefixed a Short Account of the Climate, Productions, and Inhabitants and Endemical Distempers of that Island,* 4th ed. (London: T. Cadell, 1779). A treatment of the traditional feasts and festivals of Minorca are to be found in the *Quaderns De Folklore* series published in Journals 1 through 18 (Mahon, Menorca, 1990–95).

33. C.O. 5/557:473; C.O.5/557:435–36; C.O. 5/557:454–55.

34. As late as the Depression years of the 1930s, some of the colonial descendants supplemented their sparse diets with acorn broth. Significant material on agriculture, food, and the culinary arts in eighteenth-century Minorca are to be found in Armstong, *History of Minorca,* and Cleghorn, *Observations.* A discussion of Minorcan agriculture, cooking, and recipes of past centuries are included in Janet Sloss, *La Cocina Menorquina* ([London]: Sloss Publications, 1987). Traditional New World Minorcan foods and preparation are outlined in an oral-history tape by Will Manucy, 1975 (in possession of the author).

35. While it has been thought that datil peppers were brought to the New World by the Minorcans, it is probable that the plant was imported from the West Indies in the First Spanish Period. The Old World Minorcan diet is much blander than the diet adopted in the New World. See Cleghorn, *Observations,* 11–12, 61–62, for descriptions of crops and diet in Minorca.

36. Deposition of Rafel Ximenes, C.O. 5/557:454–55. The proprietor's rejoinder to Bernard Romans and others can be found in Andrew Turnbull, "A Refutation of a Late Account of New Smyrna" in *The Columbia Magazine* (Charleston, S.C.), December 1788.

37. These Cuban fishermen carried letters from Father Camps to the Catholic Bishop in Havana, and the bundles sent by them sometimes enclosed documents from Spanish spies regarding the fortifications and troops maintained by the English in Florida (Santo Domingo [hereafter cited as SD] 2673, No. 1, 2, 2a, 3, 4, Archive of the Indies, Seville, Spain [hereafter cited as AGI]).

38. Armstrong, *History of Menorca,* 205.

39. Mart A. Stewart, *What Nature Suffers to Groe: Life, Labor, and Landscape on the Georgia Coast, 1680–1920* (Athens: University of Georgia Press, 1996), 77–81; Legg, *Pioneer in Xanadu;* Co. 5/557:430; Turnbull, "Refutation."

40. Memorials of Thomas and William Grenville and Lady Mary Duncan, 1784, reprinted in Wilber Henry Siebert, *Loyalists in East Florida, 1774 to 1785* (Boston: Gregg Press, 1972), 2:297–304.

41. Father Camps to the Bishop of Havana, January/March 1770, SD 27, Doc. 1, AGI (microfilm at the P. K. Yonge Library of Florida History, University of Florida, Jeannette Thurber Connor Collection). Turnbull Family Papers, in the possession of John D. Corse, Charlottesville, Virginia, reveal that Maria Gracia Dura Bin Turnbull was not of Greek ancestry, but it is unclear where the family originated.

42. Cowkeeper's group included some of the Lower Creeks from the Alabama and Georgia area who poured into the peninsula after the English incursions at the beginning of the eighteenth century and who, by the time of the New Smyrna plantation, were living around Paynes Prairie, near present-day Gainesville, mainly engaged in cattle-raising (as Brent R. Weisman discusses in chap. 7 of this volume). C.O. 5/552:97.

43. C.O.5/549:284.

44. For a fuller description of the political situation at the end of the British period in East Florida, see Daniel L. Schafer, "'Not So Gay a Town as This . . .'" in *St. Augustine: Saga of Survival,* ed. Jean Parker Waterbury (St. Augustine: SAHS 3), 91–123.

45. John Bartram, *Diary of a Journey through the Carolinas, Georgia and Florida from July 1,1765 to April 10,1766* (Transactions of the American Philosophical Society, 33, Part 1),54; Francis Fatio to Manuel Zéspedes, March 18, 1785, trans. in *East Florida 1783–1785: A File of Documents Assembled and Many of Them Translated,* ed. and trans. Joseph B. Lockey (Berkeley: University of California Press, 1949), 479.

46. Landsdowne manuscript, vol. 88, f.157. In all probability, he was using one or more of the bucket-leveraging systems in use on the Nile—the *shadoof, sakia,* or the Archimedes screw.

47. A. E. Douglass, "1881–1885 Florida Diaries," unpublished manuscript, copy in P. K. Yonge Library of Florida History, 24; In 1896, C. B. Moore, another amateur archaeologist, gave a similar report of his excavations near New Smyrna (Clarence B. Moore, *Additional Mounds of Duval and Clay Counties, Florida. Mound Investigation on the East Coast of Florida. Certain Florida Coast Mounds North of the St. Johns River* [1896], privately printed, Philadelphia, 18).

48. See Griffin, *Mullet on the Beach,* table 6.1, p. 87.

49. C.O. 5/556:105.

50. C.O. 5/557:39.

51. C.O 5/556:767.

52. For a second time, Father Pedro Camps followed his whole parish to a new destination, although he was detained briefly in New Smyrna to care for the sick and dying and to prepare to move the accouterments of the church. For a good description of the last days of the colony, see Kenneth H. Beeson, Jr., "Fromajadas and Indigo: The Minorcan Colony in Florida," M.A. thesis, University of Florida, 1960.

53. Bernard Bailyn, *Voyagers to the West: A Passage in the Peopling of America on the Eve of the Revolution* (New York: Random House, 1986), 451–61; Bernard Romans, *A Concise Natural History of East and West Florida* (New York: Author, 1775; facsimile edition, Gainesville: University Press of Florida, 1962). Romans relied on information furnished by his assistant, Juan Purcell, who traveled to the New World with his family aboard one of Turnbull's ships. Although the Purcell family was never a part of the colony, Juan Purcell spoke the language and kept close contact with his fellow countrymen. An opposite view is presented by the Florida historian Carita Doggett Corse, who, it should be noted, was a descendent of Andrew Turnbull. In the introduction to the 1967 revision of her 1919 book, Corse concludes that the "extravagant charges" against Turnbull were made for political reasons and that Turnbull disproved them in court. While acknowledging some of the barbaric episodes recorded in the depositions, she blamed the unprincipled overseers rather than Turnbull (Corse, *Dr. Andrew Turnbull*, 12). The colonists' depositions contain elaborate detail and corroborating accounts. Juan Purcell was one of the translators, and in his 1788 "A Refutation of a late Account of New Smyrna," Turnbull accuses Purcell of exaggerating the testimony—a charge that does have some merit (Turnbull, "A Refutation," 687).

54. For information on recent archaeological investigations, see Roger T. Grange, "The Turnbull Colonist's House at New Smyrna Beach: A Preliminary Report on 8VO7051," unpublished paper in possession of the author, 1997; personal observation of flora and fauna near New Smyrna Beach by Dorothy L. Moore and Griffin.

3

Success through Diversification

Francis Philip Fatio's New Switzerland Plantation

SUSAN R. PARKER

A 10,000-acre plantation with twelve miles of riverfront; two stables with fourteen horses; twenty-seven cabins to house eighty-six slaves; thirty-four pounds of household silver; Chinese vases in the library with its gold-fringed silk curtains and marble tables: For a late eighteenth-century context, such a litany of material goods are typically associated with an enterprise presided over by the gentry on the banks of a Virginia tidewater or perhaps by some nabob of the South Carolina low country.[1] But these items were, in fact, part of the assets of the New Switzerland plantation of Francis Philip (or Francisco Phelipe) Fatio, which he established on the frontier along the St. Johns River in East Florida.

Fatio's success was launched during the British tenure in the colony and continued through the Spanish regime that followed. He possessed a supranational viewpoint and business style that allowed him to readily adapt to the national requirements of shifting governments in Florida. He experienced a series of sovereigns, and although he recognized the necessity for overt obeisance and fealty to each, Fatio probably also viewed royal figures and their regimes as tools for his use. A native of Switzerland, he did not mature to notions of membership in a surging nation-state with a colonial empire as did his contemporaries in Spain, France, or Great Britain. As a member of the Swiss guards, he fought with the French against the British in the War of Austrian Succession (1743–48), later moved to Sardinia, and then to England, and finally to British East Florida. During the American Revolution, he rendered his services to British forces fighting in the southern American colonies.[2] When Great Britain ceded East Florida back to Spain after the Revolution, Fatio and his family remained in the Spanish colony after 1784 and took advantage of the tumult of both in- and out-migration of people and governments. Thus a flexible attitude toward national affiliation allowed Fatio to make decisions that were the most advantageous.

But Francis Fatio was no maverick. He subscribed to many of the ideas and practices propounded by bigger, better-connected British investors who dreamed of an Atlanticwide commerce and limitless possibilities in their newly acquired lands. Bernard Bailyn argues that Florida's sheer exoticism fueled many of their schemes; no exception, Fatio had been in England only a short time before succumbing to "Florida fever."[3] In 1772 David Courvoisie took title of lands on the south bank on the St. Johns River as the agent of Fatio and his partners, Thomas Dunnage, John Francis Rivas, and a Mssr. Neville. Sometime before the American Revolution, Fatio purchased the interests of his associates and became sole owner of New Switzerland. Nonetheless, whether as part of those business arrangements, expected behavior, or affection, Fatio continued a close relationship with his former partners. Isaac Rivas, a bachelor, resided at Fatio's plantation at New Switzerland and was buried in the family cemetery. "Miss Charlotte Courvoisge" (*sic*) also lies in a tomb at the plantation, and her name suggests a kinship to Fatio's agent.[4]

Like other investors, Fatio arrived in East Florida planning to follow the popular wisdom and began planting indigo. He soon changed his mind about tying his fortune to a wealth-producing staple and monoculture. Fatio thus exhibited his appreciation of capitalism, which Peter Coclanis argues is characterized by a willingness to "shift resources" in an economically rational manner.[5] Residing on the land enabled Fatio to assess the problems of development within the Florida environment, and thus either to employ or to reject ideas circulating in England. Some of the first British enterprises in Florida had already proved disastrous, and Fatio might have well learned from those failures. Moreover, his lack of nationalistic or metropolitan focus freed him to chart his own economic course. Fatio invested in additional slaves and expanded and diversified the plantation. Several of his most important exports required little change to the land, and, unlike many of his contemporaries, he avoided becoming caught up in the goal of being an "improver." As David Hancock has shown, eighteenth-century English businessmen ascribed to a "neo-Baconian belief in the possibility of bettering man's condition by promoting character, agriculture, industry and commerce; and they acted on this belief."[6] Fatio apparently did not link his status in society to "improving." Nor are there references to his using indentured white workers as a labor force.

Fatio chose, instead, to turn his attention and energies to crops well suited to the environment and thus less vulnerable to the vagaries of weather. Fatio had neither an anachronistic understanding of ecology nor a temporally uncharacteristic reticence toward altering the natural environment. Rather, he recognized that naturally occurring crops and products constituted the most cost- and labor-efficient choices. Crops or animals that flourished without continual close attention or massive reconfiguring of the growing area permitted diversification. Additionally, his choices of products did not require the intensive expenditure of labor prior to planting or fragile seasonal requirements of concentration of labor. Thus Fatio created a flexible labor regime, which allowed him to maximize his sizable work force with the least amount of risk. Other contemporary investors and speculators in Florida might have had further-reaching businesses, larger labor forces, and more land under speculation at some time, but Fatio's wise choices enabled him to outlast many of his contemporaries who were undone by the periodic frontier violence that devoured capital improvements in Florida. Fatio profited in East Florida under British and then Spanish rule and established a financial and family network that would flourish in Florida for generations. More than two centuries after the arrival of the Fatio family in 1771, Fatio descendants still wield influence in Florida.

One of Fatio's greatest assets, in fact, were sons who were active and able, not profligate, lazy, or injudicious. Hancock points out the necessity for loyal managers in overseas locations and that nephews often served in that capacity. Historian J. H. Soltow found nephews serving in Virginia back-country trading stores, where they accepted crops and products in exchange for payment or acted as agent for the farmers. Contemporary Mexican businessmen also looked to nephews, usually coming from Spain, to provide managerial skills in the multifaceted shopkeeper role, according to historian David A. Brading.[7] Fatio was able to take advantage of an even stronger kinship bond—that of father and son. His sons were vigorous and highly competent in their roles in the family business. Fatio's eldest son, Louis, served family interests in a variety of foreign locations. He conducted business for his father in Havana and after 1792 tended to family affairs in Sardinia. Fatio's youngest child, Philip, served in the Spanish diplomatic service in Philadelphia and New Orleans, forging important high-level connections in those cities. Francis Fatio, Jr., stayed closer to home, having resigned from the British service to assist in his father's business operations. An additional stroke of fortune was the acquisition of a competent son-in-law, with his daughter's marriage to George Fleming.

Fleming arrived in East Florida with business experience and worked closely with his father-in-law. Fleming built his own plantation, Hibernia, directly across the St. Johns River from New Switzerland.[8]

The historical literature on the Southeast is, however, unlikely to include few, if any, references to the successful Fatio family or any other mention of Florida's economy or productivity. Florida has been dubbed the region's "short-lived component," but this conceptually confines Florida's economic history to its two British decades.[9] Although rarely noted by historians, the Spanish had established enterprises along the river; British loyalists who sought compensation from the Crown for their abandoned Florida assets described old Indian fields and plantations established in the first Spanish colonization. Thirty years before Fatio's arrival, the Spanish governor remarked on the orange groves flourishing along the St. Johns, but little is written on that earlier economic activity in rural Florida. Spanish production in the hinterlands had expanded and contracted in response to assaults by American Indians and by British colonists from South Carolina and Georgia.[10] Ultimately, historians assessed the two decades of British rule from 1763 to 1784 positively, and portrayed the period when the province returned to Spanish possession in 1784 until the 1821 cession to the United States as economic disasters. In 1925, Florida historian Thomas Frederick Davis, writing a history of the port city of the St. Johns River, Jacksonville, asserted that with the departure of the British from Florida as well as from the colonies to its north at the end of the American Revolution, civilization vanished, plantations "sank back into the wilderness [and] rank weeds . . . grew about the empty houses of the planters and quarters of the slaves, where only savages and wild beasts roamed."[11] Like many others, however, Davis based his assessment of the Spanish periods in Florida on English-language documents.[12]

Bernard Bailyn disputes the claims about British success in this "exotic periphery" of the empire in *Voyagers to the West*. He attributes the glowing assessments of modern historians to the real-estate hype and propaganda published in Great Britain soon after the acquisition of Florida, and asserts that many plans for Florida enterprises never materialized despite generous land grants by the Crown. Bailyn attributes some of Florida's failure to defective land-title procedures but primarily to the "necessary character of the labor force"—that is, slaves, for the early entrepreneurial schemes relied upon white indentured servants.[13] In the first two chapters of this volume, Daniel L. Schafer and Patricia Griffin dispute Bailyn's assessment and offer evidence supporting initial successes by the British planters.

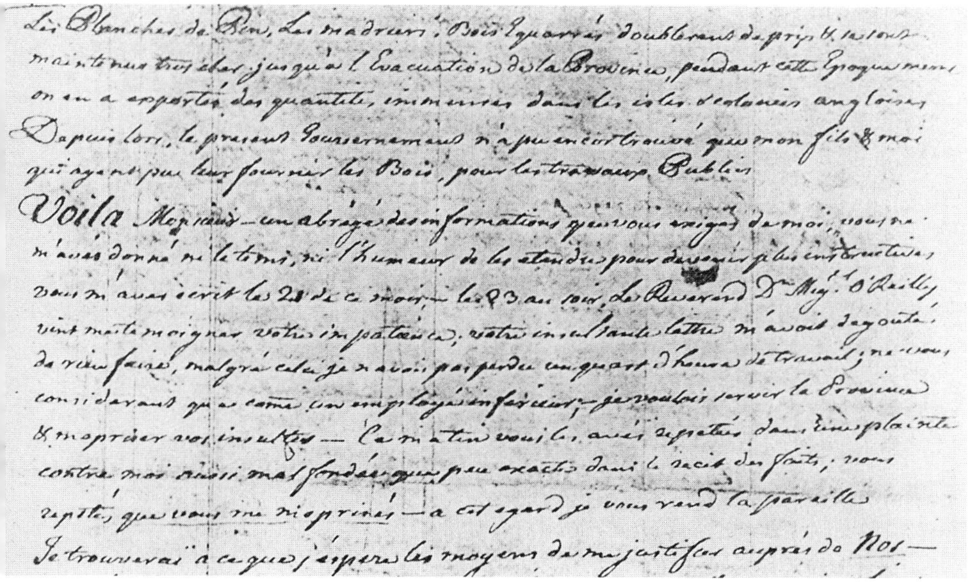
Les Planches de Bois, Les madriers, Bois Equarries doubleront de prix & se sont
maintenues très cher, jusqu'à l'Evacuation de la Province, pendant cette Epoque meme
on en a exporté des quantités immenses dans les isles et colonies angloises
Depuis lors, le present Gouvernement n'a pu en avoir trouvé que mon fils & moi
qui ayant pu leur fournir les Bois, pour les travaux Publics
Voila Monsieur — un abrégé des informations que vous exigez de moi, vous ne
m'avez donné ni le temps, ni l'humeur de les étendre pour devenir plus instructives
vous m'avez écrit le 28 de ce mois — le 23 au soir, Le Reverend Dn Migl. O'Reilly
vint me témoigner votre impatience, votre insultante lettre m'avoit degouté
de rien faire, malgré cela je n'avois pas perdu un quart d'heure de travail; ne vous
considerant que comme un employé inferieur — je voulois servir la Province
& mépriser vos insultes — Ce matin vous les avez repetées dans une plainte
contre moi aussi mal fondée que peu exacte dans le recit des faits; vous
repetez que vous me meprisez — a cet egard je vous rend la pareille
Je trouverai à ce que j'espere les moyens de me justifier auprès de Nos—

Fig. 3.1. Letter signed by Francis Philip Fatio. "Voila, Monsieur." "Take that, sir," wrote Francis Fatio in his native French to the Spaniard Lt. Rio Cosa. Fatio flaunted his standing in East Florida by not writing official correspondence in the official language of Spanish. Rio Cosa had to await a translation. *Source:* East Florida Papers, Library of Congress, Bundle 98. The full document appears in the appendix to this book. Photo commissioned by Susan R. Parker.

When Great Britain retroceded Florida to Spain in 1784, Fatio remained at New Switzerland to welcome the incoming Spanish regime. Among the British Period residents who remained in Spanish Florida, Fatio was among the most prosperous, and it is reasonable to assume that a man who was noted for his fine library and love of learning would have also maintained records of his enterprises and letter books of his correspondence. Sadly, Georgian "Patriots" burned Fatio's plantation house during the rebellion of 1812, and his extensive library and other records no doubt were consumed by the flames. Censuses, land-grant claims, and the correspondence among the Spanish rural military posts offer clues about Fatio's estate and those of his neighbors along the river.[14] But Fatio's correspondence with Spanish governmental officials, archived by the Spanish Florida government and subsequently retained by the United States in a collection known as the East Florida Papers, must serve in the absence of plantation journals and other records, which he surely generated.[15]

Such correspondence, however, is not without problems. Fatio censored information about his endeavors and demurred in disclosing any information that he thought would benefit potential competitors. To defend his purse and pride, Fatio related information in great and tedious detail; however, if he chose not to answer the Spanish governor on a sensitive topic, he would portray himself as ignorant or uninformed. Fatio spared no words to defend himself when the frontier militia commander, Carlos Howard, suggested that Fatio used a skimpy measure on the amount of corn delivered to the government and wanted to examine it. Fatio minutely bombasted upon the variations of peck measures in the commercial world and upon the provenance of his own measure.[16]

But his memory could fail very conveniently. At census time he could not recall the number of slaves he owned, although slaves constituted the most valuable property in the colonial South. And his recall failed when he was queried about information on natural resources which would benefit the general development of the colony and perhaps aid others—others who might try to get an entree into Fatio's production and markets. Fatio presented contrasting and contradictory images about his experience and knowledge of forestry products. He especially guarded his knowledge and experience about technology and marketing.

Fatio understood the significant wealth to be harvested from the forests of Florida. In 1782 he urged the British Crown to retain the East Florida colony as a source of ship lumber and naval stores and supported his petition with quantitative evidence regarding the size of the forests, the dimensions of the trees, and thus their potential through both size and inherent quality to provide various shipbuilding elements. Fatio and his son Francis, Jr., later promoted Florida forest production to the Spanish monarch and instructed the resident Spanish engineer on how best to deploy his laborers as they harvested timber for the government. But when a visiting Spanish naval lieutenant, José del Río Cosa, toured the river region of Florida to report on its potential, Fatio became evasive and accused del Río of ineptitude, for which Fatio did not intend to compensate. He claimed that he had put samples at the disposal of the lieutenant, but that the latter had failed to avail himself of the information. Fatio even composed his report in his native French, so that the officer could not read it upon receipt, but had to have it translated.[17]

When Governor Quesada himself asked Fatio as well as other residents to report on the potential of the various varieties of trees growing along the freshwater rivers in the province, Fatio deflected the request with uncharacteristic (and surely facetious) humility, claiming that he could not reply with exactness because he was "a decrepit old man with little instruction in botany and less in medicine." He claimed only minimal knowledge and dissembled by offering advice that resin mixed with rum, brandy, or "Jamaican Spirits" would cure bad colds if taken for several weeks.[18] In guarding his commercial position, Fatio has limited the information about his enterprise for use by later generations.

Fatio knew exactly how to profit from forestry and quickly put his knowledge into practice. He assigned part of his labor force to cutting lumber for building and ship construction. Pine trees that became boards and barrel staves previously had served to supply turpentine, resin, pitch and other naval stores. British merchant ships had begun taking naval stores out of East Florida in 1776, with wartime production peaking in 1782 at 50,000 barrels exported. Fatio advised that this resource in Florida could supply "enough tar and pitch for the whole Spanish navy, if the king would buy it."[19] Fatio owned the only turpentine still on the St. Johns and benefited from making it available to his neighbors with smaller enterprises, for whom he also acted as agent. Fatio's equipment and access to markets, in turn, contributed to the success of neighbors, such as Angus Clark, from whom Fatio bought lumber. Clark needed a way to send his product inexpensively to market, and the deal enabled Fatio to make up the shortfall in his own timber supply in order to fulfill a government contract.[20]

Fatio also profited from another traditional and low-investment Florida crop—citrus. Floridians had been sending citrus to South Carolina for at least half a century before Fatio shipped 1,500 gallons of orange juice (*agría*) to Charleston in 1786. Residents also shipped whole fruits to Savannah.[21] Spanish circum-Caribbean colonies were located in areas with warmer weather than Florida and could grow their own citrus. Thus, Florida orange growers had to look to foreign colonies to sell their surplus, and the British and then-American areas north of Florida eagerly purchased the fruit. Even a few trees in the residential yards of St. Augustine could generate at least small amounts of cash. The guardian of the orphaned Mestre children reported that sale of the oranges from trees at their deceased mother's residence yielded 131 pesos in 1807, which paid for the support of the young children. The previous year, the guardian had arranged for repairs to the roof of a rental house belonging to the orphans in exchange for 29 pesos of oranges. Growers like Fatio, planted whole orchards of oranges and limes as "commercial" groves and made larger profits. Like cattle and timber, citrus was a crop from which all strata of society could profit because of low labor and capitalization requirements.[22]

Fatio also dealt in the low-labor and low-capitalization cattle trade. Cattle grazed often on Crown land as well as on granted parcels. Timbering and cattle-raising were complementary endeavors. Yearly burnings, necessary to keep the brush down in the pine orchards, encouraged the growth of adequate forage for cattle. This interrelated system of naval stores, timbering, and cattle-raising in place in the eighteenth century would be even more extensively practiced in the nineteenth and twentieth centuries.[23] Up to the time of butchering, cattle required little labor expenditure. Three men, one on horseback and two on foot, could drive a herd of 100. Fatio bid on the government contract to supply beef to the Spanish soldiery in Florida while the price paid by the government was high, but lost interest in participation as the unit price the government would pay fell drastically. In 1788 and 1794, he agreed to furnish beef at twelve pounds per peso (twenty-four ounces per *real* in the contract). The Spanish government required more than 400 pounds of fresh meat per day to feed the troops and officials, with ordinary soldiers allotted twelve ounces of fresh beef per day and officers and hospital patients entitled to a larger ration. Additional food would have been needed for the convict laborers assigned to Florida, but the numbers regarding the laborers were not included in the documentation. At the time, meat contractors probably sold cattle for 250 percent more than they paid, if they had purchased the animals, and surely enjoyed a higher profit if the beeves came from their own herds. Fatio fulfilled his contract with animals from his own herd and probably the herds of neighbors and with animals brought in from Georgia and South Carolina, possibly as in-kind payments of debts he was owed. He also bought cattle from the Seminoles, with free blacks acting as agents in the negotiations.[24]

Fatio's established presence in East Florida at the time of the change of sovereigns in 1784 put him in the position to make himself nearly indispensable to the incoming Spanish. He had profited during the British era by supplying military needs and remarked that the demand for naval stores had encouraged planters to abandon the cultivation of indigo.[25] Fatio was able to supply the needs of the new Spanish government from his own lands or with his own imports, and was in the financial position to extend credit to a government with a cash-flow problem. Even after the American Revolution, the Spanish Crown was amenable to funding, or at least to subsidizing, the existence of the Florida colonies for strategic reasons:

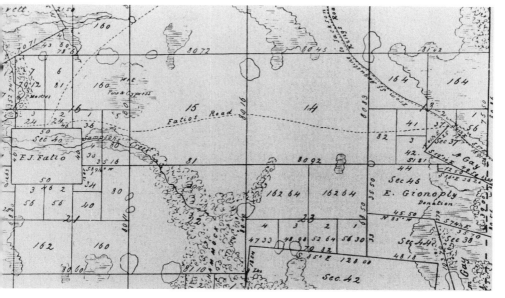

Fig. 3.2. Fatio's Road as it appeared on an 1835 Township map. Much of the portion shown here is in use today as the roadbed between U.S. 1 and an exit on I-95 (between sections 37 and 54). *Source:* Township Maps, Florida Department of Environmental Protection. Photo commissioned by Susan R. Parker.

They served to protect silver-rich Mexico. Using Allan Kuethe's words about Cuba to describe the Florida colonies: They "commanded a military significance far greater than their economic resources could justify." But the arrival and disbursement of the Crown funds was often problematic, and Florida governors continued the plaint of their First Spanish Period predecessors that the lack of sufficient flour and meat was more vexatious than lack of weapons and ammunition.

Fatio could ingratiate himself and thus accrue favors by supplying to the hard-pressed officials on credit, goods that he produced and those that he imported. Fatio also maintained a stock of supplies outside of the Spanish Florida borders, which he could offer to the government in times of shortage but which would not be subject to appropriation by the beleaguered colonial government. Sometimes the problem was both the lack of funds and the shortage of food. Much of this problem, not unlike today, arose from the governmental procedures themselves. Frequently, it was not the lack of supplies but the system of supplying that kept soldiers literally wondering where their next meal might come from. Also typical of governments over the centuries was the concern for purchasing within the nation or empire even though it might mean higher prices. For example, Capt. Manuel de los Reyes, posted at the mouth of the St. Marys River, lamented that his men had to "make do" with beans provided by the Spanish army during the Christmas season, while just across the river, barrels of flour were affordable at the store on Cumberland Island in the new United States. Fatio had supplies of corn on Cumberland Island, which he could readily bring into East Florida with official complicity such as special concessions or suspension of mercantile regulations. Recognizing a certain administrative flexibility in the Spanish, Fatio issued his own pass for the vessel on which he was sending lumber out of the colony, rather than securing one from the government and paying export fees. The commander at the post near the mouth of the St. Johns River was scandalized at the illegality and the high-handed, usurpatious behavior. But the governor, who was concerned with feeding the colony's soldiers, told the commander to overlook the entire episode, for Fatio's vessel would return with foodstuffs which were "worth more than money." Fatio might also have served as a source for civilians in the colony, but the available documentation deals only with government supplies.[26]

Fatio also supplied the timber and shingles—again on credit—to be used in essential repairs to the governor's house in St. Augustine, which housed both a residence and executive offices. Thus was Governor Zéspedes personally indebted for his own comfort to Fatio, and the chief Spanish official did not forget the favor when Fatio's boats and products attempted to skirt the regulations on departing the province.[27]

Although Fatio gained favor and leverage with the Spanish government, he was not able to gain entree into the Indian trade. He and other entrepreneurs saw that the stranglehold that control of the meat supply could create for the government might serve as a potential avenue into acquiring the governor's permission for trading stores, but the British-based firm of Panton, Leslie and Company maintained that monopoly nevertheless.[28]

As other essays in this volume discuss, armed expeditions into Spanish Florida by cattle rustlers, filibusterers, and U.S. troopers devastated many of the agricultural enterprises in Florida in 1794–95 and 1812–14. Conflict between Native Americans and U.S. settlers expanding westward in the Carolinas and Georgia also spilled southward over the international border into Florida. In Spanish Florida, Indian groups raided plantations out of need and frustration, and in October 1785 Indians cut off the ear of a rural child. This attack portended larger losses to come in the persistent Indian hostilities that followed. Seminole Indians raided New Switzerland in 1801 and stole away thirty-eight slaves, causing Francis Fatio, Jr., to travel hundreds of miles through the Indian country in a futile attempt to recover them.[29] Although humans and animals suffered in such raids, forest products and citrus were much less vulnerable to these attacks and usually were left unharmed by the destruction. Fatio's granddaughter Susan L'Engle noted that when she and her family returned to New Switzerland, probably in 1822 after a decade's absence, the orange trees still stood, outlining where slave cabins had stood before the Seminoles had burned the little houses. Surely the stands of pine and live oak remained as well.

Francis Fatio was able to live like a baron in East Florida by astutely adhering to many of the practices and following ideas held by the ascendant cadre of British traders and entrepreneurs engaged in transoceanic and multicontinent ventures while tempering and adjusting to local conditions. Fatio's reliance on environmentally economic crops permitted him and his family to withstand setbacks to their physical assets better than those who relied on more-mechanized or land-altering practices. He engaged in activities that anthropologist Kenneth Lewis identified as frontier economies: cattle-raising, timbering, and extractive industries such as naval stores. There is irony in the fact that the very crops that served Fatio so well could quite reasonably be considered egalitarian ones. Persons of all economic classes engaged in timbering, cattle-raising, and citrus-growing. Sugar and rice—which made many rich and broke many more—were crops that took substantial investment in machinery or improvements to land as well as a sizable labor force; thus, only those who could amass capital could participate in these crops. Monoculture or investment in highly profitable crops required stability in the growing region, and East Florida was permitted few periods of quiet in the rural areas.

Fatio's achievements in both the British and Spanish periods mark him as unique and exemplary in employing the contemporary tenets and procedures for plantation management, yet creatively adapting them to the Florida context. Recognition and examination of his enterprises illustrate that rural Florida was, in fact, genteelly settled in the Spanish Period and that the colony could support the material comfort of those who correctly analyzed what actions and adaptations were needed to succeed in that physical and political environment.

Notes

1. Confirmed Claim F12, Spanish Land Grants Collection, Florida Division of Historical Resources, Tallahassee (microfilm by Florida Department of Agriculture, former repository for claims); Susan Fatio L'Engle, *Notes of My Family and Recollections of My Early Life* (New York: Knickerbocker Press, 1888), 6–8; Gertrude N. L'Engle, *A Collection of Letters, Information and Data on Our Family* (Jacksonville, Fla.: private pub., 1951), 1:27; Margaret Curson [Memories of Louisa Fatio], April 18, 1817, Journal of Samuel and Margaret Curson for 1816–1818, Houghton Library, Harvard University; Allan Kulikoff, *Tobacco and Slaves: The Development of Southern Cultures in the Chesapeake, 1680–1800* (Chapel Hill: University of North Carolina Press, 1986). Daniel L. Schafer generously shared the information contained in the Curson diary. Relation of the Family of Don Francisco Phelipe Fatio, February 27, 1801, bnd. 136E11, no. 63, East Florida Papers, Library of Congress Manuscript Division, microfilm copies (hereafter cited as EFP).

2. L'Engle, *Notes of My Family*, 6, 11.

3. Bernard Bailyn, *Voyagers to the West; A Passage in the Peopling of America on the Eve of the Revolution* (New York: Alfred A. Knopf, 1986), 430–74. According to Fatio's descendant, the glowing accounts of Florida "so captured his ardent imagination" that he and his family migrated in 1771 to the newly British province, which they discovered had been "untruly pictured as an earthly paradise" (L'Engle, *Notes of My Family*, 12).

4. Statement by Sophia Fleming (Fatio's daughter), land grant from Acting Governor John Moultrie to David Courvoisie, January 10, 1772, filed in dossier for Confirmed Claim F12, Spanish Land Grants Collection; L'Engle, *Notes of My Family*, 10–11, 16. The 1784 census of "countryfolk" lists Rivas as residing at New Switzerland (Censuses, bnd. 323A, EFP).

5. Peter A. Coclanis, *The Shadow of a Dream: Economic Life and Death in the South Carolina Lowcountry, 1670–1920* (New York: Oxford University Press, 1989), 57.

6. David Hancock, *Citizens of the World: London Merchants and the Integration of the British Atlantic Community, 1735–1785* (Cambridge: Cambridge University Press, 1995), 279–85, quote on 284.

7. J. H. Soltow, "Scottish Traders in Virginia, 1750–1775," *Economic History Review*, 2d ser., 12 (1959): 86; David A. Brading, *Miners and Merchants in Mexico City, 1763–1810* (Cambridge: Cambridge University Press, 1971).

8. G. L'Engle, *Collection of Letters*, 1:37, 41, 48–49.

9. Joyce E. Chaplin, *An Anxious Pursuit: Agricultural Innovation and Modernity in the Lower South, 1730–1815* (Chapel Hill: University of North Carolina Press, 1993), chap. 7.

10. Wilbur Henry Siebert, *Loyalists in East Florida, 1774–1785*, 2 vols. (DeLand: Florida State Historical Society, 1929); Manuel de Montiano to Juan Francisco Güemes y Horcasitas, February 23, 1740, bnd. 37, no. 187, EFP; Susan

R. Parker, "The Second Century of Settlement in Spanish St. Augustine, 1670–1763," Ph.D. diss. University of Florida, 1999.

11. Thomas Frederick Davis, *A History of Jacksonville, Florida, and Vicinity* (St. Augustine: The Record Company, 1925), 51.

12. Language was often an impediment that early historians of North America made no attempt to overcome. Thus they restricted their sources largely to British- or American-era works or to works by English-speaking writers. The omission and negativity regarding Florida are part of a larger cultural and historiographical situation that has been so well synthesized by David Weber: Anglo-Americans, among them historians, saw a defective Spanish character intimately existing with, shaped by, and contributing to a malignant Spanish Catholicism. One inevitable result of this combination, they thought, was the misgovernment of the territories under Spanish control. In the nineteenth century, the Spanish and their Hispanic heirs were seen as inimical to U.S. territorial ambitions. Downplaying the accomplishments taking place in coveted territories governed by the Spanish helped to justify their annexation to the United States for the benefit of the residents of the backward areas. See *The Spanish Frontier in North America* (New Haven: Yale University Press, 1992), 336–38.

13. Bailyn, *Voyagers to the West,* chap. 12, quote on 471.

14. Susan R. Parker, "Men without God or King," Master's thesis, University of Florida, 1990, and "Men without God or King: Rural Settlers of East Florida, 1784–1790," *Florida Historical Quarterly* 69 (October 1990): 135–55.

15. Fatio's granddaughter recalled in her memoirs the fame of her grandfather's collection of books and how much time he spent in their presence. The books composed a notable part of subsequent claims for losses arising from the 1812 depredations (L'Engle, *Notes of My Family;* EFP).

16. Statement of John LeindertLem (*sic*], May 25, 1794, no. 242; Carlos Howard to Gov. Juan Nepomuceno de Quesada, May 29, 1794, no. 250, Fatio to Quesada, June 5, 1794, all in bnd. 126S10, EFP.

17. Lt. José del Río Cosa to Gov. Zéspedes, June 26, 1787, no. 42; Fatio to del Río, June 26, 1787, both in bnd. 98G8, EFP.

18. Fatio to Government Engineer, January 4, 1786, bnd. 66A6; Fatio to Quesada, March 31, September 24, 1792, bnd. 23J2, no. 2, EFP.

19. Francis Philip Fatio, "Considerations on the Importance to East Florida to the British Empire . . . By Its Situation, Its Produce in Naval Stores, Ship Lumber and the Asylum It May Afford to the *Wretched and Distressed* Loyalists," December 14, 1782, Public Records Office, Colonial Office 5/560, 911–18, typescript copy in P. K. Yonge Library of Florida History, University of Florida, Gainesville; Francis Philip Fatio, "Description of East Florida," March 18, 1785, cited in Joseph Byrne Lockey, *East Florida, 1783–1785: A File of Documents Assembled and Many of Them Translated* (Berkeley: University of California Press, 1949), 479–82.

20. Fatio to José del Río Cosa, June 26, 1787, bnd. 98G8; Estate of Angus Clark, bnd. 303, EFP.

21. Antonio Delgado to Governor Zéspedes, July 24, 1786, bnd. 118A10, EFP.

22. Accounting of 1806 and 1807, Estate of Catalina Nicles Mestre, bnd. 312, EFP; Joyce Elizabeth Harman, *Trade and Privateering in Spanish Florida, 1732–1763* (St. Augustine: St. Augustine Historical Society, 1972), 20–25.

23. James M. Smith and Stanley C. Bond, Jr., *Stomping the Flatwoods: An Archaeological Survey of St. Johns County, Florida* (St. Augustine: Historic St. Augustine Preservation Board, 1984), 119.

24. Meat Contracts, bnd. 297O12, EFP. Fatio also held a meat contract in 1792, but no price was listed (Gonzalo Zamorano, Report of the Pounds of Daily Fresh Meat, January 2, 1781, bnd. 67B6, EFP; José Taso to Governor, March 11, 1790, bnd. 121D10, no. 19[?], and Richard Lang to Governor, June 19, 1790, bnd. 120C10, no. 71, EFP).

25. Lockey, *East Florida*, 479.

26. Manuel de los Reyes to Governor Zéspedes, December 27, 1785, bnd. 118A10, no. 145; Juan Francisco Garzes to Zéspedes, October 1, 1785, bnd. 118A10, no. 98; Gregorio Castillo to Zéspedes, November 10, 1781, bnd. 119B10, no. 131, EFP.

27. Engineer's Report for 1786, bnd. 170, EFP.

28. Governor Juan Nepomuceno de Quesada to Luis de las Casas, January 2, 1794, bnd. 24, EFP.

29. Nicolás Valderas to Governor Vicente Manuel de Zéspedes, October 27, 1785, bnd. 118A10, no. 117, EFP; Kenneth Coleman, ed., *A History of Georgia* (Athens: University of Georgia Press, 1977), 52–95; Parker, "Men without God or King" (thesis), 30–35; G. L'Engle, *Collection of Letters*, 48–49; John Forrester to Governor Enrique White, August 31, 1801, bnd. 115K9, no. 204; Governor White to Governor Vicente Folch, September 12, 1801, bnd. 115K9, no. 216, EFP.

4

Francisco Xavier Sánchez, *Floridano* Planter and Merchant

JANE G. LANDERS

One of Florida's most successful planters was Francisco Xavier Sánchez, whose life and career spanned three separate colonial regimes. His family's early acquisition of prime Florida lands gave Sánchez his start, but he expanded upon what he inherited and created a group of interrelated, if not contiguous, plantations which allowed him great diversity and produced great wealth.[1] The Sánchez empire stretched along the Diego Plains, north of St. Augustine almost to the St. Marys River and west to the St. Johns River. Sánchez's main plantation on the east bank of the St. Johns, the San José, comprised over 1,100 acres. Just south of the San José lay the Ashley, a plantation of about 500 acres, and to the east on the Diego Plains lay Sánchez's original homestead, the San Diego, of another thousand acres. Below the San Diego, along the North River, lay the smaller homesteads of Capuaca and Santa Barbara. All around these were other Sánchez holdings devoted to pasturage and forests; like all large Spanish landholders, Sánchez maintained a variety of town properties as well.[2]

Sánchez's plantations and land holdings produced a wide variety of agricultural products and fed large herds of cattle. His vast tracts of forests yielded rich harvests of valuable hardwoods and timber products. Just as he diversified production, Sánchez also developed diverse mercantile connections which illustrate the patterns James G. Cusick discusses in this volume.[3] Sánchez conducted trade with U.S. merchants in Baltimore as readily as with British merchants in the Bahamas, with merchant firms in his native Cuba as readily as with the Seminoles of the Florida hinterlands. His enterprises also included a trade in human beings. Not only did he serve as a factor for various Anglo conspirators needing to depart the province hastily, but his ships transported enslaved Africans between Cuba and Florida, in both directions.

Earlier recipients of royal largesse in Florida had enjoyed only usufruct of the land, for Spain had been reluctant to create a landed elite among the *criollos* (a person of Spanish descent born in the New World). By the seventeenth century, however, Spain was experiencing serious challenges to its sovereignty in Florida, including pirate raids and the establishment of an English colony at Charleston in Spanish-claimed territory in 1670. The Crown knew that in order to hold Florida, it would have to populate it. Spain began to grant title to lands and permit officials to engage in local development efforts. During this period, about a dozen local families rose to prominence in Florida, dominating the bureaucracy and acquiring huge tracts of land, on which they raised herds of valuable black cattle. Among them was that of Diego Espinosa, whose lands lay north of St. Augustine on the Diego Plains.[4]

The rise of such landed families was at the expense of native inhabitants, whom they displaced; thus, throughout the seventeenth century, the Spaniards had to fend off attacks by embittered Indians and pirates attracted by the new wealth.[5] Then, in the disastrous years between 1702 and 1706, Col. James Moore of Carolina destroyed the large ranches of the interior grasslands of north central Florida, such as La Chua belonging to the Menéndez Márquez family, as well as the Franciscan mission chain which ran westward from St. Augustine to Apalachee Province (modern-day Tallahassee).[6] One of the few cattle ranches to escape the general devastation of the colony belonged to the Espinosas, and their fortunes and those of the Sánchez family would later intertwine.

The Sánchez family emigrated to Cuba from southern Spain in the seventeenth century, and at the beginning of the eighteenth century Francisco Xavier's father and the patriarch of the Florida Sánchezes, Joseph Sánchez de Ortigosa, relocated to St. Augustine. Joseph Sánchez married into a local family with important assets in Florida. The family of his bride, Juana Theodora Pérez, also originated in southern Spain, but had resided in St. Augustine since the middle of the seventeenth century.[7] Sánchez earned profits and royal gratitude through corsairing, an activity which helped supply St. Augustine in years of privation and English attacks. Joseph Sánchez finally retired from the corsairing life and sold his sloop to Governor Manuel de Montiano, who refitted it for use by a more famous corsair, Don Juan de León Fandiño.[8]

By this time, Joseph Sánchez had a sizable family of eight children, the youngest of whom, Francisco Xavier, was born in 1736. Sánchez supported this family on a royal grant of land in the Diego Plains.[9] In 1756 Diego Espinosa's daughter, Antonia, married Francisco Sánchez's elder brother, Joseph, enabling the Espinosa and Sánchez families to pool their resources and practice economies of scale, thereby increasing both families' wealth and influence.[10]

The Espinosa and Sánchez holdings had escaped the early damage wrought by the Moore invasions; however, once the sources of cattle and Indian slaves dried up in central Florida, later raiders from the north swept down the coast and focused on St. Augustine. The Espinosa-Sánchez holdings lay directly across their paths and suffered repeated encroachments. The families converted the Espinosa ranch into a fortified stronghouse, known as Fort San Diego, and ranch hands and government militias tried to protect what everyone in the colony recognized was a main source of sustenance. Despite these precautions, the combined Carolina, Georgia, and Indian troops led by Gen. James Oglethorpe overran Fort San Diego in 1739–40. Oglethorpe's forces devoted much of their energy to rounding up prize black cattle and horses running loose on the Diego Plains, which they stole away. Oglethorpe's siege also cost the life of some of Fort San Diego's multiracial ranch hands and soldiers. When Oglethorpe's troops finally withdrew, the colony was devastated.[11] Over the next years, the Espinosa and Sánchez families slowly rebuilt their Diego Plains estates, but British-inspired Indian raids continued to be a problem throughout the 1750s.[12] The Anglo/Spanish rivalry in Florida was only resolved in 1763 when Spain ceded Florida to England in order to reclaim the more valuable Havana.[13]

In the evacuation that followed, most Spaniards departed for Cuba with their government, but the twenty-eight-year-old Francisco Xavier Sánchez, remained in Florida, as permitted by treaty, to manage the family estates. From the Diego Plains, Sánchez now provided the English with meat and firewood. He made the most of his British government contracts and used his profits to acquire more land from Florida's new rulers, securing title to over 1,000 acres in the Diego Plains during the brief twenty years the English held the colony. However, his relationship with the British was strained when in 1779 Spain and England once more went to war.

Governor Patrick Tonyn distrusted Sánchez for his Spanish heritage, and Sánchez made his loyalties quite clear when he aided a group of Spanish soldiers held prisoner in St. Augustine. The Spaniards had been part of an expedition sent from Cuba to capture the Bahamas Islands. On the way, they were captured by British corsairs, endured a shipwreck, and were finally taken to St. Augustine, in pitiable circumstances. Sánchez provided his compatriots with food and clothes while they were imprisoned in Florida and, at war's end, shipped them back to Havana on two of his ships, a brigantine and a schooner. Such gestures may well have been motivated by compassion, but they were also calculated to generate appropriate Spanish recognition and reward in the future. While Sánchez balanced on his unsteady political tightrope, Florida became a haven for Loyalist planters from Charleston and Savannah who, as the Revolution progressed, attempted to transfer their operations southward. The planters imported as much property and as many slaves into Florida as they could evacuate from cities taken by the Patriot forces. This rapid influx of population and capital created a boom in Florida, from which Sánchez undoubtedly prospered. However, it also destabilized the colony, which was unprepared for such rapid growth. Critical socioeconomic links between Florida and the British Caribbean were strengthened during this Loyalist era, and Sánchez was able to make use of these later. Florida's Loyalist boom, however, was short-lived, for once again the fortunes of European war dictated Florida's history.[14]

The Treaty of Paris, which ended the American Revolution, retroceded Florida to Spain. Francisco Xavier Sánchez carried the happy news to Cuba in 1783, astutely combining business with diplomacy. While in Havana, Sánchez offered his services (and his cattle) to Florida's incoming governor, Vicente Manuel de Zéspedes, who soon came to appreciate the offer.

In Sánchez's absence, law and order in Florida had broken down completely. Groups of renegades—white, black, and Indian—many of them displaced by the American Revolution, took advantage of the political turmoil of the transition to raid outlying properties and cart away slaves, cattle, and other movable property. A band of 700 "banditti" camped on the Sánchez property and killed over 400 head of his cattle while he was absent in Cuba. Only one person was ever punished for this crime.

Realizing, on his return, that protection would not be forthcoming, Sánchez withheld his meat from the British government and began to deal instead with the effective power on the frontier—Daniel McGirtt, a South Carolinian, formerly of Brown's Rangers. McGirtt was perhaps the most notorious of the banditti and owned a farm on the St. Johns River where many of the Anglo renegades gathered. Sánchez not only sold McGirtt cattle, arms, and provisions, but he also bought and resold forty-six of McGirtt's slaves, fifteen horses, and other plantation tools and supplies, which were supposed to have been forfeited to the British king. These business deals infuriated Governor Tonyn, who charged that the Spaniard owed "everything he possesses to the indulgence of the British government, under which he rose from a state of obscure poverty to a degree of wealth seldom attained."[15]

When Governor Zéspedes and his entourage finally arrived to take possession of St. Augustine in the summer of 1784, Tonyn attempted unsuccessfully to force Sánchez's arrest, charging that he had received stolen slaves from McGirtt. The changes in sovereignty and populations in Florida led to many such acrid and tangled property disputes, but Sánchez maintained that his dealings with McGirtt and others unpopular with the British regime were legitimate. Although Zéspedes eventually deported McGirtt to Havana, Sánchez continued to act as McGirtt's agent in Florida, and it can be assumed that Sánchez's family connections in Havana also assisted McGirtt. When McGirtt later migrated to Providence in the Bahamas, he and Sánchez continued their partnership. Sánchez now could exploit his Spanish family and trade connections in Havana and also tap into the British trade circuit in Providence, while his sloop, the *Frolic*, continued to ply the coastal trade between St. Augustine, Savannah, Charleston, and Baltimore.[16]

Even before McGirtt's exile, the partners had expanded their investments into a new venture in the slave trade. Benjamin Guerard, the governor of South Carolina, charged that Sánchez's schooner, the *Flying Fish*, had carried over 100 stolen black slaves from the St. Johns River plantations to Havana in June 1783. He informed the governor of Cuba that McGirtt and Sánchez were thieves and demanded that the Spanish government control them. He also asked for the return of the slaves already sold in Havana, but there is no evidence that Cuba's Governor acted upon Guerard's request.[17]

Despite the charges of both Anglo governors, Zéspedes recognized Sánchez's value to Florida and pragmatically took a charitable view of his enterprises. He ignored Tonyn's demand for Sánchez's arrest and instead initiated a government meat contract with the accused. During his initial inspection tour of Florida, Zéspedes had found a colony in decay. Anticipating their departure, the British had neglected town properties and had left plantations unplanted. Sánchez's San Diego plantation was one of only two still operating in the province; Governor Zéspedes quickly posted soldiers on the property to protect the valuable estate from further vandalism.[18]

In 1784 the San Diego comprised over 1,000 acres, on which Sánchez kept a herd of 800 to 900 cattle, thirty to forty horses and pigs, and thirty-four slaves. When Sánchez was away on business, his trusted Guinea-born slave and the skilled butcher of his cattle and pigs, Felipe Edimborough (more commonly Edimboro), acted as overseer of the San Diego.[19] It was much to oversee. The San Diego encompassed the main dwelling and assorted ranch buildings, such as a cook house, stables, granaries, storehouses, houses for the overseer and slavehands, carpentry and iron-working shops, a millhouse, and a slaughterhouse. Slaves tended the horses, oxen, and cattle and prepared dried meat, hides, and tallow for sale to markets in St. Augustine and beyond. Slaves also raised and processed corn, cotton, and other garden crops. Like most other contemporary plantations, Sánchez's was a largely self-sufficient operation.[20]

In the eighteenth century, cattle cost only about three pesos a head (when a peso was equivalent to the U.S. dollar of the day), but a prime cattle hand or skilled slave could bring 300 to 500 pesos. Although cattle and slaves constituted his major assets, Sánchez also owned tools, equipment, gristmills, tack, and a variety of watercraft ranging in size from *piraguas* to brigantines to carry his products to market. Despite this obvious wealth, Sánchez was accused of cheapness in provisioning the slave population, which provided the labor on his large ranches. One slave complained in a court suit about the corn diet Sánchez fed his slaves, the hard work he expected of his field hands, and the fact that he habitually kept the *jornales* (wages slaves earned hiring themselves out on free time, a common practice in the Spanish colonies).[21] Other slave suits also support the allegation that Sánchez was rather miserly in his treatment of slaves, permitting them free time only on Sundays and Christmas, unlike more-lenient masters in Florida.[22]

Sánchez's thrift no doubt contributed to his success and ensured him official beef and firewood contracts from the Spanish government. And when the government payrolls failed to appear from Havana, Sánchez was able to sell on credit. This, too, was common practice in the Spanish colonies and was a form of obligation that wealthy Spanish colonists often used to ensure continued business, positions, land grants, and other favors from a grateful and perpetually hard-pressed government.[23] In addition to the critical supplies of fresh meat and timber that Sánchez sold the government, he also sold major stores of flour, rice, and corn.[24]

But Sánchez was not dependent upon the public contracts alone. By 1786 Sánchez owned several plantations and many slaves, a two-story stone house on St. Charles Street, and another house on Marina Street in St. Augustine. Sánchez had also became an associate in the important Florida merchant house *Miranda y Sánchez,* which operated retail stores in St. Augustine. Their general store in the lower floor of the house on St.

Charles Street offered a wide array of merchandise including laudanum, gun flints, hyson tea, ladies shoes, Jamaican rum, and cloth of various kinds. The company's ships imported merchandise from a wide variety of ports, and resold the government merchandise such as pork in brine, linseed oil, lampblack, and candles.[25] Sánchez's store accounts show that he extended credit to a wide array of individuals on the government payroll, including military officers, soldiers, sailors, artisans, and hospital employees.[26]

After 1790, Spain lifted mercantile restrictions on Florida (many of which had long been quietly ignored), and merchants like Sánchez were freed to trade legally with U.S. ports.[27] The firm of *Miranda y Sánchez* tapped into the U.S. trade in a time-honored fashion—through the marriage of Sánchez's daughter to Samuel Miles, of the Andrew Dewees Company of Baltimore. Another of Sánchez's daughters married Philip Dewees of the company, further consolidating those links. Sánchez imported trade goods such as knives, blankets, pots and pans, and munitions from the Andrew Dewees Company, which he began to sell to the Lower Creek and Seminole Indians of the interior. This opportunity opened for Sánchez when Florida's governor rescinded the Indian trade monopoly held since 1786 by the British-owned firm of Panton, Leslie and Company.[28] The ships of *Miranda y Sánchez* plied an important trade with Havana—of which St. Augustine was, in effect, a hinterland—but also sailed regularly between St. Augustine, St. Marys, Savannah, and Charleston.[29]

Sánchez's extensive landholdings and wealth made him a respected and influential member of the Spanish community, and his status devolved on his families, white and black. Sánchez raised two large families over the course of his life. Sánchez lived with his common-law wife, María Beatriz Piedra (also known as Stone), a free mulatto born in Charleston, for almost twenty years on the San Diego plantation. There the couple raised Sánchez's first family—three sons and five daughters. Sánchez recognized all these children when they were baptized in the Catholic church, and his influential friends served as their godparents. When they grew older, Sánchez moved his quadroon children into town, and they lived in St. Augustine attended by slaves of their own. Sánchez's sons attended the public school in St. Augustine, and his daughters also received an education (perhaps from a home tutor), for they were literate. Two of the boys, Antonio and Francisco Mateo Sánchez, died suddenly on the same day in 1804, perhaps of an epidemic illness. Sánchez's surviving son, Joseph, named after his paternal grandfather, eventually married Lucía Ysnardy, the free and propertied quadroon daughter of St. Augustine's royal trea-

surer, Miguel Ysnardy. With their father's blessings and official dispensation from the bishop, three of Sánchez's biracial daughters married white
peninsular Spaniards and began their own households, while his twin
daughters remained unmarried and lived together in the townhouse provided by their father.[30]

In 1787, at the age of fifty-one, Sánchez married María del Carmen
Hill, the seventeen-year-old daughter of a wealthy South Carolina family
from the 96 District. This marriage brought new commercial connections,
but also a social elevation for Sánchez, whose common-law wife, María
Beatriz Piedra, died three years later. Although María Beatriz's testament
records that she left no property "due to her poverty," this formulaic
phrase denotes her legal rather than actual condition, for as his treatment
of his illegitimate children substantiates, Sánchez would have been shamed
by such a failure of community-sanctioned responsibility. Sánchez's marriage to María del Carmen produced four legitimate sons and six daughters, the last of whom was born days before her father's death in 1807.
María del Carmen and her children apparently enjoyed a close relationship with the children of Sánchez's first union and served as godparents
many times over for their children.[31]

Meanwhile, Sánchez's fortunes kept pace with his burgeoning family
obligations. Sánchez's government meat contract was renewed many
times, despite the rise in his prices over time. Sánchez petitioned for and
was granted more land. He also contracted to cut thousands of cords of
cedar and oak of specified dimensions for the needs of the presidio. The
wood was harvested from royal lands, and Sánchez had only to transport
it to the banks of the North River. From that point, it was the government's
responsibility to get the wood to St. Augustine. Sánchez's entrepreneurial
skill is evident in this venture, for the only expense he accrued was in the
maintenance of his own slaves and equipment.[32]

If Sánchez prospered in peacetime, he did even better in times of war. In
1793 the minister of the new French republic, citizen Edmund Charles
Gênet, arrived in Charleston and began to instigate plots to revolutionize
North America. Gênet raised an army of backwoodsmen with promises of
land, money, and titles, and Spanish Florida prepared for the expected
invasion. In the face of the French-inspired threat, Governor Juan Nepomuceno de Quesada, who succeeded Zéspedes, raised and posted new
militias on the northern frontier to protect St. Augustine from invasion.
Sánchez grandly offered twenty armed black slaves for government service, whose maintenance he would provide. However, when the governor
actually organized slave militias in 1794, Sánchez reneged, claiming his

slaves were too busy planting corn. The governor disgustedly condemned Sánchez's behavior in his military reports, but the planter's corn was indeed important to the well-being of the province. It fed the townspeople and the Indians, whose friendship the Spanish had to retain as a "human barrier" to invasion.[33]

Governor Quesada recognized that despite the organization of the new militias, his troop strength was insufficient to protect the vast colony. In a most unpopular move, Quesada ordered the northern settlements evacuated and all the homes north of the St. Johns River burned.[34] Quesada's war council voted to arm all the free blacks and mulattoes in the province, and Spain sent regular army reinforcements from Catalonia, Havana, and Mexico to shore up Florida's defenses. These war preparations increased the number of dependents employed in government business and entitled to government rations, as well as Sánchez's profits. His beef fed the new recruits, but in view of the crisis, Lt. Col. Carlos Howard was incensed that Sánchez insisted on charging the same price on the frontier as he did for cattle herded all the way to St. Augustine. Although Howard protested what he viewed as Sánchez's greed, he had no option but to buy his beef. That year Sánchez sold the government over 19,000 pounds of fresh meat, for which he was paid 1,612 pesos.[35]

In the summer of 1795, the plotters who hoped to liberate Florida from monarchical rule began their attacks and seized several of the colony's northern outposts. The Spaniards and their black and Indian allies engaged the enemy in several land and naval battles and eventually were able to dislodge the invaders. Although the invasion plot failed, several of Florida's Anglo planters had taken part, and the Spanish government embargoed their property as punishment. When these goods were sold at public auction, Sánchez was able to buy land, slaves, and other property at rock-bottom prices. At one auction, Sánchez bought four slaves (three adults and one child) formerly owned by the rebels for only 600 pesos.[36] Other Anglo planters, not involved in sedition, nevertheless deemed it wise to leave the province, and Sánchez obligingly bought them out, too. In other cases, Sánchez simply "held in trust" the valuable slaves of absent Anglos, whom he put to work alongside his own.[37]

The numerous political transitions, intrigues, and episodes of violence in Second Spanish Period Florida—the British exodus, the exile of the banditti, the French plot of 1795, followed by Indian raids instigated by Augustus Bowles in the early 1800s—resulted in depressed prices and desperate sellers. Moreover, the *situado* (an annual government subsidy) arrived irregularly and belatedly after 1800. There were few solvent buyers within the colony, and fewer without, who would risk an investment in the turbulent area. It was Sánchez's market, and he made the most of it. His entrepreneurial talents generated badly needed capital for the depressed colony. And when international embargoes sparked renewed prosperity in St. Augustine—through which merchants trans-shipped goods from the Atlantic seaboard to ports as diverse as Lisbon, Rotterdam, Liverpool, and St. Petersburg, to name only a few—Sánchez went right on making money. The U.S. embargo on the slave trade, which was to take effect in 1808, also prompted many Anglo merchants and planters to buy southward, where slave introductions were still permitted—in St. Augustine and its new ancillary port at Fernandina, on Amelia Island.[38]

Francisco Xavier Sánchez missed the possibilities of these later political disturbances and the profits they generated. He died intestate on October 3, 1807, and was buried in the Tolomato cemetery in St. Augustine. When Spanish officials probated Sánchez's estate, it comprised nine plantations including the San Diego, the San José, the Ashley, the Capuaca, the Araguey (also known as the Santa Barbara), the lands at Royal Palm, the Laurel de Sánchez, the Swamp, the Consejero, and the Sabana General. In addition, Sánchez owned slaves, cattle, nine town houses and lots, and commercial interests. His holdings were valued at over $32,000.[39]

After Sánchez's death, his widow, María del Carmen, managed his multiple estates, carefully recording income and expenses for each, as required for the division among the many heirs. These accounts describe the harvests of the various plantations, the wages earned by slaves who were working for themselves or hired out to others, expenses for slave clothing and medical care, as well as gifts of rum and tobacco for the slaves at Christmas.[40] Sánchez had instructed María del Carmen to see that his five natural children, all adults, were provided for, and she complied with his wishes. María and her eight young children could afford to be generous to the illegitimate children with whom they were closely linked: Sánchez's biracial children inherited houses, lands, and slaves valued at over 7,000 pesos. When María del Carmen died in 1813, her legitimate son, Joseph Simeon, inherited the bulk of the Sánchez estates, which he continued to hold intact despite the series of political disturbances that repeatedly devastated the province during the final years of the Spanish tenure.[41]

The empire that Francisco Xavier Sánchez built over the course of a lifetime was a cornerstone of colonial Florida's economic development. Sánchez weathered the political storms that buffeted Florida and, in the most adverse conditions, created prosperity. His cattle, timber, and agricultural harvests sustained three separate administrations, and his varied commercial interests buoyed Florida's fragile economy. Sánchez's vast holdings on the Diego Plains remained within the family when the colony became a territory of the United States, and his descendants, following the pragmatic lead of their patriarch, became loyal and energetic supporters of the new government. Sánchez's oldest son, Joseph Simeon Sánchez, served in the new territorial army and became a ferocious Indian fighter during the Second Seminole War, winning the gratitude and favors of the U.S. government. His fervor may have been inspired by the mass escape of some of his slaves to the Black Seminole village on the Suwannee River in 1818.[42]

The influx of U.S. settlers soon changed Florida in many ways, and one of the most significant alterations was to history. All that came before the introduction of Anglo-Saxon industry and "improvement" into Florida was soon forgotten or depreciated, ethnocentrically recast as belonging to a lethargic Spanish doldrums. As this essay and the others in this volume hope to demonstrate, this is an inaccurate portrayal. No social, economic, or political history of the colonial Atlantic or circum-Caribbean is complete without the inclusion of Florida, and rich and available archival materials await the interested scholar for such work.[43]

Notes

1. An earlier version of this essay appeared in *Spanish Pathways in Florida*, ed. Ann L. Henderson and Gary R. Mormino (Sarasota, Fla.: Pineapple Press, 1991), 168–87. I also delivered a section of this essay at the 1994 Southern Historical Association conference, on which Alan Gallay offered very thoughtful comments. I am in his debt.

2. Some of that expansion came through intermarriage and purchase, but Sánchez also acquired "public" land from several governments that were in his debt. Sánchez's estates included: the original homestead, the San Diego, on the Diego Plains (1,000 acres); five additional pieces on the Diego Plains, including the Laurel de Sánchez, the Swamp, the Consejero, and San Francisco Afuiqui (300 acres), which Sánchez acquired at later dates; Governor Vicente Manuel de Zéspedes's grant of the San Nicolás on the St. Johns River (1,000 acres); Governor Juan Nepomuceno de Quesada's 1791 grants of the San José and the Santo Domingo on the east bank of the St. Johns River (1,130 acres); the Capuaca and Torope savannahs, along the west bank of the North River, which Sánchez purchased at the Jessie Fish auction in 1792 (599 acres); lands known as Santa Barbara or Araguey, also along the North River; Governor Enrique White's 1801 grant of lands at Monte de Puercos (100 acres); and the Ashley plantation (300 acres), on the east bank of the St. Johns River, which Sánchez bought from Juana Ashley in

1809 (*Spanish Land Grants in Florida, vol. 5 Confirmed Claims* (hereafter cited as *SLGF*) [Tallahassee: Historical Records Survey, 1940], 25–48; Bruce S. Chappell, "A Report on Documentation Relating to the History of the Diego Plains Region in the Second Spanish Period," typescript on file at the P. K. Yonge Library of Florida History, University of Florida, Gainesville (hereinafter cited as PKY); Inventory and appraisal of the estate of Francisco Xavier Sánchez, October 1808, Testamentary Proceedings, microfilm reel 141, East Florida Papers (hereinafter cited as EFP), PKY.

3. Also see James G. Cusick, "Across the Border: Commodity Flow and Merchants in Spanish St. Augustine," *Florida Historical Quarterly* 69, no. 3 (1991): 277–99.

4. Amy Bushnell, "The Menéndez Márquez Cattle Barony at La Chua and the Determinants of Economic Expansion in Seventeenth-century Florida," *Florida Historical Quarterly* 56, no. 4 (April 1978): 407–31; Charles W. Arnade, "Cattle Raising in Spanish Florida, 1513–1763," *Agricultural History* 35 (July 1961): 116–24.

5. Bushnell, "Menéndez Márquez Cattle Barony."

6. Verner W. Crane, *The Southern Frontier, 1670–1732* (Westport, Conn., 1977); Bushnell, "Menéndez Márquez Cattle Barony"; *The Spanish Missions of La Florida*, ed. Bonnie G. McEwan (Gainesville: University Press of Florida, 1993).

7. The Sánchez family originated in Ronda, and the Pérez family in San Lucar de Barrameda, Spain. Sánchez Family Papers, PKY); I. B. Hebel, *The Sánchez Family of St. Augustine, Florida* (Daytona Beach, 1957), transcript in the P. K. Yonge Library of Florida History, Gainesville.

8. Governor Manuel de Montiano to Captain General Juan Francisco de Güemes y Horcasitas, January 2, 1741, *Letters of Montiano, Siege of St. Augustine*, Collections of the Georgia Historical Society (Savannah, Ga., 1909), vol. 7, part 1, 54–55; Fandiño triggered the War of Jenkins's Ear by mutilating that English corsair, but he also captured at least thirty-eight prizes for the Spanish in his long career (Joyce Elizabeth Harmon, *Trade and Privateering in Spanish Florida, 1732–1763* [St. Augustine: St. Augustine Historical Society, 1969], 39).

9. Sánchez Family Papers, PKY; Hebel, *The Sánchez Family.*

10. The couple married on August 4, 1756 (Hebel, *Sánchez Family*); Chappell, "Report on . . . the History of the Diego Plains," PKY.

11. Manuel de Montiano to the king, December 27, 1740, Santo Domingo (hereinafter cited as SD) 2658, Archivo General de Indias, Seville, Spain (hereinafter cited as AGI); John Jay TePaske, *The Governorship of Spanish Florida, 1700–1763* (Durham, N.C.: Duke University Press, 1964), chap. 5.

12. TePaske, *Governorship of Spanish Florida*, 154–58.

13. Robert L. Gold, *Borderland Empires in Transition: The Triple-Nation Transfer of Florida* (Carbondale: Southern Illinois University Press, 1969); Evacuation Report of Juan Joseph Eligio de la Puente, January 1764, SD 2595, AGI.

14. Justification of Francisco Xavier Sánchez, March 8, 1785, cited in Joseph Byrne Lockey, *East Florida, 1783–1785: A File of Documents Assembled and*

Many of Them Translated, ed. John Walton Caughey (Berkeley: University of California Press, 1949), 473–76; J. Leitch Wright, Jr., *Florida in the American Revolution* (Gainesville: University Press of Florida, 1975); Franklin W. Knight, "The American Revolution and the Caribbean," in *Slavery and Freedom in the Age of the American Revolution,* ed. Ira Berlin and Ronald Hoffman (Charlottesville: University of Virginia Press, 1983), 237–61; Wilbur Henry Siebert, *Loyalists in East Florida, 1774–1785,* 2 vols. (DeLand: Florida State Historical Society, 1929).

15. Patrick Tonyn to Vicente Manuel de Zéspedes, July 5, 1784, and Francisco Xavier Sánchez's Justification, March 8, 1785, cited in Lockey, *East Florida, 1783–1785,* 214–17, 473–76; Edward J. Cashin, *The King's Ranger: Thomas Brown and the American Revolution on the Southern Frontier* (Athens: University of Georgia Press, 1989).

16. Lockey, *East Florida;* For more on the Anglo residents of Florida, see Susan R. Parker, "Men without God or King: Rural Settlers of East Florida, 1784–1790," *Florida Historical Quarterly* 69 (October 1990): 135–55; Accounts of the Royal Hacienda, Cuba 2636, AGI.

17. Benjamin Guerard to Luis de Unzaga, August 2, 1783, Manuscript Box 45, PKY.

18. The other plantation belonged to Francis Philip Fatio, about whom Susan R. Parker writes in chapter 3 of this volume (Vicente Manuel de Zéspedes to Bernardo de Gálvez, June 29, 1785, cited in Lockey, *East Florida, 570–73).*

19. For more on Edimboro's work and life and his lengthy manumission suit against Sánchez, see Jane G. Landers, *Black Society in Spanish Florida* (Urbana: University of Illinois Press, 1999), and "Felipe Edimboro Sues for Manumission," in *Colonial Lives: Documents on Latin American History, 1550–1850,* ed. Geoffrey Spurling and Richard Boyer (Oxford: Oxford University Press, 1999).

20. Inventory of the Sánchez estate, October 1808, Testamentary Proceedings, microfilm reel 141, EFP, PKY.

21. Catalina Mariana Morales, the slave of Bartolomé Morales, made that charge in court when she was trying to force Sánchez to sell her husband, Francisco Sánchez, to her own owner (Petition by Francisco Xavier Sánchez and Response by Bartolomé Morales, October 23, 1802, microfilm reel 156, EFP, PKY).

22. Coartación suit of Felipe Edimboro, July 10, 1794, Notarized Instruments, microfilm reel 152, EFP, PKY.

23. Accounts of the Royal Hacienda, SD 2635 (1784–95) and 2636 (1796–1819), AGI.

24. Sánchez won fresh meat contracts on August 28, 1784, March 1, 1785, December 30, 1793, November 6, 1794, March 6, 1802, February 27, 1806, June 6, 1806 and a firewood contract on September 1, 1787. These represent only a sample of his contracts (To and From the Intendant of the Exchequer, microfilm reel 24, EFP, PKY).

25. Accounts of F. X. Sánchez in U. B. Phillips and J. D. Glunt, eds., *Florida Plantation Records from the Papers of George Noble Jones* (St. Louis: Missouri

Historical Society, 1927). For sales by Miranda and Sánchez to the government on March 3, 1797, see Accounts of the Royal Treasury, SD 2636, AGI.

26. Juan Nepomuceno de Quesada, List of the Employees Indebted to Don Francisco Xavier Sánchez, March 28, 1792, Cuba 407, AGI.

27. Cusick, "Across the Border."

28. Chappell, "Report on Documentation Relating to . . . the Diego Plains," PKY. On the Panton, Leslie and Company, see William S. Coker and Thomas D. Watson, *Indian Traders of the Southeastern Spanish Borderlands: Panton, Leslie & Company and John Forbes and Company, 1783–1847* (Pensacola: University of West Florida Press, 1986).

29. Accounts of the Royal Hacienda, SD 2635 (1784–95) and 2636 (1796–1819), AGI; Allan J. Kuethe, "Havana in the Eighteenth Century," in *Atlantic Port Cities: Economy, Culture, and Society in the Atlantic World, 1650–1850*, ed. Franklin W. Knight and Peggy K. Liss (Knoxville: University of Tennessee Press, 1991), 13–39, provides background on Havana and its booming economy but makes little reference to Florida. Linda K. Salvucci and James Lewis also discuss the role of Anglo merchants in Cuba in the eighteenth century in Jacques A. Barbier and Allan J. Kuethe, eds., *The North American Role in the Spanish Imperial Economy, 1760–1819* (Dover, N.H.: Manchester University Press, 1984).

30. The baptisms of María Beatriz Piedra's children are recorded in the Cathedral Parish Records, Diocese of St. Augustine Catholic Center, Jacksonville, Fla. (hereafter cited as CPR), Black Baptisms, vols. 1–3, on microfilm reel 284 J, PKY. The baptisms of Sánchez's legitimate children are recorded in vols. 1–4, on microfilm reel 284 I, PKY. For marriages, see Black Marriages, CPR, vol. 1, on microfilm reel 284 L, ibid.

31. Black Baptisms, CPR, on microfilm reel 284 J, PKY. For more on these families see Landers, *Black Society*.

32. Contract between F. X. Sánchez and Vicente Manuel de Zéspedes, September 1, 1787, microfilm reel 24, EFP, PKY.

33. Carlos Howard to Juan Nepomuceno de Quesada, enclosed in Juan Nepomuceno de Quesada to Luis de Las Casas, April 21, 1794, Cuba 1439, AGI.

34. On the burned plantations, see Claim of Francisco Pellicer, August 20, 1802, microfilm reel 11, EFP, PKY.

35. Howard informed the governor that Sánchez had paid no more than seven pesos a head for cattle for which he now charged the government almost twenty-five pesos, a profit Howard considered exorbitant (Carlos Howard to Juan Nepomuceno de Quesada, November 6, 1794, microfilm reel 51, EFP, PKY). Government payments to Sánchez for meat in 1795 are in SD 2635, AGI. In 1797, after the extra troops had left the province, Sánchez sold the government less than 1,500 pounds of meat (SD 2636, AGI).

36. Sánchez bought Paris, who had once belonged to Jorge Knolls, and Waley, her son, and Waley's mother Paty, who had all belonged to Guillermo Jones (Receipt of 600 pesos from Don Francisco Xavier Sánchez, December 20, 1798, microfilm reel 129, EFP, PKY). Detailed property inventories and the disposition of

the properties are included in Criminal Proceedings, Rebellion of 1795, on microfilm reels 128–29, EFP, PKY.

37. In 1795 Sánchez "held" five slaves belonging to Juan Macandos, worth 1,500 pesos, and five belonging to Reden Blunt, worth 750 pesos (Report by Lt. Juan de Pierra of Slaves Owned by the Inhabitants in 1795, microfilm reel 154, EFP, PKY).

38. Accounts of the Exchequer, SD 2636, AGI. Also see Christopher Ward, "The Commerce of East Florida during the Embargo, 1806–1812: The Role of Amelia Island," *Florida Historical Quarterly* 68, no. 2 (1990): 160–79. Investors such as Zephaniah Kingsley, Fernando de la Maza Arredondo, Daniel Hurlburt, and James Cashen now sent ships to Sierra Leone, the "Guinea Coast," and even Mozambique, for slaves. Some slaves were unloaded in Havana, but others were sold in Florida to Anglo planters and mercantile companies such as Hibberson and Yonge. On the slave sales, see Landers, *Black Society,* chap. 7.

39. Inventory and Appraisal of the Estate of Francisco Xavier Sánchez, 1808, microfilm reel 141, EFP, PKY.

40. Testamentary Proceedings of F. X. Sánchez, Accounts by María del Carmen Hill, January 31, 1809, microfilm reel 141, EFP, PKY.

41. Probate of estate of María del Carmen Hill, May 2, 1816, microfilm reel 141, EFP, PKY.

42. Unfortunately for the slaves, Andrew Jackson's invasion force attacked that settlement the same year (Joseph Simeon Sánchez, typescript dated November 15, 1938, Sánchez Family Biography Box, PKY); Alexander Arbuthnot to John Arbuthnot, April 2, 1818, cited in *Narrative of a Voyage to the Spanish Main in the Ship "Two Friends,"* facsimile of 1819 ed. (Gainesville: University Press of Florida, 1978), 216–18.

43. One who questions how North American history came to exclude the Caribbean is Alison F. Games, "The Importance of Caribbean History in U.S. History Courses: Some Thoughts on the Early Modern Atlantic World," paper delivered at the Association of Caribbean Historians, San German, Puerto Rico, March 1994. The untapped sources for the eighteenth-century Atlantic world include literally thousands of microfilmed folios on trade into and out of Florida. Other particularly rich sources that should be of interest to colonialists include the testamentary and land claims records and papers related to the Indian trade and diplomacy. The complete notarial archive of the Spanish government for East Florida (1784–1821) is available as the East Florida Papers on microfilm in the Library of Congress and in various repositories in the United States, including the PKY.

5

Zephaniah Kingsley's Laurel Grove Plantation, 1803–1813

Daniel L. Schafer

On the morning of June 4, 1810, white members of the colonial militia of Spanish East Florida raided slave quarters at plantations along the St. Johns River. Experiencing "little interruption while the Negroes were at work in the field," the mounted raiders confiscated forty-one guns.[1] Two influential plantation owners were incensed by the raids. George Fleming, a prominent Irish-born planter and militia officer who had been in East Florida since 1790, and María del Carmen Hill Sánchez, the widow of wealthy Florida-born planter and merchant Francisco Xavier Sánchez (about whom Jane Landers writes in this volume), wrote to Governor Enrique White demanding compensation for lost weapons. Fleming claimed the armaments confiscated at his plantation were for "defense and security [against] savage indians, [and] animals eating corn." Sánchez warned of "dangers now due to lack of firearms," and said her enslaved workers "must have weapons to keep animals away from planted seeds."

A bolder challenge came from two black slaves, Abraham Hannahan and Peter [Kingsley]. Hannahan, the mulatto manager of Zephaniah Kingsley's Laurel Grove Plantation, confronted militia members as they searched the plantation's slave quarters and confiscated eleven guns. According to one of the militia men, Abraham used "improper language . . . [and] conduct." When told that the militia acted under government orders and must be obeyed, Abraham said he would "go and see Mr. [William] Craig [the judicial official in charge of the St. Johns River district] and that if he did not give him satisfaction that he would go to governor White, that he would speak his mind to him and that he might send him to the guard house to the fort or to the Devil that he did not care."[2]

Abraham went the following day to the home of Andres Maclean to "repeat that he was going to the governor and that he did not fear going to the stocks nor anywhere else for he would have his gun."[3] Andrew Atkinson heard Abraham declare that neither "Mr. Craig, the governor or anybody else had any right to interfere with his master's plantation." With another slave manager, named Peter, Abraham continued the protest on June 6, at a meeting of area planters and militia members to discuss the raids, which was held at the Cowford Ferry. Peter boldly demanded the return of his personal weapon and became irritated when the white men refused, declaring "things would take a turn and . . . Negroes would yet have their arms."[4] This was more black protest than the white planters and slaveowners could tolerate. After hearing "the very improper and disrespectful expressions used in the [presence of the white men] by a Mulatto man named Abram . . . and the expressions of disrespect and insubordination uttered by an old Negro man named Peter," Craig had the men manacled and marched to St. Augustine.[5]

Craig also dismissed the protests from white slaveowners. He had ordered the militia raids of June 4 in an atmosphere of hysteria prompted by rumors of a pending slave insurrection in Georgia. The rumors had begun circulating through Northeast Florida in April. Hurried investigations produced reports of a "secret correspondence subsisting betwixt the Negroes and a mulatto man named Morris who had lately come in from Georgia, and from whence it since appeared he had been driven on account of his being an active encourager of the intended Insurrection there." Even more ominous were reports of more than 100 slaves who owned guns (some "were purchasing a second") and comments that slaves had been "more Insolent and disobedient than usual." Convinced they had stemmed a potential disaster, militia members brushed aside protests from whites as well as blacks and made plans for further raids on plantations where no weapons had been found. Further raids were justified by reports of "the Negroes having received some intimation of what was going to take place, in others the owners refused to have their Negro's houses examined or their arms taken from them."[6]

As for the black protesters, Abraham told a judicial tribunal at the provincial capital that his actions were justified by the authority placed in him by his owner when he was absent from the plantation. As first manager (Peter was second manager), he was responsible for Kingsley's estate and his 100 enslaved Africans; nonetheless, the soldiers had demanded "keys to all the habitations from a female slave in charge of all the interior interests of our master and as she . . . did not have it in her power in our [Abraham and Peter's] absence, they . . . broke the doors of the houses of the Negroes [and destroyed] as much as it was their pleasure to trample."[7]

The governor's tribunal sided with the militia and sentenced Abraham and Peter to "fifty lashes to each one" and "forced labor for one month in chains or shackles," a punishment deemed necessary to "make them understand and observe due submission and respect."[8]

The events surrounding the militia raid of 1810 reveal a troubled and divided community of white residents. Slaveowners throughout the Americas had grown increasingly apprehensive in the years after the American Revolution, especially following the slave revolt in Saint Domingue that drove the French from that island and ushered in the free black state of Haiti.[9] In East Florida, settlers experienced economic hardship and chronic instability after Spain resumed control following the postwar British evacuation in 1784. Governor Juan Nepomuceno de Quesada reacted in 1794 to a threat of invasion from Georgia with a scorched-earth policy that devastated settlements north and west of St. Augustine, weakening the new settlers' loyalty to Spain. Free black militia companies were effective in stemming that threat and also helped to defeat invaders led by William Augustus Bowles in 1800–1803. To the white settlers, however, dependence on nonwhite militia was fraught with peril, especially after Gen. Jorge Biassou arrived in St. Augustine from Saint Domingue in 1796. Biassou, a former slave, had commanded an army of 40,000 men. Even Touissant Louverture had been his subordinate. Biassou allied with the Spanish government of Hispaniola, on the western portion of the island; but after Spain and France agreed to peace terms in 1795, Biassou and his closest followers were sent to the troubled East Florida frontier. Historian Jane G. Landers has described the effective military service that Biassou and his black troops provided. Nevertheless, Landers writes, the presence of a "decorated, militant, independent, and propertied" black man, one who "had fought his way out of slavery in the hemisphere's bloodiest revolution," greatly alarmed Florida slaveowners.[10] They feared that the example would incite unrest among their own slaves.

Spanish governors also relied on Seminole warriors from the nearby Alachua prairie, which further troubled the province's white planters. The Seminole nation was seen as a potential threat, especially to migrants from Georgia who had experienced troubles with Creek Indians in their former homes. Other settlers feared that slave runaways who had previously found sanctuary in Seminole territory would raid plantations and tempt other slaves to abscond. East Florida in 1810, therefore, was a promising frontier area with huge reserves of undeveloped land, but it was still dependent on black militia and Indian allies for security—an unsettling prospect for white planters.[11]

In the decade preceding the militia raid of June 4, 1810, however, planters experienced record prosperity, based on exports of lumber, cotton, and rice. The slave population had increased dramatically following the 1790 decision by Spanish officials to open East Florida's borders to foreign and non-Catholic immigrants and to grant them fifty acres of unclaimed land for every family member or worker (free or slave) they brought into the colony. Within months, 300 whites and their 1,000 enslaved blacks became new Florida residents. Between 1790 and 1804, approximately 750 immigrant heads of family took loyalty oaths in St. Augustine, 270 of them slaveowners claiming nearly 5,000 bondsmen. More than 80 percent were born in a British North American colony (by then part of the United States), or in England, Scotland, or Ireland. Another 10 percent were of French ancestry, including refugees from the slave rebellion in Saint Domingue.[12]

In 1809, John Fraser, a Scottish-born slave trader with an African family at Rio Pongo, West Africa, transported 370 Africans to his East Florida rice and cotton plantations. John H. McIntosh imported more than 200 slaves from his estates in Georgia. The lure of land and profit prompted numerous adventurers to move to East Florida, including African slave traders who moved from English, Danish, and U.S. ports after these nations banned the international trade in slaves. The Spanish possessions were among the few remaining places where the slave trade could continue under a protective flag. The combination of huge reserves of unclaimed land, a booming agricultural export market, and the availability of inexpensive African laborers resulted in black and enslaved population majorities at St. Augustine, Amelia Island, and along the St. Johns, St. Marys, Nassau, and Mosquitoes Rivers. Planters in need of laborers eagerly purchased the Africans arriving at Fernandina and St. Augustine, but other settlers feared the new Africans would prompt slave rebellions. Fear could easily become hysteria at remote frontier estates with black slave majorities.[13]

Zephaniah Kingsley did not share these fears. At his Laurel Grove Plantation, located at Doctors Lake and the St. Johns River, approximately forty miles upriver from the Atlantic Ocean, 100 enslaved Africans were at work, often without a white man in residence. Abraham Hannahan, a man of mixed-race origins born in the Kingsley home in Charleston (the same man who had protested the June 4 militia raid at Laurel Grove) was in charge of a major plantation while his owner captained a ship in the West Indies and African slave trade. Even Kingsley's sailors were slaves: When one of his schooners was seized in 1808 for possible violation of Spanish tax laws, Kingsley was its captain and six black slaves were its crew. His domicile at Laurel Grove was managed by Anta Majigeen Ndiaye, a thirteen-year-old Wolof girl whom Kingsley had purchased in Havana in 1806 and who later became his wife and the mother of four of his children. At a time when other planters were fearful of slave insurrection, eleven of the guns confiscated in the 1810 raid were owned by Kingsley's bondsmen. He must have been as controversial in 1810 as he seems atypical today.[14]

Kingsley was born in 1765 in Bristol, England, to a Scot mother and an English-Quaker father. The family moved in 1770 to Charles Town, South Carolina, where the elder Kingsley became a successful merchant before being banished in 1784 for Loyalist activities during the American Revolution. In 1793 Zephaniah Kingsley, Jr. returned to Charleston and swore to an oath of naturalization. Between 1793 and 1797, when the slave rebellion was underway in the French colony of Saint Domingue, Kingsley lived for a year at the town of Jeremie, purchasing and exporting coffee. He took another oath of loyalty in 1798, this time to Denmark, and found employment as a ship captain at the port of Charlotte-Amalie on the island of St. Thomas. In March 1802 he sailed his own ship from St. Thomas to Havana, Cuba, with a cargo of 250 Africans.[15]

On September 24, 1803, Kingsley took his third oath of loyalty in a decade, becoming a Spanish citizen at St. Augustine, East Florida. Already a wealthy man, possessing properties worth 67,160 pesos, Kingsley purchased Laurel Grove Plantation and began importing African laborers. Although Florida would be his primary residence for the next four decades, his inveterate travels continued. He was away from Florida from July 1804 to November 1806—twenty-eight consecutive months—traveling to England, Africa, and the West Indies, serving as supercargo (business agent) of a ship that sailed from Savannah to Liverpool; from there he sailed to Mozambique and Zanzibar Island to purchase slaves for the Charleston market. In July 1806, Kingsley sent sixteen East Africans from Charleston to his Florida plantation before traveling to Havana to sell other Africans and to purchase sugar, rum, and coffee. When Kingsley finally returned to Laurel Grove Plantation in November 1806, he was accompanied by *tres negras bozales* (three African females), one of whom is believed to have been the Wolof woman Anta Majigeen Ndiaye, who became his wife and was known in Florida as Anna Kingsley.[16]

Laurel Grove Plantation had been under Kingsley's ownership for only three years. He purchased the property from Rebeccah Pengree in 1803 for 5,300 pesos. With a subsequent purchase of 300 adjacent acres, Kingsley became the owner of nearly 3,000 acres of prime land situated on East Florida's principal waterway. By March 1808 sixty-six additional "new Negroes" selected from the slaves Kingsley purchased in Africa had arrived and begun work under the supervision of Abraham Hannahan and Peter [Kingsley].[17]

Kingsley divided his Africans into three work groups and housed them at three separate agricultural villages at Laurel Grove. The main export crop was long-staple cotton. Citrus, an important secondary crop, was grown at Laurel Grove and at Drayton Island (also owned by Kingsley), located twenty miles further upriver. Hay meadows scattered in clearings amidst the uncleared reserves of pine and oak forests produced fodder for the draft animals; fields of corn, peas, and sweet potatoes provided foodstuffs for the laborers and for commercial sale. The custom at the time was to assign each worker five or six acres of cotton, six acres of corn and peas (planted together), and four acres of sweet potatoes. Under the task system of labor utilized by Kingsley, the workers tended one-quarter increments of cotton and other crops as assigned daily by the overseer/manager. When tasks were completed, workers were able to organize their own time for hunting, fishing, recreation, or for cultivating vegetables, corn, and other items in the garden spaces Kingsley provided each family.[18]

The largest of the three agricultural villages was the Laurel Grove settlement, an elaborate complex of 1,800 acres extending north and south along the St. Johns River for two miles, and west along Doctors Lake for one mile. Two dwelling houses were standing in July 1812. One had been newly built that year for a retail store on the first floor and a family residence on the second. Its probable location was on the St. Johns River north of Doctors Lake, near the present site of Club Continental at Astor Street, south of Kingsley Avenue, in the city of Orange Park. The store/dwelling was a thirty-six-by-forty-foot framed building covered with "cedar shingles" and fitted "with brick chimneys." The comfortable family quarters held "a quantity of furniture and beds, valuable books, charts, and crockery ware." Kingsley said the retail store "contained a large supply of every article for plantation and family use and was kept for the supply of the surrounding country." An inventory of the store done in July 1812 valued the supplies at $2,685 (a value of at least $83,400 today).[19] A nearby twenty-six-by-thirty-foot framed warehouse was stocked with 1,500 bushels of salt and 120 gallons of Jamaican rum, sugar from Havana, barrels of gunpowder, and other items valued at $2,780. A seven-foot post and clapboard cedar fence enclosed the retail store/dwelling house; somewhere inside were ten muskets and bayonets, two four-pounder cannons with carriages, and cartridges, iron balls, and grapeshot.

The second dwelling house at Laurel Grove was "a good frame building measuring thirty by thirty-five feet with double piazzas and brick chimneys" containing "a large quantity of household and kitchen furniture, beds and [miscellaneous] . . . and one spring shuttle loom." A detached kitchen stood near the dwelling house. A framed cotton house, thirty by forty feet, stored the cotton harvested from all the fields at the estate. During July 1812 there were sixty bales (21,000 pounds) from the 1811 crop awaiting export. With long-staple cotton selling for fifty cents a pound, Kingsley expected the bales to bring $10,500. An additional 30,000 pounds of "unginned" seed cotton from the 1810 crop was on

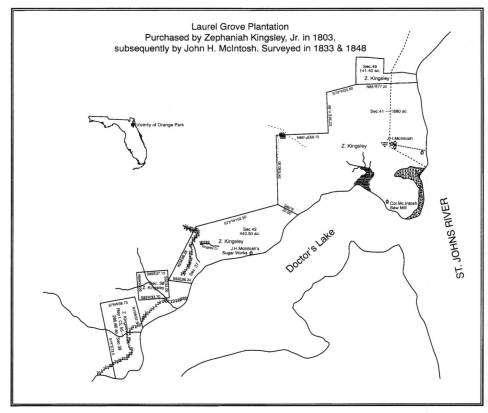

Map 5. An artist's conception of Laurel Grove Plantation, 1812. Computer generated by Teresa St. John. Based on K-10, Zephaniah Kingsley, Spanish Land Grant Maps, Series 990, Florida State Archives, Tallahassee.

Fig. 5.1. Artist's conception of Zephaniah Kingsley's Laurel Grove Plantation in 1812, by Nancy Freeman. By permission of Nancy Freeman.

hand, estimated to be worth only $.15 a pound (or $4,500) before ginning. Only 200 acres were planted in cotton in 1812, but the predicted yield was 200–300 pounds per acre—or 40,000 pounds, worth $20,000 after ginning.

Kingsley invested heavily in machinery and barns and other storage structures. Three double-sized cotton gins, each worth $250, cleaned the seeds from the fiber. A large water wheel outside the gin house, measuring forty feet in diameter, provided power for the cotton gins and for two stone grinding mills and one large steel mill. That power must have come from water diverted from the small creek via a dam and reserve pond and a mill race, although the exact location has not been found. A frame carpentry shop measuring thirty by forty feet held an extensive inventory of saws, drills, axes, hatchets, and carpentry adzes. The blacksmith shop contained bellows, anvils, and tools under the control of Morton, whom Kingsley labeled "a very prime young man" and valued at $1,000. The remaining structures included a new barn measuring twenty-five by forty feet stocked with 800 bushels of corn and 300 of peas; a fodder house; a cart house with three carts, three plows and harnesses; and twelve "good Negro houses" with clothing and furniture.

Citrus was also a valuable crop at the Laurel Grove settlement. A nine-acre citrus grove with 750 choice Mandarin orange trees was located near the dwelling houses, surrounded by a 2,000-foot "bearing orange hedge," which in turn was enclosed by a twelve-foot-high cypress picket fence. Two men worked for three months installing the picket fence around the grove. They also worked for another four months constructing a rail fence which extended for thirty miles around the fields and buildings at Laurel Grove and beyond to the other two agricultural settlements.

The second agricultural village, called both Ship Yard and Canefield in the records, was on Doctors Lake, approximately two miles west of the St. Johns River and adjacent to the southwestern boundary of Laurel Grove settlement. The shipyard revolved around a twenty-by-thirty-foot workshop equipped with a large steaming stove and kettle. Adjoining posts in the ground extending to the water launched newly completed ships and facilitated repair of the plantation's work boats. A dwelling house, a store house, a twenty-by-thirty-foot blacksmith shop, three grindstones and stands, and nine slave houses—all surrounded by ornamental live oak trees—completed the structures at Ship Yard settlement. The dual names— Ship Yard and Canefield—suggest that sugarcane was planted on the north shore of Doctors Lake, a practice followed by the owner of the property in the 1850s, John H. McIntosh.[20]

Springfield settlement was west of Ship Yard at the northwest corner of Doctors Lake. It was devoted to provisions and cotton cultivation under the supervision of Peter, a "mechanic and valuable manager" valued by Kingsley at $1,000 (the same man who confronted militia members in 1810). Buildings at Springfield included a large framed house for Peter, a storehouse stocked with 700 bushels of corn and 400 of peas, fifteen "new Negro houses," and a mill house. Also at Springfield in July 1812 were four stacks of fodder, 150 hogs, and fifteen dozen ducks and chickens.

The three settlements at Laurel Grove Plantation were completed in less than a decade. With four dwelling houses, thirty-six slave houses, two blacksmith shops, a shipyard, retail store, barns and other storage buildings, stocks of poultry, hogs, cattle and horses, and a network of roads and fences, citrus grove, provisions and cotton fields, Laurel Grove was a considerable achievement created by the labor of enslaved Africans. Like dozens of planters in the province, Kingsley experienced record profits until July 1812, when the prosperous times ended abruptly.

In March 1812 land-hungry invaders from Georgia—encouraged and financed by United States authorities and directed and supported by the U.S. troops who covertly accompanied them—brought destruction to East Florida and an end to its booming export economy. Calling themselves "Patriots," the invaders were joined by residents of the Spanish province in an insurgency aimed at annexing it to the United States. Kingsley and other influential planters who opposed the rebellion were captured and held in a detention camp for several months. In July, after the insurgents established siege lines outside St. Augustine, Governor Sebastián Kindelán ordered his Seminole allies to attack the outlying settlements, hoping to force rebel planters back to their vulnerable homes and families.

Governor Kindelán's strategy succeeded, but it also resulted in the destruction of dozens of East Florida's formerly thriving plantations. Laurel Grove Plantation was plundered and destroyed in July 1812. Only the dwelling house on the St. Johns River, surrounded by a stockade fence, escaped the general conflagration of crops and buildings. Occupied by bands of "Patriot" invaders, the fortified dwelling survived until November 1813, when it was destroyed in a spectacular fire ignited by Anna Kingsley, Zephaniah's wife and household manager.

The full story of this daring incendiary act is told in my monograph *Anna Kingsley*. Anna was the same Wolof teenager known as Anta Majigeen Ndiaye, whom Kingsley had purchased in Cuba in 1803 and brought to Laurel Grove as his wife. Kingsley manumitted Anna and her three children in March 1811, when she was eighteen years old. In 1812, she moved across the St. Johns River and established a home of her own in Mandarin on land granted by the Spanish government. Also living at Anna's Mandarin homestead were twelve enslaved African Americans. Anna Kingsley had become a slaveowner.

The "Patriot" invaders represented a dire threat to Anna after the invasion quickly degenerated into a plundering expedition. Bands of guerrilla marauders looted plantations, stealing slaves and other property and thoroughly disrupting social and economic conditions in Northeast Florida between 1812 and 1815. Free African Americans captured by the marauders were manacled and marched to Georgia and sold into slavery. Although the exact sequence of events is not known, there is evidence that Anna returned to Laurel Grove after placing her children and her slaves aboard a Spanish gunboat anchored in the St. Johns River. She also placed aboard the vessel several Africans she had secreted away from Laurel Grove. She then returned by canoe to the wharf, slipped into the fortified dwelling house, and placed in the building an incendiary device that ignited after she had returned safely to the gunboat. Saying that "her master" would be pleased when he learned that the fortified stronghold occupied by hostile forces was burned to the ground, she left the gunboat for a second time to torch her own homestead on the eastern shore of the river, denying another potential sanctuary to the invaders. By these brave actions, Anna saved herself and children from reenslavement. The gunboat commander praised her noble acts of patriotism, writing: "[S]he has worked like a heroine, destroying the strong house with the fire she set so that the artillery could not be obtained, and later doing the same with her own property."[21]

Laurel Grove Plantation was almost totally destroyed by the Seminole attack of July 1812 and Anna's incendiary action of November 1813. In what a U.S. Treasury Department official later judged a conservative estimate, Kingsley totaled his financial losses at $110,753 (over $3.3 million today).[22] Kingsley wrote of the tragic incident:

> After a few years, this pleasant and profitable state of harmony was interrupted by the revolution of 1812. A war party of Seminole Indians attacked the plantation in my absence; caught, bound, and carried off, or killed, forty of them [actually forty-one], whose reluctance in going with the invaders may be imagined from the following circumstance. The wife of a young man they had tied and were driving off, that her husband, who was too strong to be handled, and who had his young child in his arms, might follow; but this he absolutely refused, handing over the child to his wife, and saying that she knew best how to take care of it, but that his master should never say that he was a runaway negro; upon which the Indian shot him, and he died next day.[23]

The strong young man killed by the Seminoles was Morton, the blacksmith. Also killed that day was Peter, the manager at Springfield. An additional forty-one men, women, and children were abducted by the Seminoles. Over the next thirty years, none returned to Kingsley's employ, casting doubt on the patriarchal view of slave life at Laurel Grove which he propagated in a pamphlet published in 1828, *A Treatise on the Patriarchal or Cooperative System of Society as it Exists in Some Governments and Colonies in America, and in the United States, under the Name of Slavery, with Its Necessity and Advantages.*

> About twenty-five years ago, I settled a plantation on St. Johns River, in Florida, with about fifty new African negroes, many of whom I brought from the coast myself. They were mostly fine young men and women, and nearly in equal numbers. I never interfered with their connubial concerns, nor domestic affairs, but let them regulate these after their own manner. I taught them nothing but what was useful, and what I thought would add to their physical and moral happiness. I encouraged as much as possible dancing, merriment, and dress, for which Saturday afternoon and night, and Sunday

morning were dedicated; and, after allowance, their time was usually employed in hoeing their corn, and getting a supply of fish for the week. Both men and women were very industrious. Many of them made twenty bushels of corn to sell, and they vied with each other in dress and dancing, and as to whose woman was the finest and prettiest. They were perfectly honest, and obedient, and appeared quite happy, having no fear but that of offending me; and I hardly ever had occasion to apply other correction than shaming them. If I exceeded this, the punishment was quite light, for they hardly ever failed in doing their work well. My object was to excite their ambition and attachment by kindness; not to depress their spirits by fear and punishment. I never allowed them to visit, for fear of bad example, but encouraged the decent neighboring people to participate in their weekly festivity, for which they always provided an ample entertainment themselves, as they had an abundance of hogs, fowls, corn, and all kinds of vegetables and fruit. They had nothing to conceal from me, and I had no suspicion of any crime in them to guard against. Perfect confidence, friendship, and good understanding reigned between us; they increased rapidly.[24]

Kingsley's nostalgic and patronizing ruminations no doubt fail to reflect reality as understood by his enslaved Africans; yet from an owner's perspective, his interpretation is plausible. It is doubtful that the level of development achieved at Laurel Grove by 1812 could have been possible in an atmosphere of rebelliousness bordering on insurrection.[25] In a unique inventory, Kingsley documented the property he lost, listing ages and gender, family affiliation, and either ethnic or regional derivation for most of the Africans carried off by the Seminoles. The inventory makes it possible to reconstruct some features of Kingsley's first slave community and to visualize what must have been a complex process of cultural adjustment and culture-building at a major colonial plantation.[26]

One striking feature of the inventory is the youthfulness of the laborers. Ages of the adults ranged from twenty-six years to forty-eight, with a median age of twenty-eight. Eight of the fifteen males were between the ages of twenty-four and thirty, four between thirty-two and thirty-six, and three between forty and forty-eight. The nine adult females were all between the ages of twenty-five and thirty. Twelve boys and seven girls ranged in age from two to eight. All of the adults, with the exception of the three men ages forty and older, were classified as either "prime" or "very prime" workers. It was a young and valuable slave community which was steadily increasing in number through natural reproduction. Eight males and eight females living in household units were listed on the inventory as parents of one to four children, ranging in age from one to eight. Only one couple was childless. Two men were carpenters, one was a driver, and another was a sailor. The women as well as the men were field laborers.[27]

The other noteworthy feature of the labor force is that the majority of the adults were born in Africa, hailing from distant nations on the continent. Nearly half of the twenty-two adults retained African names, while all but two of the twenty-nine children were given Anglicized names. Eight adult males were listed as natives of southeastern Nigeria in West Africa: three were Igbo, two New Calabar, and three Calabari. Two males (both carpenters) and one female were Zinguebari, probably reflecting origins in East Africa and Kingsley's purchase of them at either Zanzibar Island or Zanguebar, on the coast of what today is Tanzania. Three males were from Guinea, on the West African coast: two men were "SooSoo" (generally SuSu today), an ethnic group living near the Pongo River; a woman listed as "Rio Pongo" may also have been SooSoo, or from the neighboring Baga, Landuman, or Nalu people. The name Martin McGuinda is written as if McGuinda were a nationality or an ethnic name. The historian George Brooks, has suggested that "Cabo Mouse" may have been a head boatman, with the name combining the Portuguese word *cabo,* for chief or headman, and the French word *mousse,* for cabin boy or ship boy.[28]

The inventory supports Kingsley's claim that he encouraged his workers to live in family units. Living arrangements, judging from the ages of the nineteen children abducted, must have been made soon after the Africans arrived at Laurel Grove. Jack, a carpenter listed as "Zinguebari," and Tamassa lived together with their two sons and two daughters. The name of their youngest son, M'toto (the Swahili word for boy), suggests that the parents were from East Africa. The name of another carpenter from "Zinguebari" is even more suggestive: M'Sooma has been tentatively identified as a "Kamba," possibly from a village located at the headwaters of the Tana River, whose residents today are well known as wood carvers.[29]

Jacob and Camilla made up one of the family units: he was an Igbo, she was from Rio Pongo. One wonders what language or languages their son Jim learned growing up in the slave quarters. For each family unit other than Jacob and Camilla's, only the male was assigned an African identity, prompting the conclusion that when an ethnic title or geographic location was not listed for the wife, the husband and wife shared a common background. If this assumption is correct, then two more New Calabar, two Zinguebari, two Calabari, and one Eabo should be added to the Creole "melting pot." Diversity must have been the key feature of the slave quarters, with a proliferation of languages being spoken and great variety in food preparations, clothing and hair styles, songs and musical instruments, and facial markings a daily staple of life. It is unfortunate that no further records exist of the cultural creolization process underway at Laurel Grove in 1812.

It is also regrettable that only minimal information exists concerning the laborers left behind when the Seminole warriors departed. A Spanish census taken June 2, 1814, lists Kingsley with only twenty-one slaves still in his possession; others must have been away on temporary assignments. It is known that at least two of Kingsley's enslaved women were Wolof, from today's Republic of Senegal, West Africa: One was Kingsley's wife Anna, the other was Sophy Chidgegane, the wife of Abraham Hannahan. The names of other Kingsley slaves listed on 1840s inventories—Carpenter Bonafy, Qualla, Abdalla, Bella, Tamassa, Comba, Coonta, Tamba, Penda, Nassebo, Yamba, and Jenoma—suggest the continuing influence of Africans at Kingsley's estates.[30]

Anna Kingsley was not at Laurel Grove when the Seminoles raided in 1812; she had been emancipated in 1811 and had moved to her own home on the east side of the St. Johns River. Abraham Hannahan was still at Laurel Grove in 1812 but not as manager. That position had been assigned to John Ashton, a white man, perhaps as a result of pressure from the colonial government following the insurrection hysteria of 1810. Abraham had survived the "fifty lashes" and "forced labor . . . in chains or shackles" ordered by the judicial tribunal, and had returned to Kingsley's plantation. Zephaniah emancipated Abraham in 1811 and gave him land on the river at Laurel Grove. John M. Bowden, a white neighbor, said that Hannahan "marked off and called his own place" a plot of land, where he built a home and outbuildings.[31]

As a free man, Hannahan became an independent farmer and a traveling merchant, selling plantation supplies from Kingsley's retail store to settlers along the river. Another neighbor, Rebecca E. Read, said that she had known Hannahan since his arrival in Florida in 1804 and that she had always considered him "a good Spanish subject." Hannahan's property was destroyed by the Patriots in 1812, and he was forced to pilot the insurgent's supply vessels on the St. Johns River. After peace was restored, Hannahan received land from the colonial government and established a new estate upriver near Fort Buena Vista. A close relationship between the former slave and his owner continued, with Hannahan becoming father-in-law to Kingsley after Flora, his and Sophy Chidgegane's daughter, became one of Kingsley's wives.[32]

Kingsley restored only the shipyard at Laurel Grove Plantation follow-ing the 1812–14 insurgency. Fort George Island at the mouth of the St. Johns River became his principal residence for the next two decades. He also acquired several other East Florida plantations and more than 200 slaves. His involvement in the African slave trade and his merchant activi-ties had ended by the time the United States acquired East Florida in 1821. His only known source of income thereafter was the profit derived from agricultural exports. Laurel Grove may have been leased to another planter or cultivated periodically by workers from Fort George Island; the record is incomplete.

Neither Kingsley nor the Africans who labored at Laurel Grove fit the image most Americans have of slaveowners and their human property. Kingsley believed that coerced labor of Africans was necessary to prosper from agriculture in Florida's semitropical climate. Only Africans were able to work and flourish amid the heat and disease; their pale European coun-terparts sickened and died under these conditions. Kingsley wrote: "Na-ture has not fitted a white complexion for hard work in the sun, as it is evident that the darkness of complexion here is a measure of capacity for endurance of labor."[33]

Coercing Africans carried the risk of rebellion, however, which con-vinced Kingsley to advocate a humane and patriarchal system of labor. Kingsley's Africans lived in family units, practiced African customs, worked under a task system, and were permitted to own small properties and work for themselves after completing their assigned duties. He estab-lished another measure of protection by creating a caste of black allies. If white patriarchs were to survive and prosper, Kingsley believed, liberal manumission policies were needed to convince "the free colored popula-tion to be attached to good order and have a friendly feeling towards the white population." He believed that the loyal and talented leaders among the slaves should be identified and emancipated and given personal and property rights to ensure that they became allies of white slaveowners. "Color ought not be the badge of degradation," Kingsley argued; "the only distinction should be between slave and free, not between white and colored." Closing off access to manumission would turn free blacks into "enemies by degrading them to the rank of our slaves."[34]

While Spain controlled East Florida, with its flexible three-caste system of race relations, Kingsley's views were generally in accord with govern-ment policy. Events like the militia raids of 1810 suggest, nevertheless, that seeds of discontent with the three-caste system were sown early by settlers moving to East Florida from Georgia and South Carolina. After the United

States took over in 1821, Spanish racial policies were replaced by a rigid set of laws based on the assumption that all black persons—whether slave or free—were uncivilized and inferior to white persons and could not exist peacefully outside the bonds of slavery.[35]

As a member of the American Territorial Council, Kingsley resisted the passage of the racially restrictive laws, then watched in despair as the rights of free persons of color were curtailed. He sold most of his Florida properties and purchased several plantation tracts in the free black Republic of Haiti, where Anna Kingsley and her sons George and John Maxwell, along with other Kingsley co-wives and children and fifty slaves, settled in 1837. Kingsley urged two daughters who remained in Florida (both were married to prominent white men) to emigrate "to some land of liberty and equal rights, where the conditions of society are governed by some law less absurd than that of color."[36]

Kingsley increasingly endorsed abolitionist doctrines in his later years, but he was still a major slaveowner when he died in New York City in September 1843. Lamenting only his previous involvement in the African slave trade, Kingsley proudly advocated his ideas on plantation management and race and marital relations even after legislators drafted laws that made them illegal. Undaunted, he published in 1828 a unique pamphlet, *A Treatise on the Patriarchal or Cooperative System of Society*, to persuade others of the merit of his views. A centerpiece in the argument advanced there was the great success achieved by his slave managers and African laborers at Laurel Grove Plantation before it was destroyed in 1812–13. About Laurel Grove Kingsley was undoubtedly correct. After 1821, however, his new U.S. neighbors emphatically rejected his system of race relations.

Author's note

I want to thank Joan E. Moore, my wife, for her constant love and support and for reading and editing countless versions of this essay. I also thank Jane Landers for several valuable suggestions. The recommendations of Jean Parker Waterbury, a great copyeditor and a kind friend, greatly improved the text.

Notes

1. The incident is documented in Reel 125, Bundle 28902 document 1810, no. 4, The East Florida Papers (Spanish archival records for 1784–1821, hereafter EFP R125 B28902). Originals are in the National Archives of the United States, micro-

film copy is at P. K. Yonge Library of Florida History, University of Florida (hereafter PKY). Numerous letters dated April to July 1804 written by individuals mentioned in the text are in the file, as well as commentary by Governor White and other Spanish officials and residents of Georgia. Quotations correspond to parties named in the text unless otherwise noted.

Militia members specifically named were Andrew Atkinson and Nathaniel Hall, Reuben Hogan, William Lawrence, George Morrison, George Cook, Andrew McClean and Joseph McCullock (names Anglicized by the author). Hogan and Hall were counted in the Spanish census of 1789. Hall and McCullough swore loyalty to Spain in 1790, Atkinson in 1791, Craig and Lawrence in 1799, and Morrison in 1804. Cook arrived from Georgia with his mother and stepfather, Rebeccah and William Pengree, in 1787. Atkinson was born in Ireland; Lawrence, in Scotland; the others, in the United States, probably Georgia. See James Cusick, comp., "East Florida Papers Oaths of Allegiance, 1793–1804," unpublished manuscript based on the *Padron de los Estrangeros* and accompanying index. Copy at PKY. I thank Dr. Cusick for my copy.

2. Testimony of George Cook, July 19, 1810.

3. Testimony of Andrew Maclean, July 19, 1810.

4. Craig to White, June 22, 1810.

5. Ibid.

6. Craig to Governor White, June 23, 1810.

7. Testimony of Abraham Hannahan Kingsley, no date.

8. Tribunal to Governor White, July 31, 1810.

9. A recent volume edited by David Barry Gaspar and David Patrick Geggus, *A Turbulent Time: The French Revolution and the Greater Caribbean* (Bloomington: Indiana University Press, 1997), explores the rebellion's impact on colonies of the greater Caribbean, including East Florida. See especially Geggus, "Slavery, War and Revolution in the Greater Caribbean, 1789–1815," 1–50. See also James Sidbury, "Saint Domingue in Virginia: Ideology, Local Meaning, and Resistance to Slavery, 1790–1800," *Journal of Southern History* 63, no. 3 (August 1997): 531–52.

10. Landers, "Rebellion and Royalism in Spanish Florida: The French Revolution on Spain's Northern Colonial Frontier," in *A Turbulent Time*, ed. Gaspar and Geggus, 156–77.

11. One scholar who has examined anxieties among Southern slaveholders is Michael Mullin, *Africa in America: Slave Acculturation and Resistance in the American South and the British Caribbean, 1736–1831* (Urbana: University of Illinois Press, 1992), chap. 9. Gerald W. Mullin, *Flight and Rebellion: Slave Resistance in Eighteenth-Century Virginia* (New York: Oxford University Press, 1972), 140–63, is insightful for Virginia. Joyce E. Chaplin, *An Anxious Pursuit: Agricultural Innovation and Modernity in the Lower South, 1730–1815* (Chapel Hill: University of North Carolina Press, 1993), chap. 8, discusses expansion of slavery from coastal to interior Georgia and South Carolina; the white fears of new Africans; acculturated Creole slaves who migrated with their owners; runaways and

maroons on the Indian frontier; and the transition from task to gang systems of labor. Her conclusions seem appropriate for East Florida in 1810. Also important are Allan Kulikoff, "Uprooted Peoples: Black Migrants in the Age of the American Revolution, 1790–1820"; and Philip D. Morgan, "Black Society in the Low-country, 1760–1810," in *Slavery and Freedom in the Age of the American Revolution,* ed. Ira Berlin and Ronald Hoffman (Charlottesville: University of Virginia Press, 1983), 83–141, 147–52; Jeffrey D. Crow, "Slave Rebelliousness and Social Conflict in North Carolina, 1775 to 1802," *William and Mary Quarterly,* 3rd ser., 37 (January 1980): 79–102; Ira Berlin, "Time, Space, and the Evolution of Afro-American Society on British Mainland North America," *American Historical Review* 85 (1980): 54–67; Michael P. Johnson, "Runaway Slaves and the Slave Communities in South Carolina, 1799 to 1830," *William and Mary Quarterly,* 3rd ser., 38 (1981): 418–41; and Jane Landers, "Gracia Real de Santa Teresa de Mose: A Free Black Town in Spanish Colonial Florida," *American Historical Review* 95 (1990): 9–30.

12. Cusick, "Oaths of Allegiance."

13. Daniel L. Schafer, "'A Class of People Neither Freemen nor Slaves': From Spanish to American Race Relations in Florida, 1821–1861," *Journal of Social History* 26, no. 23 (Spring 1993): 587–609. Of great importance for slavery and race relations in East Florida is Jane G. Landers, *Black Society in Spanish Florida* (Urbana: University of Illinois Press, 1999). See also Susan Parker, "Men without God or King: Rural Settlers of East Florida, 1784–1790," *Florida Historical Quarterly* 69 (October 1990): 135–55. For a general study, see David J. Weber, *The Spanish Frontier in North America* (New Haven: Yale University Press, 1992), 265–301. For John McClure, Joseph Hibberson, James Wilson, Daniel O'Hara, James and George Taylor, James English, and other slave traders who moved to Florida, see my "Family Ties That Bind: Anglo-African Slave Traders in Africa and Florida, John Fraser and His Descendants," *Slavery and Abolition* (December 1999).

14. Kingsley emancipated Anta and three of her children in 1813, when she was eighteen years of age. She, herself, came to own a plantation and slaves. See Daniel L. Schafer, *Anna Kingsley,* rev. ed. (St. Augustine: St. Augustine Historical Society, 1997). Other published work includes Philip S. May, "Zephaniah Kingsley, Nonconformist," *Florida Historical Society* 23 (January 1945): 145–59; Charles Bennett, "Zephaniah Kingsley, Jr.," in *Twelve on the River St. Johns* (Jacksonville, 1989), 89–113; Jean B. Stephens, "Zephaniah Kingsley and the Recaptured Africans," *El Escribano; The St. Augustine Journal of History* 15 (1978): 71–76; Karen Jo Walker, "Kingsley and His Slaves: Anthropological Interpretation and Evaluation," *Volumes in Historical Archaeology* 5 (Columbia: South Carolina Institute of Archaeology and Anthropology, 1989). Folk legends of Kingsley are in Carita Doggett Corse, *The Key to the Golden Islands* (Chapel Hill: University of North Carolina Press, 1931); and Branch Cabell and A. J. Hanna, *The St. Johns: A Parade of Diversities* (New York: Farrar & Rinehart, 1943).

Kingsley wrote *A Treatise on the Patriarchal or Cooperative System of Society as it Exists in Some Governments and Colonies in America, and in the United States, under the Name of Slavery, with its Necessity and Advantages* (1828; reprint, Freeport, N.Y.: Books for Libraries Press, 1970). Published anonymously, "By an Inhabitant of Florida," *Treatise* went through four editions between 1828 and 1834. Daniel W. Stowell has analyzed the various editions in his "'To Balance Evils Judiciously': Zephaniah Kingsley's Antiracist Defense of Slavery in Territorial Florida," unpublished manuscript, 1996, 36–37. See also Kingsley's "Address to the Legislative Council of Florida on the Subject of Its Colored Population," typescript, no date, Florida State Park Service, Tallahassee; and *The Rural Code of Haiti; Literally Translated from a Publication by the Government Press; Together with Letters from That Country Concerning Its Present Condition, by a Southern Planter* (Middletown, N.J.: George H. Evans, 1837; 2d ed., 1838).

15. The elder Kingsley resettled at St. John, New Brunswick. Birth records are in Bristol Record Office, Book 1517–71, p. 290. Quaker background is in Digest Registers, Births, 1773–4–11–12 (823/32), Friends House Library, Euston Square, London, and Temp MSS 933, Lincolnshire Friends Registers 1618–1837, Vol. 1, Births and Marriages. For the elder Kingsley in South Carolina and Nova Scotia, see "Royal Gazette and New Brunswick Advertiser," December 18, 1787, January 16, 1789, Ward Chipman Papers, H. T. Hazen Collection; Andrew S. Beyea, "A History of French Village," unpublished manuscript, 66, all at the New Brunswick Museum, St. John; and Zephaniah Kingsley, Loyalist Claim, in Alexander Fraser, "Second Report of the Bureau of Archives for the Province of Ontario" (Toronto, 1904); Brent H. Holcomb, *Probate Records of South Carolina*, 2 (Easley, S.C.: Southern Historical Press, 1978), 177, 213, 216, 262, and *South Carolina Naturalizations, 1783–1850* (Baltimore: Genealogy Publishing Co., 1985), 93; James W. Hagy, *People and Professions of Charleston, South Carolina, 1782–1802* (Baltimore: Genealogy Publishing Co., 1992).

Kingsley's Danish "Burger Brief" (oath of loyalty) at St. Thomas, is in Danish National Archives, RA, GTK, Udskrift af St. Jan og St. Thomas, Søpasprotokoller, 1788–1807. For Danish maritime trade, Notarial Protocol (St. Thomas), 1804–6; GTK, Adskrift af St. Jan & St. Thomas Søpasprotokoller, 1788–1807; VL, West Indian passport and citizenry registers, St. Thomas Police Station, registers of persons arriving 1805–99; VRR, St. Thomas, Toldregnskaber, November 7, 1802, Liquidations Beregning; and VL, Harbormaster Reports. I am indebted to Svend E. Holsoe for help with Danish records.

Residence at Jeremie is in Kingsley, *Treatise on the Patriarchal*, n. 8. See also David P. Geggus, "Sugar and Coffee Cultivation in Saint Domingue and the Shaping of the Slave Labor Force," in Ira Berlin and Philip D. Morgan, *Cultivation and Culture: Labor and the Shaping of Slave Life in the Americas* (Charlottesville: University Press of Virginia, 1993), 73–98.

16. Naturalization in Florida is in Book 4, Oaths of Allegiance of New Settlers, East Florida Papers, Microfilm Reel No. 164, Bundle 351 U5 (hereafter EFP R 164 B 351 U5). Kingsley owned houses, money, and slaves equal in value to 67,160 pesos. For the 1802 Cuba voyage, see Herbert S. Klein, comp., "Computerized

Data on Slave Ships Arriving at Havana, 1790–1821," Audiencia de Santo Domingo, "legajo" 1835. AGI (magnetic tape, University of Florida Libraries).

See Schafer, *Anna Kingsley,* for recapitulation of the African voyage and details on Kingsley's wife. Another version appeared as Schafer, "Shades of Freedom: Anna Kingsley in Senegal, Florida and Haiti," in *Slavery and Abolition,* special issue, ed. Jane L. Landers (April 1996), later published as *Against the Odds: Free Black Slaves in the Slave Societies of the Americas* (London: Frank Cass & Co., Ltd., 1996). The sixteen East Africans arrived in Florida aboard Capt. Joel Dunn's ship *El Pele* in July 1806. See EFP R114 B270 & R147 B323. For Kingsley at Havana in 1806, see EFP, Reel 97 Bundle 231J18 and R172 B231N21; arrival at Florida R163 B350U4 & R133 B300 (October 21, 1806), and *Charleston Courier,* September 23, 1806. See also Kingsley, *Treatise on the Patriarchal,* n. 12.

Much later, in 1826, Kingsley reminisced on the early years of his life: "[I]t has been my lot in the earlier portion of my life, to travel in Africa, nay more, to be engaged and concerned in the odious commerce of the slave trade . . . [and] to have visited all the West India colonies, and resided in the most of them—I spent several years in Cuba, and St. Domingo, as well as on the Main Land of South America." See a letter to the editor entitled "To the Legislative Council of the Floridas" in the *St. Augustine East Florida Herald,* December 26, 1826. The author of the letter is identified as "Rationalis," apparently a pseudonym for Kingsley. There is another letter by Rationalis (Kingsley) in the December 12, 1826, issue of the *Herald.* I am grateful to Daniel W. Stowell for bringing these sources to my attention.

17. In Kingsley, *Treatise on the Patriarchal,* n. 13, Kingsley said he selected the Africans himself. See also my *Anna Kingsley,* chap. 2. It was customary for super-cargoes to receive a percentage of the cargo as partial payment for services. William and Rebeccah Pengree were British settlers in East Florida until 1784. They moved to Georgia, but fear of Indian attacks prompted their return. They acquired Laurel Grove in 1787 and, with forty-eight slaves, cleared 400 acres for provisions and cotton cultivation. By 1794 they had built a home, barns, and slave quarters, all destroyed in military insurgency. After William's death in 1794, Rebeccah was unable to return the estate to profitability. See Testamentary Records (probate file) of William Pengree, January 18, 1974, microfilm reel 136, No. 25. William's estate, valued at 12,442 pesos, was divided between Rebeccah and two adult children.

18. Philip D. Morgan, "Work and Culture: The Task System and the World of Lowcountry Blacks, 1700 to 1880," *William and Mary Quarterly* 3d ser., 39 (October 1982): 563–99, best explores the nature of slave labor under tasking. Specific information for Kingsley and tasking can be inferred from policies of his nephew, Kingsley Beatty Gibbs, who learned plantation management while living with his uncle at Fort George Island. See Jacqueline K. Fretwell, *Kingsley Beatty Gibbs and His Journal of 1840–1843* (St. Augustine: St. Augustine Historical Society, 1984). For a differing system, see Michael P. Johnson, "Work, Culture, and the Slave Community: Slave Occupations in the Cotton Belt in 1860," *Labor History* 27 (1986): 325–55. Yields of provisions at Laurel Grove were generally twenty-five

bushels of corn to the acre, and between five and eight bushels of both peas and sweet potatoes—more than enough to feed the Laurel Grove community.

19. I multiply by thirty to correlate prices of most commodity goods circa 1812 to prices today. Circa 1812, pesos and dollars were equal in value, and £1 British Sterling was worth 4.4 pesos. My own study of commodity prices found in Northeast Florida newspapers and probate records, traced across several decades, led to the conclusion that $1 in 1812 would have value today of at least $30, probably closer to $35. The "Composite Commodity Price Index" found in Scott Derks, ed., *The Value of A Dollar: Prices and Incomes in the United States, 1860–1989* (Detroit: A Manly, 1994) values U.S.$1.00 in 1860 at $30.84 in 1989 (see p. 2).

The following analysis of structures and crops at Laurel Grove in 1812 is from Records of the Superior Court, District of Northern Florida, on permanent loan to the St. Augustine Historical Society. See Patriot War Claims, 1812–46, the Case of Zephaniah Kingsley: Manuscript Collection 31. The more complete "Petition to Honorable Raymond Reid, Judge of the Superior Court," East Florida Claims, Superior Court Files, Box 131, Folder 16, was used for analysis and quotations in this text. The slave inventory discussed later is included in both files. For the "Patriot" insurgency that destroyed Laurel Grove, see Rembert Patrick, *Florida Fiasco: Rampant Rebels on the Florida-Georgia Border, 1810–1815* (Athens: University of Georgia Press, 1951).

20. See Original Spanish Land Grant Files, John H. McIntosh, Record Group 599, Florida State Archives, Tallahassee.

21. In addition to *Anna Kingsley,* see José Antonio Moreno to Don Tomas Llorente, November 24, 1813, EFP, R62 B149F12.

22. Kingsley Claim, EFC, Superior Court. Total included African laborers, cotton and provisions already in storage, the unharvested 1812 crop, buildings and furnishings, tools, retail goods, livestock, and miscellaneous. Kingsley's losses at Drayton Island were estimated at $2,657. My comparative current value is undoubtedly distorted, since Kingsley's total included the value of his lost slaves.

23. Kingsley, *Treatise on the Patriarchal,* n. 13.

24. Ibid. Kevin Mulroy considers the black slaves who joined Indian villages "Seminole Maroons," a distinct people who "established communities under their own leaders, developed unique cultural forms, and pursued their own political agenda." See "Ethnogenesis and Ethnohistory of the Seminole Maroons," *Journal of World History* (Fall 1993): 287–305. Further study is needed of the specific African backgrounds of the Seminole Maroons and the creolization process that produced their unique culture and historical consciousness. See also Jane Landers, "Free and Slave," and John K. Mahon and Brent R. Weisman, "Florida's Seminole and Miccosukee Peoples," in *The New History of Florida,* ed. Michael Gannon (Gainesville: University Press of Florida, 1996), 167–206. Still useful is Kenneth Wiggins Porter, *The Negro on the American Frontier* (New York: Arno Press, 1971).

25. The discussion and examples of slave life at lowcountry plantations in Morgan, "Work and Culture: The Task System," lend credence to Kingsley's state-

ment. Flexibility in determining the duration of labor, independence, and incentive to acquire labor skills and property ("measure[s] of autonomy" to Morgan) were intended to minimize resistance to slavery. Morgan quotes Georgia planter Rufus King: "'[N]o Negro with a well-stocked poultry house, a small crop advancing, a canoe partly finished or a few tubs unsold, all of which he calculates soon to enjoy, will ever run away,'" and concludes: "[O]n a much reduced scale, there were lowcountry slaves who resembled the protopeasants found among Caribbean slaves" (597). Tasking may have originated in Africa; see Judith A. Carney, "From Hands to Tutors: African Expertise in the South Carolina Rice Economy," *Agricultural History* 67 (Summer 1993): 1–30; and Daniel C. Littlefield, *Rice and Slaves: Ethnicity and the Slave Trade in Colonial South Carolina* (Baton Rouge: Louisiana State University Press, 1981).

26. For an intriguing introduction to the African slave trade and African culture in the Americas, read John Thornton, *Africa and Africans in the Making of the Atlantic World, 1400–1680* (Cambridge: Cambridge University Press, 1992). See also David Eltis and David Richardson, eds., *Slavery and Abolition*, special issue, 18, no. 1 (April 1997).

27. For analysis of labor and slave life, see Ira Berlin and Philip D. Morgan, "Labor and the Shaping of Slave Life in the Americas," and John Campbell, "As 'A Kind of Freeman'?: Slaves' Market-related Activities in the South Carolina Up Country, 1800–1860," both in *Cultivation and Culture: Labor and the Shaping of Slave Life in the Americas,* ed. Ira Berlin and Philip Morgan (Charlottesville: University Press of Virginia, 1993), 1–45, 243–74.

28. In Kingsley, *Treatise on the Patriarchal,* n. 13, Kingsley says he brought many of his workers from Africa himself and that one voyage was to the East Coast of Africa. The numbers of Igbo, Calabari, and New Calabar entries on the inventory, suggest that Kingsley also traveled to Nigeria. I thank George Brooks for the personal correspondence (August 1, 1998) mentioning Cabo Mouse.

29. A Kenyan living in Miami made the identifications. I am indebted to Dr. Svend E. Holsoe for conducting the interview.

30. See Schafer, *Anna Kingsley,* for the Wolof information. Note that Anna had been freed by 1811. Also, Anna's statement that she was a native of Senegal in her Patriot War Claims, MC 31–58, June 2, 1835, SAHS; and emancipation entries for "Sophy Chidgegane, a woman of Jalof, thirty-six years of age, about five feet high, black complexion," and Flora Hanahan Kingsley, "a mulatto-colored woman of 20 years of age, a native of Florida and daughter to Sophy Chidgigaine . . . five feet high," in Deed Book H, March 17, 1828, St. Johns County Courthouse. The 1840s slave inventories are in the 1843 and 1846 probate files for Zephaniah Kingsley and George Kingsley in Duval County Records, 1203 and 1205.

31. EFP: R62 B144F12 has the emancipation file for Hannahan. See Schafer, *Anna Kingsley,* and Patriot War Claim of Abraham Hannahan, MC 31, Box 124, Folder 24, Superior Court Files, SAHS.

32. Kingsley's last will and testament left a generous bequest for Flora and her

children. See Duval County Probate No. 1203 for the bequest, and Archibald Abstracts of Historical Property Records, Duval County, Book B, 10–12, for property deeds.

33. Kingsley, *Treatise on the Patriarchal*, 1.

34. Ibid., 7.

35. I explore this question in "'A Class of People Neither Freemen nor Slaves,'" and conclude that one reason East Florida retained the flexible three-caste system of race relations was the colonial administration's dependence on free colored militia as allies against U.S. invaders. Had the booming economy not been interrupted by invasions, East Florida may have followed the pattern of Cuba: huge profits from sugar exports, massive slave imports, brutal use of enslaved Africans, and a sharp decline in the status of free people of color. See Robert L. Paquette, *Sugar Is Made with Blood: The Conspiracy of La Escalera and the Conflict between Empires over Slavery in Cuba* (Middletown, Conn.: Wesleyan University Press, 1988).

36. See Kingsley's Will, Duval County Probate File 1203. John Maxwell Kingsley's date of birth was November 22, 1824 (Cathedral Parish Records, Baptisms [microfilm roll 3, entry 650, January 30, 1829]).

6

Free Black Plantations and Economy in East Florida, 1784–1821

JANE G. LANDERS

Poised between the North American and Caribbean worlds, Spanish Florida was buffeted by the revolutions of the late eighteenth century, as well as by annexation plots, invasions, and Indian wars in the early nineteenth century. Throughout the chaos, free blacks in Spanish Florida struggled to create homesteads and participate in the economic life of the province despite the great challenges on a volatile frontier.[1]

After a British interregnum of twenty years, the Treaty of Versailles retroceded Florida to Spain in 1784. English settlers who chose to remain in Florida could do so and keep their property if they swore loyalty oaths to Spain, and some *Floridanos* (persons born in Florida under the first Spanish regime) returned from Cuba to reclaim their original homesteads.[2] But after twenty years, many former Floridians preferred to stay in Cuba, and Spanish administrators complained frequently about problems of underpopulation in the vast province, which by 1784 was bordered by the fledgling United States of America. Spain's frontier commander called this neighbor "a nation, as ambitious, as it is industrious."[3]

Spain worried about its weakness in the face of such ambition and also about the failure of the United States to control its citizens on the turbulent southern frontier. For several years after the cession, assorted "banditti" stole cattle, slaves, and other movable property from planters and farmers thinly spread south of the St. Marys River. In an effort to stabilize the province, Florida's new governor, Vicente Manuel de Zéspedes, offered amnesty to those who would desist and deported those who would not, but opined that "the best fortification would be a living wall of industrious citizens."[4]

Spain tried to increase Catholic immigration into Florida by offering tax exemptions and royal subsidies to critical industries and by approving the unlimited introduction of slaves. Despite these encouragements, uncertainty about land tenure frustrated Spanish efforts to maintain a stable population in Florida. The governors warned repeatedly that the Crown would have to clarify the land titles of non-Spaniards so that those living in the province would not depart and so that new settlers might be attracted.[5]

Spain's failures to repopulate the frontier created an opportunity for an unexpected group of new immigrants. They were fugitive slaves of the Loyalists who, during the chaos of the American Revolution and the subsequent retrocession of Florida to the Spanish government, escaped from bondage and fled to St. Augustine to claim religious sanctuary. Governor Zéspedes doubted the religious motivation of the supplicants, but the seventeenth-century sanctuary decree was still in effect, and the governor was required to honor it. However, he also attempted to stabilize and account for the refugee population by ordering that all blacks and mulattoes without a known owner or papers attesting to their free status present themselves, clarify their status, and obtain a work permit, or else be apprehended as slaves of the Spanish king.[6]

More than 250 petitioners presented themselves to be registered, and they came to form the nucleus of the free black community in Second Spanish Period Florida (1784–1821). This group included skilled carpenters and masons, hostlers, hunters and fishermen, sailors and soldiers, ranch foremen, butchers, shoemakers and tanners, and field hands. Many of the newcomers quickly found employment in town. Others became paid laborers on the plantations and farms of Anglo, Spanish, and Minorcan homesteaders. Those who hired them were responsible for the good behavior of their black employees and were required to notify authorities of any problems. But their work contracts specified that all the men were free, as were their wives and children.[7]

Within a few years, the freedmen and women had begun to work the Spanish system. They usually had their children baptized quickly, and as soon as they had learned the required doctrines, they too were baptized, taking the Spanish names of their godparents. Some couples had their consensual unions validated in religious ceremonies. The men began to enlist in volunteer militia units and hire on to do public works for the government—cutting lumber, building bridges, and repairing fortifications. Some participated in building the new cathedral, donating everything from chickens to timber to cash. They learned the legal system and went to court to advance their positions or petition for redress of grievances.[8]

When, in 1790, Spain finally adopted a revised land policy (based on the British "headright" system), free blacks quickly tested their rights. According to the new policy, foreigners who wished to move to Florida were required to swear allegiance to the Spanish Crown, but previous requirements to convert to Catholicism were dropped. Each incoming head of household would receive 100 acres for himself and fifty for every person attached to his household, of whatever race. The *nuevo poblador,* or new homesteader, had ten years in which to hold and develop the land, after which time he received full title.[9] Within a few months after the new policy was announced, approximately 300 Anglo immigrants crossed Florida's northern border to take up these grants, bringing with them about 1,000 slaves.[10]

As soon as they could, free blacks also petitioned for land as new settlers. Many of the black citizens of Florida had once been considered property themselves and, in the English areas from which they fled, had few opportunities to hold property. But Spanish law and custom (which were grounded in Roman law) guaranteed slaves the right to a *peculium,* or personal property.[11] In general, the need to hold the frontier and make it productive overrode any racial qualms Florida's governors may have had, and all legitimate land requests were approved unless the land in question were already occupied. Petitioners carefully described the land they wanted, and the governor would request a recommendation from the royal engineer. The engineer often would comment on the industry of the applicant and the benefits to the plaza of having the land settled, whereupon, the governor would grant the request. If problems later arose and the land became unproductive or uninhabitable due to danger from Indian attacks, for example, the owners appeared to request exchanges for new land; these, too, usually would be granted.[12]

Prince Witten, his wife, Judy, and their children, Polly and Glasgow, are examples of how talented and determined free blacks might rise within the Spanish system. In 1786, after several failed attempts, the family escaped from slavery in Georgia and requested sanctuary in St. Augustine.[13] Witten was a skilled carpenter, and Judy was a laundress; both quickly found employment in the city. As they earned a free living, the Witten family also began to adapt to the social norms of St. Augustine. The parents and children were baptized, and the renamed Wittens, Juan Bautista and María Rafaela, were married in the Cathedral after twenty-one years of cohabitation. The elder Wittens became godparents of numerous children in the community over the next years, as did Polly and Glasgow, now María Francisca and Francisco Domingo.[14]

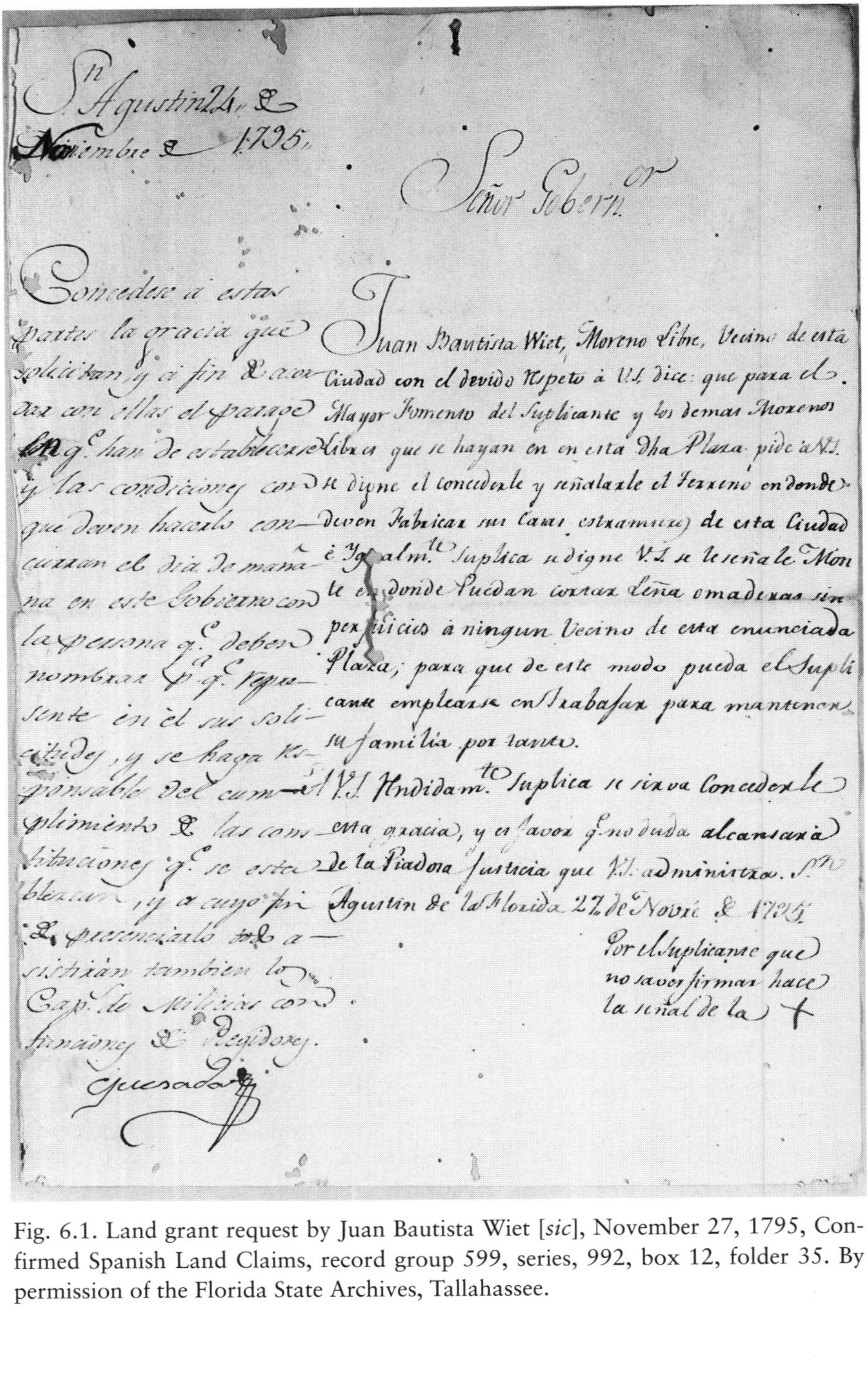

Sn Agustin 24 de Noviembre de 1795.

Señor Gobernor

Concedese a estas partes la gracia que solicitan y à fin de acordar con ellas el parage en q.e han de establecerse y las condiciones con que deven hacerlo concurran el dia de mañana en este Gobierno con la persona q.e deben nombrar p.a q.e represente en el sus solicitudes, y se haga responsable del cumplimiento de las constituciones q.e se establezcan, y a cuyo fin de presenciarlo todo asistirán tambien los Cap.s de Milicias con funciones de Regidores.

Quesada

Juan Bautista Wiet, Moreno Libre, Vecino de esta Ciudad con el devido Respeto à V.S. dice: que para el Mayor Fomento del Suplicante y los demas Morenos Libres que se hayan en en esta dha Plaza pide à V.S. se digne el concederle y señalarle el Terreno en donde deven Fabricar sus Casas extramuros de esta Ciudad è ygualm.te Suplica se digne V.S. se le señale Monte en donde Puedan cortar Leña o maderas sin perjuicios à ningun Vecino de esta enunciada Plaza; para que de este modo pueda el Suplicante emplearse en trabajar para mantener su familia por tanto.

A V.S. Rendidam.te Suplica se sirva Concederle esta gracia, y es favor q.e no duda alcansarà de la Piadosa justicia que V.S. administra. Sn Agustin de la Florida 27 de Novre de 1795

Por el Suplicante que no saver firmar hace la señal de la +

Fig. 6.1. Land grant request by Juan Bautista Wiet [*sic*], November 27, 1795, Confirmed Spanish Land Claims, record group 599, series, 992, box 12, folder 35. By permission of the Florida State Archives, Tallahassee.

The Wittens also became property holders. A census from 1793 shows the Wittens living in a house in town, with prominent white neighbors on either side.[15] Two years later, Witten petitioned the government for land outside the city walls on which to build houses for himself and the other free blacks of the community. He also asked permission to cut timber so as to be self-employed and support his family. The new governor, Juan Nepomuceno de Quesada, agreed to the request. However, as fate would have it, a French-inspired invasion from Charleston rocked the province that year, and the panicked governor ordered all the northern settlements evacuated and burned to deny them to the enemy.[16] Three years later, Witten's son Francisco signed a petition, "for my father who does not know how to write," asking for land to cultivate south of the city, which the governor granted.[17]

In 1792, another former runaway, the free English-speaking mulatto John Moore, petitioned for and received 350 acres near Trout Creek, for himself, his wife, and four grown sons. Governor Enrique White later required that same land to pasture cattle herds belonging to Panton, Leslie and Company, and in place of the grant that the governor reclaimed, Moore received an equal amount of acreage on the St. Johns River. He and his family began again and improved their claim by building a home on it, fencing the land, and cultivating fields. The family also raised cattle and seemed to be on an upward trajectory when Indian raids intervened (1800–1803). Although Moore and his wife remained on the dangerous frontier to defend their homestead, their grown sons reported for militia service in St. Augustine. After the trouble settled, the sons returned to the farm, and the Moore family held the land until after the end of the Spanish regime. In 1823 Moore sold his homestead for $1,200 to the American Elihu Woodruff.[18]

In 1796 a new group of black refugees arrived in Spanish Florida, and they, too, began to work the system and claim rights as "new homesteaders." This time they came not from the English-speaking north, but from the French-speaking Caribbean. After ceding Santo Domingo to France by the Treaty of Basle, Spain evacuated Gen. Jorge Biassou and his "family" of some twenty-six followers and their families to St. Augustine. Although the presence of this band of seasoned black soldiers who had waged unrelenting war for the previous six years disturbed many of St. Augustine's citizens (and even more, the Anglo planters to the north), before long, the new immigrants were applying for and receiving homesteading lands. Although he lived in town, Biassou was soon clearing a plantation north of St. Augustine, lending the place its name of Bayou Mulatto. When he applied for land, the black general indicated that many of his countrymen would soon be establishing themselves nearby.[19]

Almost all free blacks who applied for land received it. Among them were the free mulatto Stephen Cheves, who received 200 acres; the free blacks Tory Travers and Felipe Edimboro, who each received 100 acres; Antonio Williams and Abraham Hannahan, who received fifty acres; and Scipio, who received twenty-five acres. Free women of color could petition under the same formula, and among those who did so were Flora Leslie, who received 500 acres, and Isabella Wiggins, who received 300 acres.[20]

Another route to land ownership for free blacks was through membership in militias. As representatives of the Crown, governors could grant lands for meritorious service to the state, which included military service. By the early nineteenth century, Spain was fighting invasions at home and revolutionary movements throughout the empire and could devote very few resources of any kind to Florida. Unfortunately, Florida was also under siege much of that time. In addition to the Genet-inspired invasion (1794–95), it suffered repeated Indian attacks during the State of Muskogee's war against Spain (1800–1803); another invasion during the so-called Patriot Rebellion (1812), in which the U.S. government supported Georgians attempting to take the province; and repeated violations of Spanish sovereignty by the United States, such as the U.S. navy's attack on the Negro Fort on the Apalachicola River (1816) and Gen. Andrew Jackson's raids on the black and Seminole villages along the Suwannee River (1818). In its final years, Spanish Florida also suffered the seizure of Amelia Island by revolutionaries, pirates, and finally, the U.S. navy. Given Spain's inability to protect Florida, desperate governors had to make do with the resources at hand, and their necessity created leverage for free blacks, who saw service in all those crises.[21]

Free blacks had been organizing themselves into militia units under their own leaders in Florida since the seventeenth century, just as they had in other circum-Caribbean locales. Spanish governors paid the men for their service, and the empirewide military reforms of 1759 also entitled blacks to the military *fuero*, or exemption from civil prosecution and taxes. On orders from the governors and from white commanders of the frontier, black Floridians served as scouts, pilots, sailors, messengers, foot soldiers, and cavalrymen. They manned the frontier and river posts outside the city as well as the batteries and lines of Florida's main fort, the Castillo de San Marcos. In the eighteenth and nineteenth centuries, governors also posted black units among the Seminoles to encourage their continued loyalty to

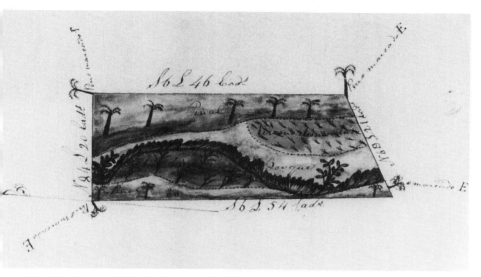

Fig. 6.2. Survey of the land grant of Felipe Edimboro, Confirmed Spanish Land Claims, record group 599, series, 990, box 11, folder E-4. By permission of the Florida State Archives, Tallahassee.

Spain. In their military correspondence, Florida's governors commented frequently on the "excellent" contributions of the black militia.[22]

The men had compelling reasons to serve. Most importantly, their interests lay with Spain, the nation that had freed them. They knew full well what would come of a U.S. takeover. Moreover, their service underscored their loyalty and citizenship and won them pay, titles, recognition, and the gratitude of the beleaguered Spanish community. During the so-called Patriot Rebellion of 1812, Sgt. Prince Witten led a black and Indian unit in an attack on the U.S. Marines, who were supporting the Patriot siege of St. Augustine; Witten's unit liberated vitally needed food supplies for the starving Spanish citizens.[23] Spain declared that it was "well satisfied with the noble and loyal spirit which animates all the individuals of this company" and promised that "each one's merit shall be magnanimously attended to and compensated with all the advantages the state can assign, and the national supreme government can support for their good services to the country."[24] Despite the rhetoric, actual cash rewards were minimal; however, such guerrilla operations provided free blacks the opportunity to enrich themselves at the expense of the enemy. Witten and the other black officers received orders specifying that they could appropriate any guns, powder, and provisions they might need from the rebels' sizable plantations. In addition, horses, cattle, equipment, supplies, clothing, and household goods went to the takers, and these spoils of war no doubt were put to good use by the militiamen.[25] More importantly, as a result of their vital service in 1812, a royal order of 1815 made black militiamen eligible for service-related land grants. Thus, many acquired land for the first time or added to their existing holdings.[26]

Florida's military dependence upon free blacks presented the militiamen with opportunities, but the ever-present danger also took its toll on black families and farmsteads. As we have seen, some black homesteaders lost their original homesteads during the invasion of 1794–95. During the Indian raids of 1800–1803, others were forced to flee for their lives to the shelter of the city. A decade later the Patriot Rebellion drove others from their land. On these occasions, the black homesteaders reported their losses to Spanish authorities, who made an attempt to relocate them to new properties.

Some years after the fact, blacks also made claims against the U.S. government, which reviewed and paid for part of the damages for which it was liable as a result of its sponsorship of the Patriot Rebellion. At least twenty-six free blacks pressed claims against the United States. Their claims ranged from a high of $3,062, for well-connected free blacks such as Abraham McQueen, to a low of $320, for "Segui, a free black" (without a surname, or presumably connections). The average claim was for approximately $2,000. The claims describe the black homesteads and the value of the losses sustained and also indicate how the free property holders worked their lands.[27]

The carpenter, Lewis Sánchez, and his wife, Diana, who had formerly belonged to Francisco Xavier Sánchez, also discussed in this volume, had a "plantation" four miles from town.[28] Their claims show they had planted eight to ten acres of corn, as well as peas, potatoes, peanuts, pumpkins, and melons in fenced fields. They owned a herd of sixty cattle, twenty-six hogs, six work horses, and a large number of poultry, housed in four chicken houses. Sánchez had built two log dwelling houses, corn cribs, poultry coops, and a cookhouse on the place. He owned considerable farm equipment and carpentry tools, and the plantation was said to be "in a flourishing state" when the family was forced to abandon it. Witnesses attested that Sánchez was an "honest and hard-working man" and a "good farmer," and supported his claims to losses worth $2625.75.[29]

The Patriots also struck the homestead of Benjamin Wiggins, the mulatto son of Job Wiggins and the free Senegalese Nansi Wiggins. Wiggins supported his family by raising cattle on a land grant west of St. Augustine. He was also a pilot for the black militia and served repeatedly in the many disturbances that shook Florida. Wiggins and his wife, Nicolasa, and their three children owned land adjacent to his father-in-law, Felipe Edimboro, and the families worked their holdings cooperatively. Wiggins owned a herd of thirty-eight cattle, two yokes of oxen, three horses, and poultry, and had planted crops of corn, potatoes, peas, and pumpkins. Once again, witnesses testified to support his compensation claims for $1196.50, stating that "the circumstances of the claimant were very good for a person of color before the rebellion," but that the family was "entirely reduced" immediately afterward. They reported that he was a man "who always had money . . . but kept it private" and that "he must have expended it for the support of his family during the siege . . . for he was actually very poor directly afterwards." Despite his losses, Wiggins's industry sustained the family in town. In addition to the pay he received as a pilot, he earned money fishing and oystering, and Nicolasa added to their income by un-specified work. Witnesses also remarked that Wiggins had inherited some income from his (white) father's estate and "is again getting up in the world."[30]

Wiggins's claims point to another means by which free blacks acquired property. He and others in St. Augustine commonly inherited from their white fathers, who may not have married their mothers but who recognized their children at baptism and provided for the mothers and their children in their wills. José Sánchez, the natural son of the wealthy cattle rancher, Francisco Xavier Sánchez, married Lucía Ysnardy, the natural daughter of the royal accountant, Miguel Ysnardy. Both received inheritances from their fathers, including houses, land, and slaves of considerable value. Sánchez also provided well for his natural daughters, leaving them houses and slaves.[31]

Finally, a free black, like any other *vecino,* or citizen, could buy property, if he or she had the resources. Juan Bautista Collins, a free mulatto from New Orleans, had entered Florida in 1770 during the British occupation. In 1792 he petitioned for and received a new settlers' headright grant of 300 acres for himself, his mother and daughter, and two slaves. He may have entered Florida with some inherited money, but once there, he also engaged in a successful commercial career. He bought and traded items ranging from butter to cattle and horses to slaves, in locations as diverse as Charleston, Havana, New Orleans, Pensacola, and the Indian nations in the interior. He won the government meat contract and spent months among the Seminoles buying cattle to be taken to St. Augustine and Pensacola. By 1793 he had bought a town home in St. Augustine for himself, his mother, and daughter.[32]

After 1808 some free blacks moved from St. Augustine to the new and fast-growing town of Fernandina, on Amelia Island. Lying just south of the U.S. border and blessed with a good harbor, Fernandina boomed as a result of the U.S. Embargo Act of 1807 and the Congressional cessation of the African slave trade in 1808. The same year, Fernandina became a free port and soon was attracting smugglers and slave traders from every Atlantic port and many Caribbean ones. The haphazard growth of Fernandina disturbed Governor White, who appointed a surveyor general, Don Jorge J. F. Clarke, to design an urban-renewal plan that would bring Fernandina into line with the Spanish urban model. To encourage the beautification program, all those who already held land and had built homes were guaranteed reimbursement for any moves or required changes to their homes, as well as title to their lots. By 1813 forty-one free blacks owned property in Fernandina and had constructed homes and businesses, some of considerable substance.[33] Jorge Clarke and his brother Carlos both had black consorts and many natural children, whom they recognized, educated, and named in their wills. The Clarkes moved their extended families to Fernandina in 1808 and seem to have functioned as patrons, sponsors, and supporters of many other free black Floridians. Some of the free blacks badly needed assistance after the brief Patriot Rebellion spread its destruction to Fernandina.[34]

The American and French revolutions had created havoc in Spanish Florida, but they had also made it possible for former slaves of the Southern colonies and of Spanish Santo Domingo to claim sanctuary and freedom in Florida.[35] Subsequent disturbances only hurt the free blacks of Florida, repeatedly undermining their hard-won prosperity. The last years of Spanish tenure in Florida were especially hard.

Only five years after the Patriot Rebellion fizzled, and as black families were beginning to recuperate from the losses of that fiasco, Gregor MacGregor, a veteran of the Napoleonic wars and of the South American revolutions, seized Fernandina, with the stated intent of freeing all of Florida from monarchy. His "Republic of the Floridas" failed to gain official U.S. support, and within months he was gone. After MacGregor came a French corsair, Luis Aury, who also claimed to be advancing the causes of liberty and republicanism. With the aid of over 100 black Haitians, Aury claimed Fernandina for the "Republic of Mexico" and also set up a government. Like the Spaniards, Aury planned to use land to reward loyalty, promising a private who would serve the republican cause for six months 320 acres of Florida land; those with longer service or higher rank would earn even more-generous bounties. Since many of his own forces included freed blacks, this offer might actually have added to black property holdings, but Aury never had a chance to deliver on his promises. The fear of lost customs' profit and potential slave flight from the southern states inspired another U.S. intervention. A naval squadron soon arrived to clear out the "pirate's den," and take Fernandina.[36] Throughout the political turmoil, black Floridians, many of whom were members of the Fernandina militia, fought bravely to defend their Fernandina homes.[37]

Free blacks and Spaniards struggled to the best of their abilities to stave off the inevitable nonetheless, in 1819 Spain conceded Florida to the United States. Once more Spain arranged a general exodus to Cuba, and on August 22, 1821, a total of 145 free blacks, including 40 men, 27 women, and 78 children boarded ships leaving St. Augustine. Like their earlier counterparts, they were resettled in Cuba at government expense and there began the arduous process of restructuring their lives.[38]

The few free blacks who trusted cession treaties and remained in the new territorial Florida, found the white-supremacist planters who immigrated into the area unable to tolerate such a challenge to the myth of black inadequacy. Over the next years, these immigrants pressured many free blacks into selling what remained of their property at rock-bottom prices. In the years leading up to the U.S. Civil War, some free blacks joined later exiles going to Cuba and Mexico, where their histories have yet to be traced.[39]

Several factors combined to facilitate the growth of a free black property-holding class in Florida, including law, custom, and Spain's geopolitical necessity to hold a frontier under constant threat. Blacks who had once been counted as chattel themselves must have valued more than most the right to be free citizens, to own and dispose of property, and to take arms in defense of their families and homes. Given the opportunity, former slaves worked hard and made good lives for themselves and their families on Florida land, and as some of the case studies above illustrate, many prospered until factors beyond their control thwarted their efforts. As long as it could, and for its own purposes, the Spanish Crown continued to reward loyal black citizens with land grants and subsidies; with that commitment in place, black Floridians repeatedly rebuilt their lives, demonstrating not only great ambition but a fierce determination to succeed against the odds.

Notes

1. An earlier version of this paper appeared in a special issue on "Free Blacks in the Slave Societies of the Americas," *Slavery and Abolition* 17, no. 1 (April 1996): 85–101, and in the hardback edition of that issue as Jane G. Landers, ed., *Against the Odds: Free Blacks in the Slave Societies of the Americas* (London: Frank Cass & Co., 1996), 85–101. For a more complete discussion, see Jane G. Landers, *Black Society in Spanish Florida* (Urbana: University of Illinois Press, 1999).

2. Susan R. Parker, "In My Mother's House: Female Property Ownership in Spanish St. Augustine," paper delivered at the Florida Historical Society, St. Augustine, 1992, on file at the St. Augustine Historical Preservation Board.

3. Carlos Howard to Luis de Las Casas, July 2, 1791, Cuba 1439, Archivo General de Indias, Seville, Spain (hereafter cited as AGI).

4. Decree of Vicente Manuel de Zéspedes, July 14, 1784, in Joseph Byrne Lockey, ed., *East Florida, 1783–1785: A File of Documents Assembled and Many of Them Translated* (Berkeley: University of California Press, 1949), 233–35; James A. Lewis, "*Cracker*—Spanish Florida Style," *Florida Historical Quarterly* 63 (1984): 202.

5. Ramón Romero Cabot, "La defensa de Florida en el segundo período Español," thesis, University of Seville, 1982, 39–44.

6. Proclamation of Vicente Manuel de Zéspedes, July 26, 1784, in Lockey, *East Florida*, 240–41.

7. Census returns, 1784–1814, bundle 323A, East Florida Papers (hereafter cited as EFP), microfilm reel 148, P. K. Yonge Library of Florida History, University of Florida (hereafter cited as PKY); Jane Landers, "Spanish Sanctuary: Fugitives in Florida, 1687–1790," *Florida Historical Quarterly* 62, no. 3 (January 1984): 296–313.

8. Landers, *Black Society in Spanish Florida*, 76–78, 87–89, 118–25.

9. To demonstrate improvements, a settler had to build a house with a suitable chimney, erect fences, and maintain a prescribed number of livestock on the land. When tenure and improvements were proved by the sworn testimony of witnesses, the homesteader would receive title. See Works Project Administration, *Spanish Land Grants in Florida* (Tallahassee, 1940), 1:xviii–xxiii (hereafter cited as *SLGF*).

10. Carlos Howard to Luis de Las Casas, July 2, 1791, Cuba 1439, AGI.

11. William D. Phillips, Jr., *Slavery from Roman Times to the Early Transatlantic Trade* (Minneapolis: University of Minnesota Press, 1985), 28, 50.

12. For multiple examples, see U.S. Board of Land Commissioners, Miscellaneous Spanish Florida Land Records 1808–1849 (hereafter cited as SFLR), Record Group 599, Series 992, Florida State Archives, Tallahassee.

13. Census Returns, 1784–1814, EFP, microfilm reel 148, PKY. The family may have been in St. Augustine for several years before being required to register.

14. Black Baptisms, Cathedral Parish Records, Diocese of St. Augustine Catholic Center, Jacksonville, Florida (hereafter cited as CPR), 1: 41, 118, microfilm reel 284 J, PKY.

15. Census of 1793, EFP, microfilm reel 148, PKY. Witten's neighbors were Don Juan Leslie, head of the Panton, Leslie and Company Indian trading house, and Don Juan McQueen, of American revolutionary fame, who was a major landholder and later a judge in Spanish Florida. His next-door neighbor, Don Manuel Fernández Bendicho, served as Prince and Judy's baptismal sponsor and patron.

16. Richard K. Murdoch, *The Georgia-Florida Frontier, 1793–1796: Spanish Reactions to French Intrigue and American Designs* (Berkeley: University of California Press, 1951); Carlos Howard to Luis de Las Casas, May 4, 1796, SD 2590, AGI.

17. Petition of Juan Bautista Wiet (*sic*), SFLR, Record Group 599, Series 992, Box 12, Folder 35.

18. *SLGF,* 5:223–24. Governor White amended the original head rights system, reducing grants to fifty acres for the head of the family, twenty-five for every child or servant over the age of sixteen, and fifteen acres for every child or servant between the ages of eight and sixteen years (ibid., xxii).

19. Petition of Juan (*sic*) Buissou (*sic*), Jul. 7, 1797, Record Group 599, Series 992, Box 1, FF 32, SFLR. After Biassou's death in 1806, his brother-in-law and military heir, Juan Jorge Jacobo, laid claim to Biassou's lands; see Jane Landers, "The French Revolution on Spain's Northern Frontier: Rebellion and Royalism in Spanish Florida," in *A Turbulent Time: The French Revolution and the Greater Caribbean,* ed. David Barry Gaspar and David Patrick Geggus (Bloomington: Indiana University Press, 1997, 156–77).

20. "Land Claims in East Florida," *American State Papers, Public Lands,* 6: 59, 70–71, 88. The complete petitions for land grants and the governmental responses are found in SFLR. Flora Leslie was the consort of St. Augustine's white surveyor, George J. F. Clarke, and Isabella Wiggins was the consort of his brother, Carlos Clarke, which may explain their large awards. Louise Biles Hill, "George J. F. Clarke, 1774–1836," *Florida Historical Quarterly* 21 (1943): 208–13. Another female property holder of substance was the former Anta Majigeen Ndiaye, whom Daniel L. Schafer discusses in this volume and in "Shades of Freedom: Anna Kingsley in Senegal, Florida and Haiti," in *Against the Odds: Free Blacks in the Slave Societies of the Americas,* ed. Jane G. Landers (London: Frank Cass & Co., 1996), 130–54.

21. Landers, *Black Society.* On the French invasion, see Murdoch, *The Georgia-Florida Frontier.* On the State of Muskogee's war against Spain, see J. Leitch Wright, Jr., *William Augustus Bowles, Director General of the Creek Nation* (Athens: University of Georgia Press, 1967); and on the Patriot Rebellion, see Rembert W. Patrick, *Florida Fiasco: Rampant Rebels on the Georgia-Florida Frontier, 1810–1815* (Athens: University of Georgia Press, 1954). See also James W. Covington, "The Negro Fort," *Gulf Coast Historical Review* 5 (Spring 1980): 78–91; and Canter Brown, Jr., "The 'Sarrazota,' or Runaway Negro Plantations: Tampa Bay's First Black Community, 1812–1821," *Tampa Bay History* 12 (1990): 5–19.

22. Landers, *Black Society.*

23. J. H. Alexander, "The Ambush of Captain John Williams, U.S.M.C.: Failure of the East Florida Invasion," *Florida Historical Quarterly* 56 (1977): 286; Patrick, *Florida Fiasco,* 179–344; Landers, *Black Society.*

24. Review Lists for the Free Black Militia of St. Augustine, 1812, Cuba 357, AGI.

25. Orders to Jorge Jacobo, Prince Witten, and Benjamin Segui, July 19, 1812, EFP, microfilm reel 68, PKY.

26. *SLGF,* xxiv–xxv. Among those receiving service grants were Antonio Proctor, 185 acres; Pedro Sively, 150 acres; Prince Patton, 300 acres; Aysick Travers, 115 acres; and Tory Travers, 125 acres.

27. Patriot War Papers, St. Augustine Historical Society, Manuscript Collection 31, Folder 96, 3. At least twenty-six free black claimants are recorded in this collection.

28. Lewis Sánchez had been making payments on his freedom, and when his owner died intestate in 1808, he continued to pay Francisco Xavier Sánchez's widow, María del Carmen Hill. In 1808 Lewis added 26 pesos to the 174 he had already paid and the widow recorded it in his account (Accounts of 1808, Testamentary Records of F. X. Sánchez, microfilm reel 141, EFP, PKY).

29. Claim of Susannah Sánchez, September 9, 1834, Patriot War Claims, MC 31, folder 69, St. Augustine Historical Society. When driven from his land, Lewis Sánchez joined the black militia and served against the invaders who ruined him.

30. Ibid., MC 31, Folder 75. Felipe Edimboro also claimed damages to his own farm in the amount of $1,624 (Sánchez Papers, Vault, MS Box, 12, PKY). Edimboro's farm was burned and his cattle, horses, and hogs robbed by the insurgents. On April 28, 1815, he asked for and received new lands (Record Group 990, Box 11, Folder 4, SFLR).

31. Marriage of José Sánchez and Lucía Ysnardy, February 2, 1805, Black Marriages, CPR, vol. 1, microfilm reel 284 L, PKY; Notarized Instruments, Testament of Miguel Ysnardy, March 2, 1803, microfilm reel 157, EFP, PKY. Testamentary Proceedings of F. X. Sánchez, November 31, 1807, microfilm reel 8, EFP, PKY. Also see Landers, *Black Society,* and Schafer, "Shades of Freedom."

32. Petition of Juan Bautista Collins, August 6, 1791, SFLR, Record Group 599, Series 992, Box 3, Folder 18; Notarized Instruments, Suits and sales by Juan Bautista Collins, September 4, 1787, March 22, 1798, May 9, 1799, June 23, 1800, January 8, 1801, and January 16, 1810, microfilm reels 166–68, EFP, PKY.

33. Census of Fernandina and Amelia Island, 1814, microfilm reel 148, EFP, PKY.

34. Hill, "George J. F. Clarke"; SFLR and *SLGF.* Clarke surveyed many land grants for free blacks and helped them document and retain these grants when the United States finally took Florida in 1821.

35. Landers, "The French Revolution on Spain's Northern Frontier."

36. David Bushnell, ed., *La República de las Floridas: Texts and Documents* (Mexico City: Instututo Panamericano de Geografia e Historia, 1986); Rufus Kay

Wyllys, "The Filibusters of Amelia Island," *Georgia Historical Quarterly* 23 (1928): 311.

37. The black unit of Fernandina was headed by Sgt. Jorge Jacobo, heir to Jorge Biassou's command and a veteran of the slave revolt of Santo Domingo. Jacobo was also a son-in-law of Prince Witten, with whom he often served. Aury's forces also included over 100 black Haitians, so Jacobo and other Fernandina troops from Santo Domingo may have faced off against some of their erstwhile country-men (Fernandina Militia List, Aug. 12, 1811, microfilm reel 51, EFP, PKY).

38. Relation of the Florida Exiles, August 22, 1821, Cuba 357, AGI.

39. Landers, *Black Society*; Ruth B. Barr and Modeste Hargis, "The Voluntary Exile of Free Negroes of Pensacola," *Florida Historical Quarterly* 17 (1938): 3–14.

7

The Plantation System of the Florida Seminole Indians and Black Seminoles during the Colonial Era

Brent R. Weisman

How and why did the Seminoles develop a plantation system? To answer these questions, we must look for evidence of changes in settlement patterns, economic practices, division of labor, and material culture, all of which would support the contention that the Seminoles were actively adapting to Florida's changing colonial economy. For the purposes of this essay, I define "plantation" as an agricultural enterprise focused on crops or animals grown or raised for export to national or international markets. If the plantation system is a useful analytical model for understanding colonial Florida, then it should also explain the changes in Seminole culture taking place during this period. Further, that the Seminoles were drawn into a network of global relationships should be evident also by the presence of European artifacts at Seminole archaeological sites across the Florida peninsula. The abundance of European artifacts evident at Seminole sites dating to the British (1763–83) and Second Spanish (1784–1821) periods attests to the economic integration and success of the Seminoles during the colonial era.

I argue in this essay that the incorporation of the so-called Black Seminoles into the Seminole agricultural system after the 1790s underpinned the Seminole contribution to the colonial economy through the creation of an agricultural surplus. The basic Seminole agricultural complex was in place well before this time, but it was essentially a self-sustaining system. Environmental constraints limited the ready expansion of Seminole agriculture, and the social, political, and economic emphases on the deerskin trade also inadvertently served to limit the economic role of agriculture. I further propose that the Seminole variant of the plantation system (which included the Black Seminole farms) developed as an adaptation to interior Florida environments and in response to changing economic conditions in colonial Florida. One crucial feature of Seminole plantation economy is that an agricultural surplus was extracted through indirect control of labor, without coercion. The available evidence concerning the Seminoles is minimally adequate to approach most of these issues; that concerning the Black Seminoles is far less so. An area greatly in need of further research is the relationship between blacks and Seminoles and the economic role of the Black Seminoles as can be addressed archaeologically.

Origins of the Florida Seminoles

The Seminole Indians are the historic descendants of prehistoric southeastern Indians who, although diverse in language and ethnicity, shared a basic cultural pattern centered around corn agriculture and a chiefdom type of political and social organization. Prehistoric settlements typically consisted of a mound center, focused on one or more temple or platform mounds associated with the chief, and a series of outlying hamlets, bound to the mound centers through both ceremonial and economic ties. Although subsistence practices revolved around corn, considerable effort was directed to hunting, fishing, and gathering; this most ancient way of life was never abandoned. This basic cultural pattern characterized many Indian societies living along the many rivers of the interior Southeast at the time of first European contact in the sixteenth century, areas that today are parts of North Florida, Georgia, and Alabama.[1] As this portion of the Southeast fell under colonial control in the centuries following European contact, practical alliances developed between the various Indian towns in order to consolidate some degree of political power when dealing with the colonists. Indians living in towns participating in these native alliances or confederacies began to be referred to by the colonial authorities as "Creeks." Further divisions were recognized between the Upper Creeks, living in central Alabama, and the Lower Creeks, of the Flint, Chattahoochee, and Apalachicola River drainages of Georgia and Florida.[2] Creek towns located in Florida eventually began to be called "Seminole" (from the Spanish *cimmarone*, or "wild one") as they became increasingly separated from the Creek Confederacy, particularly after the 1770s. The Spanish mission system in Florida had long since been smashed by British-backed Creek raids, resulting in the dispersal and extermination of the majority of the mission Timucua and Apalachee Indians who once resided in North and Central Florida. The mission Indians had been converted both to God and Crown, and formed the backbone of the agricultural base that kept the colony alive. Some mission Indians or remnant groups may have been absorbed in the proto-Seminole towns, particularly in the middle Suwannee River area. In many respects, the cultural patterns of the early Seminoles reflected continuities with the generalized Creek pattern of the interior Southeast, in which society was organized around a squareground town.[3] The squareground was the center of ceremonial, political, and social life, and like the prehistoric mound centers from which it derived, it connected the outlying dispersed households together into an integrated society.

Settlement Patterns

One fundamental question regarding settlement patterns is where and when the traditional squareground model gave way to a plantation settlement plan. By 1764, when the British gained control over the colony, Seminoles had established themselves in several locations in Central Florida, on the rim of the great Alachua savanna (present-day Paynes Prairie) and on the western bank of the Suwannee River, due west of the Alachua area in the vicinity of present-day Old Town. The Alachua band, under the leadership of the famed Cowkeeper, and the Suwannee band under White King, maintained a traditional alliance as "sister" towns, like the paired towns of the Creek Confederacy bound by social, ceremonial, and political ties. Firsthand accounts clearly indicate that these were squareground towns, similar in many respects to the squaregrounds of the Creeks and certainly derived from them.[4]

Cowkeeper and the White King were not well known to British governor James Grant and Indian agent John Stuart (and not recognized as distinctly "Seminole"). Therefore, Stuart and Grant chose to negotiate the cession of Indian lands east of the St. Johns River with representatives of the Creek Confederacy. The 1765 Treaty of Picolata accomplished two important British objectives: the cession of lands between the St. Johns River and the Atlantic coast, needed for the establishment of rice, indigo, sugarcane, and timber plantations, and securing the St. Johns River both as the primary transportation route linking the plantations to St. Augustine and as a supply route for provisioning the Indian trade.[5] By the 1770s traders were operating two stores on the west bank of the river, where the Indians could get to them easily, one south of present-day Palatka, the other further south near Astor.[6]

Despite the seeming indifference of the colonial authorities to the inte-

Map 6. Seminole and Black Seminole settlements. Map by Barbara Vargo and Brent R. Weisman.

rior Seminole presence, entrepreneurs wasted no time in venturing inland. By 1764 a Dutch trader named Barnet had established himself in the vicinity of Cowkeeper's Alachua town, and by May of that year Denys Rolle arrived at White King's town on the Suwannee.[7] The trail they traveled to Alachua probably followed the old mission spur that once had connected Spanish St. Augustine to the Potano province and then later the La Chua ranch to the colonial capital. The trail from Alachua to the Suwannee crossing did not follow the mission road, however, and may have been of Seminole making.

The Seminoles knew full well what the traders had to offer and how to use circumstances to their best advantage. Rolle intended to push on westward to St. Marks, attracting on the way any and all Seminoles he encountered to his proposed store on the lower St. Johns. White King wanted Rolle to stay on the Suwannee (like Barnet at Alachua), however, and intimated that his people would deal with Barnet if Rolle's enticements failed to meet their expectations. Artifacts found beneath the Suwannee near the bank where White King's town stood—British trade guns, military buttons, and the ceremonial spontoon-type tomahawk—suggest that further British contact with the Suwannee Seminoles continued to have a diplomatic aspect.

The focus of early British interest in the Seminoles was in their deerskin trade, although Florida yields could never compete with those from the piedmont floodplains of the interior Southeast. Nonetheless, an average figure of about forty pounds of skins per year per Seminole hunter can be estimated, each pound having an equivalent value in different quantities of trade goods such as glass beads, cloth, shirts, knives, and gunpowder.[8] This system, in which the Seminole hunters were suppliers of a commodity whose availability and abundance was beyond their control, was by definition fallible and debt-prone.

In the late 1760s, during the early years of British rule, the Seminoles were not yet true agricultural producers in economic terms and thus were not integrated into the plantation system. By the late 1770s, however, certainly by the time of William Bartram's travels among the Alachua and Suwannee Seminoles, the full Seminole agropastoral complex was in place. On this base the Seminole variant of the plantation system was to develop. The complex included not only a wide range of agricultural crops, from potatoes to rice, but also cattle, and to a lesser extent, horses and hogs. This basic agropastoral complex formed the economic template for the Seminoles through the end of the Second Seminole War in 1842, and was abandoned only under duress resulting from their forced relocation into the South Florida swamps. Bartram refers to the agricultural fields that he saw as "plantations," but also makes it clear that commercial enterprise was not their primary purpose. Referring to fields on the edge of the great prairie about two miles from Cowkeeper's town of Cuscowilla, he writes: "This plantation is one common enclosure, and is worked and tended by the whole community; yet every family has its particular part, according to its own appointment, marked off when planted; and this portion receives the common labor and assistance until ripe, when each family gathers and deposits in its granary its own proper share, setting apart a small gift or contribution for the public granary, which stands in the centre of the plantation."[9]

At a village on the St. Johns River near the location of Rolle's store and plantation, Bartram observed that the Seminoles had cleared several hundred acres around the habitations, which they had planted in corn, potatoes, beans, squash, and oranges, "abundantly sufficient for the inhabitants of the village."[10] Bartram also described Seminole women paddling canoeloads of oranges, melons, and other exotics to the St. Johns trading houses to exchange for trade goods. However, the large-scale movement of produce from Seminole farms to colonial markets had not yet begun, and the economy still centered on commercial deer-hunting, supplemented perhaps by the sale of cowhides from the Alachua herds.

By the 1790s, after the death of Cowkeeper and the ascendancy of his nephew Payne, and following the return of Florida to Spain, changes had taken place both in Seminole society and in the agricultural system in which it was embedded. Reasons for these changes are several, and all more or less speculative. Instability in the deerskin trade coupled with the change in colonial administrations may have deepened debt among the Seminoles and forced a diversification of economic efforts. The Seminoles clearly were successful in both plant and animal husbandry in the hot, humid, challenging climate of Central Florida, something never accomplished by the Europeans. Thus it would have seemed eminently practical and pragmatic for the colony to rely more heavily on the Seminoles as agricultural producers. But up to this point, Seminole yields, as bountiful as Bartram makes them appear were sufficient only to feed reliably the Seminoles themselves, and this through a communal redistribution system. What was lacking was a surplus.

At this point, we must consider the most significant factor in the development of the Seminole plantation system. Runaway African slaves filtered into Florida in increasing numbers after the American Revolution, some directly from the lowland plantations of U.S. Georgia or the Carolinas, others perhaps from their Creek masters in interior Georgia or Alabama.[11] How the Seminoles actually came to claim ownership of the runaways is not known, but by the 1790s Payne and other prominent Seminoles were slaveowners, and wealth began to be determined by the numbers of blacks owned. In 1793 Payne was reported to have twenty slaves, 1,500 head of cattle, 400 horses, and untold numbers of sheep and goats.[12] The cattle were probably descended from Cowkeeper's herd, itself descended from the cattle abandoned by the failed Spanish ranch at La Chua. But Cowkeeper had no black slaves, few horses beyond what were needed for transportation and breeding stock, and certainly no sheep or goats. In the years 1783–93, the years between the end of Cowkeeper's rule and the reign of Payne (and the passage of Florida from England back to Spain), the Seminole plantation system came into existence.

By the turn of the nineteenth century, the Black Seminoles had established themselves in a number of villages scattered from the Apalachicola River southward to Tampa Bay, autonomous but formally linked through obligations and responsibilities to the nearby villages of their Seminole masters. Although not bound by the forced-labor system of U.S. plantation slavery and essentially free to go about the business of their daily lives, the Black Seminoles were responsible for providing tribute to the Seminoles in the form of agricultural harvest. They were, as events of the later Seminole wars would prove out, considered by the Seminoles to be property.[13]

Thus, through the efforts of the Black Seminoles, the Seminoles were able to increase significantly their agricultural productivity without having to increase their own population for use as a labor force. Production of an agricultural surplus requires food yields consistently above the level needed for subsistence and stable family size. Admittedly, it is difficult to speak with certainty regarding Seminole population levels given the absence of solid documentary evidence prior to the U.S. Period, but known historical accounts do not give the impression that population pressure was a factor in Seminole settlement patterns. Rather, overall Seminole population seems to have grown as the result of band migration. By incorporating the satellite farms of their Black Seminole vassals, the Seminoles expanded their plantation system. Further, the expansion of the Black Seminoles into a variety of habitats throughout the panhandle and central peninsula allowed for maximum productive use of the environment, well beyond what the Seminoles, with their relatively low populations, could have accomplished. One such area was known as Boggy Island and was occupied by Black Seminoles owned by Sitarkey of the Alachua band. By the 1820 the Black Seminoles were growing large stands of sugarcane at that settlement.

The expansion of the Black Seminoles into diverse environments might reflect a unique cultural adaptation to Florida's mosaic natural habitats, where satisfactory soils and resource abundance tend to be tightly concentrated but widely dispersed. Likewise, as land, not hunting territory, became the resource of primary concern, settlement patterns became dispersed and the Seminoles abandoned the traditional squareground town plan of Cowkeeper and White King's time. With the corresponding decline

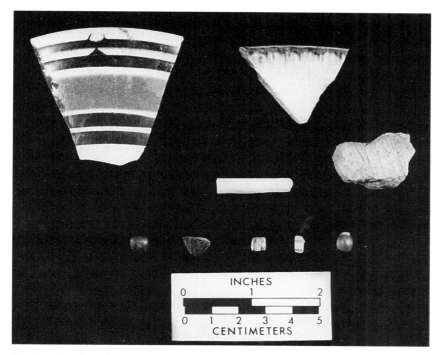

Fig. 7.1. Artifacts from early nineteenth-century Paynestown, Paynes Prairie State Preserve, Alachua County. *Top:* English pearlware ceramics; *center:* kaolin pipe stem; *middle right:* brushed Seminole pottery; *bottom:* glass beads. Photo by the author.

in chiefly authority, the central mechanism for redistributing communally produced surplus no longer existed. Production now centered on the family, which provided individual incentives to seek favorable trade relations with the colonists.

Ironically but perhaps not coincidentally, it is these post-1790s dispersed Seminole plantations that are most archaeologically visible. Payne's settlement at Paynestown, in the southeastern portion of what is now Paynes Prairie State Preserve, has been investigated archaeologically.[14] Datable artifacts indicate occupation between 1790 and 1820, although the site likely was abandoned following Payne's death in 1813. At the presumed house site, archaeologists found concentrations of English ceramics, including banded and transfer-print pearlwares and salt-glazed stoneware, glass necklace beads, smoking-pipe fragments, gun parts, and sherds of the traditional brushed pottery. Discrete artifact concentrations at some distance from the house suggested to the archaeologists the pres-

Fig. 7.2. "Negro Abraham," from Joshua R. Giddings, *The Exiles of Florida* (Columbus, Ohio, 1858). Abraham was an advisor to the Seminole chief Micanopy at Pilaklikaha.

ence of outbuildings and an overall site plan more resembling a plantation than a squareground.[15]

This basic archaeological signature is repeated at sites in the high rolling hills north of Tampa Bay, near the present Dade City. Here, at several locations in the Lake Pasadena area, trade goods of many kinds abound as surface finds. Glass beads, smoking pipes, glass bottle sherds, numerous types of European ceramics (possibly including at least one complete tea setting), and remnants of cast-iron Dutch ovens are among the artifacts that attest to the relative wealth of the former Seminole occupants. Bottle glass sherds had been chipped into scrapers, possibly for use in cleaning either deer or cow hides.[16]

The Black Seminole town of Pilaklikaha ("Many Ponds"), established between 1813 and 1820 in the hammock and prairie area of Central Florida east of Bushnell, is today marked by a dense scatter of artifacts, including creamware and pearlware ceramics and bottle glass.[17] When the merchant-diplomat Horatio Dexter visited Pilaklikaha in 1823, 100 acres in the vicinity were under cultivation in corn, rice, and peanuts.[18] Large herds of cattle also ranged in the prairies interspersed between hammocks.

These large sites, containing distinct artifact concentrations but dispersed across the landscape over an extensive area, clearly were situated to take best advantage of multiple environmental opportunities suited for providing open grazing, the growing of wet crops such as rice and sugarcane (rice perhaps introduced originally to the Creeks by African slaves), and the well-drained soils needed for corn and other crops. Driving through this area of Central Florida today in portions of Sumter, Lake, and Pasco Counties, one can easily imagine herds of Seminole cattle moving slowly across the prairies, kept from the corn and the rice by the watchful vigilance of the farmer.

What would a Seminole plantation have looked like? Opauney's settlement east of Tampa near Bartow in present-day Polk County might have been typical. Here, near the shore of a lake and in an environmental setting similar to Pilaklikaha and the other Central Florida settlements, Opauney lived in a two-story frame house, surrounded by various outbuildings including a corn crib, dairy, stable, and a "physic" house, where the sacred medicines were stored.[19] In outlying fields, Opauney cultivated corn, potatoes, peaches, and rice, the latter forming the basis of a lucrative export trade to St. Augustine. Upon Opauney's death in 1820, his son inherited $7,000 in coins and various other holdings.[20] In keeping with traditional Indian custom, however, the Seminoles destroyed the plantation buildings and crops of the deceased.[21] Opauney was not alone in sending pack trains laden with produce to St. Augustine.[22] Rice—low-maintenance, high-yielding, and nonperishable—was particularly well suited to Seminole commerce. The Seminoles used two methods of planting rice: in hills in upland settings and in wet prairies or swamps.[23]

Cultural Implications of Changes in Economic Practices

By the late eighteenth century, changes in the economic practices of the Central Florida Seminoles enabled the development of commercial agriculture, which to some degree supplanted or supplemented income derived from the deerskin trade. Historical treatments of this period emphasize increasing debt loads on the Indians as credits or advances exceeded actual profits as calculated by weights of skins, but the archaeological record suggests that the Seminoles in the area under study obtained consumer goods from the Europeans in considerable quantities.[24] Many of these items, such as the imported transfer-print tablewares and tea sets, were not strictly utilitarian in a technological sense but rather can be considered luxury items, perhaps used by the Indians to indicate wealth or prestige. These assemblages do not seem to reflect an impoverished quality of life and do not in themselves seem to be direct indicators of economic decline. Rather, these artifacts could be interpreted to suggest a degree of prosperity, reflecting the Seminoles' ability to actually purchase items. This would particularly apply to the European ceramics, which would have been obtained by purchase rather than barter. Bartram's visit to a Creek Indian named Bosten of Apalachicola Town, one of the Creeks who operated a true plantation, drew profuse comments about his wealth and ability to buy sugar, coffee (served in "china ware" cups), and other goods from white markets. This example serves as a positive comparison to our less well-documented Seminole case.[25]

If there is indeed a correlation between this period of Seminole prosperity from the 1790s through 1821 and the development of plantation agriculture, one must ask why this system developed. The shift to plantation agriculture required not only a redirection of labor but also the development of a new set of obligatory relationships with the Black Seminoles, who lived apart in their own villages but were bound to individual Seminoles through tribute. This system works if one of the objectives of the plantation economy was to maximize productivity, but it was very unlike traditional aboriginal forms of slavery, in which war captives were incorporated into society. Thus, in order for the plantation system to succeed, traditional ways of doing things had to be rethought, and in relatively short order.

What were the implications of the plantation system for aspects of Seminole society such as inheritance patterns and division of labor? There is some evidence that the accumulation of money caused a change in the path of inheritance. It was Opauney's son who was reported to have received the $7,000 inheritance rather than his nephew, as might be expected in a matrilineal society. If wealth was not being passed down by mother's brother to mother's son, then the basic unit of society during this period might have been the nuclear family, not the extended kinship group. Traditional roles of chiefly authority had greatly eroded by Payne's time, and many of the documented villages of the early nineteenth century through the early American Period were occupied by individuals or heads of small bands, not chiefs in the traditional sense.[26]

Division of Labor

If the Seminoles had to intensify their own agricultural efforts (including livestock-raising) to produce a surplus, rather than depending exclusively on the Black Seminoles, would this have required men to spend more time in the fields and less time in the forest? Seminole men never entirely gave up hunting deer for skins until the American Period after 1821, but did more farming mean less hunting? In part this answer rests on determining whether or not there was a true fall-winter hunting season in Florida, as there was in areas of the upper South. Cowkeeper claimed to be out hunting in November, which prevented him from attending the Picolata Conference; but, overall, the evidence for seasonality is limited. If the men were hunting in fall and winter, tending stock and farming fields in spring and summer (the traditional pattern among southeastern Indians of the eighteenth century), then any intensification of agricultural production would have had to rely on increased labor, not increased time. The need for increased labor would have been met most readily by reliance on the Black Seminoles, as I have previously suggested.

An increased economic role for women and children is also implied. Herds numbering in the thousands of animals would require some attention in the fall and winter, even if on free range. Tree crops such as oranges and peaches grown in Central Florida might have required fall or winter harvest, and the harvest of other fruits and vegetables may not have conformed strictly to the cycle of spring growing season followed by summer harvest. In November 1774, Seminole watermelons, oranges, and other produce arrived by canoe at St. Johns trading houses for exchange, indicating that the agricultural season did indeed extend beyond summer.[27]

The deeper question of what compelled the Seminoles to develop a unique variant of the plantation system as their means of economic interaction with colonial society must remain unanswered at present. Clearly it reflects an innovative cultural response to a period of economic instability and stress, if the documentary and historical record is to be believed. In their agricultural efforts, the Seminoles were perhaps too successful, in that they demonstrated to the United States that interior Florida could be made agriculturally productive and thus held lands worth coveting. When Florida came under U.S. control in 1821, an Indian policy of removal was quickly put into effect. This policy also required that the bond between Seminole and Black Seminole be severed, a condition that became one of the flashpoints leading to the Second Seminole War. After the Second (1835–42) and Third (1855–58) Seminole Wars, the remaining Seminoles (fewer than 200) retreated to the hammock islands of the Big Cypress Swamp and the Everglades, growing crops in small family plots and taking up life as hunters and gatherers.

Notes

1. J. Leitch Wright, *Creeks and Seminoles* (Lincoln: University of Nebraska Press, 1986), 20–21.

2. William G. Sturtevant, "Creek into Seminole," in *North American Indians in Historical Perspective*, ed. Eleanor Burke Leacock and Nancy Oestrich Lurie (New York: Random House, 1971), 93–98.

3. Ibid., 98–103.

4. William Bartram, *The Travels of William Bartram*, ed. Mark Van Doren (New York: Dover Publications, 1955); Denys Rolle, *The Humble Petition of Denys Rolle* (1765; facsimile reprint, Gainesville: University of Florida Press, 1977).

5. John Bartram, *Diary of a Journey through the Carolinas, Georgia, and Florida from July 1, 1765 to April 10, 1766*, ed. Francis Harper, Transactions of the American Philosophical Society 33, no. 1; James W. Covington, *The British Meet the Seminoles* (Gainesville: Contributions of the Florida State Museum, Social Science, 7, 1961).

6. John M. Goggin, "A Florida Indian Trading Post, Circa 1763–1784," *Southern Indian Studies* 1, no. 1 (1949): 35–37; Kenneth E. Lewis, Jr., "History and Archaeology of Spalding's Lower Store (Pu-23), Putnam County, Florida," Master's thesis, University of Florida, 1969.

7. Rolle, *Humble Petition*.

8. Wright, *Creeks and Seminoles*, 59.

9. Bartram, *Travels*, 96.

10. Ibid.

11. Wright, *Creeks and Seminoles*, 83–85.

12. James W. Covington, *The Seminoles of Florida* (Gainesville: University Press of Florida, 1993), 29.

13. William Simmons, *Notices of East Florida with an Account of Seminole Nation of Indians by a Recent Traveller in the Province* (Charleston, S.C.: privately printed, 1822); Kenneth W. Porter, *The Black Seminoles* (Gainesville: University Press of Florida, 1996).

14. Nancy Mykel, "Seminole Sites in Alachua County," manuscript on file in Department of Anthropology, Florida Museum of Natural History, Gainesville, 1962; Sue Ann Mullins, "Archaeological Survey and Excavations in Payne's Prairie State Preserve," Master's thesis, University of Florida, 1978.

15. Mullins, "Archaeological Survey"; Brent Richards Weisman, *Like Beads on a String: A Culture History of the Seminole Indians in North Peninsular Florida* (Tuscaloosa: University of Alabama Press, 1989), 77–78.

16. Ibid., 69–74.

17. Jordan Thomas Herron, "The Black Seminole Settlement Pattern, 1813–1842," Master's thesis, University of South Carolina, 1994.

18. Mark F. Boyd, "Horatio S. Dexter and Events Leading to the Treaty of Moultrie Creek with the Seminole Indians," *The Florida Anthropologist* 11 (1958): 65–95; Weisman, *Like Beads on a String,* 68.

19. Boyd, "Horatio S. Dexter"; Weisman, *Like Beads on a String,* 69.

20. James Glunt, "Plantation and Frontier Records of East and Middle Florida," Ph.D. diss., University of Michigan, 1930. Particularly relevant to this essay are the sections dealing with Horatio Dexter.

21. Simmons, *Notices of East Florida.* Simmons's work also contains an account of Payne's death.

22. John Griffin, "Some Comments on the Seminole in 1818," *The Florida Anthropologist* 10 (1957): 41–49.

23. William C. Sturtevant, "The Mikasuki Seminole: Medical Beliefs and Practices," Ph.D. diss., Yale University, 1954, 470.

24. Wright, *Creeks and Seminoles,* 54–60.

25. William Bartram, "Observations on the Creek and Cherokee Indians, 1789," Transactions of the American Ethnological Society 3 (1853): 1–81.

26. Charles H. Fairbanks, *Ethnohistorical Report on the Florida Indians* (New York: Garland, 1974). This publication is Fairbanks's study of Florida Seminole origins conducted for the Indian Claims Commission and is a crucial source for Seminole history prior to the 1823 Treaty of Moultrie Creek.

27. Bartram, *Travels,* 250; Gregory A. Waselkov and Kathryn E. Holland Braund, eds., *William Bartram and the Southeastern Indians* (Lincoln: University of Nebraska Press, 1995). Thorough annotations make this volume extremely valuable for Seminole studies.

8

The Cattle Trade in East Florida, 1784–1821

SUSAN R. PARKER

Southern soils nourished more than cotton, but the historical literature seldom reminds us that cattle left their hoofprints on the land before there was a cotton belt or that cowpens predated the dikes in the rice country of Carolina. The cattle zone stretched across developing southern North America, for wherever Europeans brought their own version of civilization, cattle accompanied them. Cattle, horses, and slaves constituted the bulk of declared wealth in British America, where houses and furniture mattered little. Well aware of contemporary attitudes, naturalist John Bartram extolled in promotional literature (1765) the "tolerable good grass" that newly British East Florida offered for grazing.[1] Documents continued to imply the value of cattle after Spain repossessed East Florida in 1784. Census takers counted the beasts, testators willed them and appraisers evaluated the animals in postmortem inventories, border officials certified incoming stock, and rustlers of every racial group stole them.

"Scandal, government intervention, and mutual recriminations" have characterized the history of the red-meat industry throughout the United States, according to Jimmy Skaggs. Spanish East Florida was no exception, although Skaggs does not include the Spanish colony in his examination of an industry that is a "microcosm of American economic development."[2] An examination of this microcosm of Spanish East Florida's society indeed acquaints us with all strata of the province's populace—Indians, slaves, free blacks, government officials, small ranchers, and the rancher-planters at the apex of influence. Cattle's ubiquity throughout the society and the geographical area allows us to touch upon the histories of all sorts of persons. Racial lines and national boundaries were ignored in the goal of selling or acquiring beef.

Here we can examine the nature of the cattle trade in the borderlands and the sociocommercial relationships of the participants. Spanish military officers assigned to rural defense posts in East Florida oversaw a frontier settled by a largely Anglo or Northern European population. The officers' almost daily reports provided details of a sort generally unavailable for the less-regulated frontier territories of the United States. Such accounts of events and the observations on social relationships are almost impossible to tease from censuses, probate proceedings, and ledgers. While contemporary livestock-raising in regions farther north became an increasingly hands-on occupation, East Florida's cattlemen paid little attention to the animals themselves. Instead they invested their energies in the competition for the cattle trade.

Although Frank L. Owsley in 1949 pointed out the omission of cattle-raising from the South's historiography, he quickly let the herdsmen slip back into oblivion. A quarter of a century later, Forrest McDonald and Grady McWhiney accused specialists of continuing to ignore livestock in the South's history and then blazed their own trail in the interpretation of southern graziers.[3] Historians who had paid attention to livestock in colonial Florida usually did not get it right because they relied on English documents for information about a Spanish colony. Lewis C. Gray, in his classic study of southern agriculture, turned to reports written during the period of British control in Florida (1763–84), that were hostile to Spain. George H. Dacy (1940) and Joe Akerman (1976) repeated Gray's errors. Dacy, like many other historians, collapsed the first two centuries of Spanish rule in Florida into one generic era, then concluded that "[t]he cattle business never attained much significance under Spanish rule"—a viewpoint that Charles W. Arnade and Amy Bushnell later would refute. Dacy praised British-era development of the cattle industry and rued that "[t]he unfortunate feature about the buildup was that it went to seed as soon as the Spaniards repossessed Florida." Bernard Bailyn's recent investigation of the "exotic" periphery of the British Empire has, however, challenged the myth of the long-touted economic success of the British in East Florida.[4]

In the last years of the American Revolution, beleaguered Loyalist refugees and their slaves moved into British Florida from Georgia and South Carolina. They attempted to remake their lives in British Florida, but Georgian raiders scattered their herds and made life on the frontier hazardous. Further disruption of lives and economy came in 1784, when Spain regained Florida and most of the population chose to relocate to other parts of the British empire rather than remain under incoming Spanish rule.[5] Too much has been made of the cattle and horse thievery of the eighteen-month evacuation period as the source of the colony's lawless frontier element. Emphasis upon the cultural bases of brigandage has obscured less-ballad-worthy economic factors. The escapades of a Loyalist horse thief bearing whipping scars for his crime might sustain legend and song for many years, but not the prolonged economic problems of Florida.[6]

For more than two centuries, costly though it was for Spain, occupation of Florida was a strategic necessity, "command[ing] a military significance far greater than its economic resources could justify."[7] As during the first Spanish tenure, a significant portion of Florida's military budget paid for fresh meat to feed those on the government payroll, although during shortages tinned or salted meat had to substitute. The Spanish government was the largest consumer and purchaser of meat in the province and encouraged cattle production by allowing Spanish settlers owning cattle to supplement their own pasturage by feeding their stock on Crown land, the colonial counterpart of public land. The land might be miles from their farms, and such feeding arrangements encouraged theft; nonetheless, profitable production depended on cheap forage—either free grass or cheap grain.[8] Although the allotted military force and the colonial budget both shrank as Spain's financial situation worsened yearly, the Crown clung to a mercantilist policy, ignoring pleas from its colonies, including East Florida, for free trade. Limited trade meant limited revenue. Then, in 1808, Napoleon's conquest of the Iberian Peninsula left Spain's American colonies to their own devices.

Meanwhile, the United States threatened Spain's possession of Florida. Incursions and invasions and the preludes to them disrupted settlement in the beleaguered colony and brought widespread destruction to the hinterland. Native Americans' anger over U.S. expansion also spilled over the border into Florida, and Creek Indians attacked and burned many Florida plantations and homesteads.[9]

Despite the chronic frontier violence, Spanish Floridians depended on international trade across the St. Marys River or negotiations with the Seminole Indians to obtain cattle. At Spanish military posts near the border, drovers from Georgia arrived with cattle for well-to-do businessmen in St. Augustine, such as Francisco Xávier Sánchez (discussed by Jane G. Landers in chapter 4) and Miguel Ysnardy. Sánchez, one of the few Spanish subjects to remain in East Florida during the British Period, retained ownership of his family's cattle ranches, which had been established by the early part of the eighteenth century. Ysnardy also engaged in foreign commerce by virtue of holding one of only three special licenses issued by the viceroy. The two other license holders, Pedro Cosifacio and Francis Fatio (discussed by Susan R. Parker in chapter 3) also acquired cattle from Georgia and South Carolina, often in conjunction with other negotiations. The cattle for these buyers arrived in lots of about 100, usually guided by one man on horseback and two footmen.[10] Lesser men had to make the journey to Georgia themselves. Artemis Elliott Ferguson reported that he and two slaves traveled to Georgia to take advantage of the lower prices there for cattle, sheep, and hogs that had originally been bred in Carolina.[11]

Still other colonists brought their own small herds with them when they moved into East Florida to settle. Georgians fleeing Indian raiders sought refuge in Florida with their families, slaves, and cattle and remained in the province after the threats subsided. William Pengree crossed his 110 cattle and numerous slaves into East Florida to avoid their loss in 1786. Charlton Mazell's family fled to East Florida in 1788 with 17 cattle as well as other possessions. In 1790 the Spanish crown finally permitted foreigners to homestead in Florida and required new settlers to maintain livestock in order to establish a valid claim. Newcomers, signing pledges of their fealty to the king of Spain, reported the number of cattle that they were importing as well as their household members, slaves, boats, and cash.[12]

Cattle thus integrated new Anglo settlers into the colonial economy and the empire. As Brent Weisman also argues in chapter 7, cattle did the same for the Seminole Indians. The Indians, whose herds fed the Florida soldiers, occupied one end of a money trail that began in Veracruz. Taxes collected in that Mexican port to fund the Florida military post eventually arrived in the Seminole towns to buy cattle to feed the colony's troops. Trade with the Indians relied especially upon the work of free blacks and mulattoes, who rode to the Alachua prairie (near present-day Gainesville) to negotiate the transactions. The Indians sold the cattle at monetary rates rather than using some simpler form of exchange. Barter, gift-giving, or other forms of nonmonetary exchange still took place, nonetheless, as a part of some sales. These transactions did not necessarily involve the exchange of specie or even drafts, but they did signify that the Seminoles understood the concept of exchange-value and employed it. The unit of exchange was the chalk, or chalkmark (*raya* in Spanish), equivalent to two *reales,* or about twenty-five cents.[13] J. Leitch Wright, Jr., on the other hand, states that no money changed hands. He asserts that it was all a matter of marks in ledgers, where the value of peltry offset the price of manufactured goods that the Indians acquired at trading stores. Wright focuses on the practices of Panton, Leslie and Company and its successors, who held a virtual monopoly on the legal Indian trade in East Florida. His conclusions rely on the company's account books and correspondence of Creek traders and United States Indian agents.[14]

However, the Seminoles also did business outside of such a narrow and regulated structure of sales to the government and to licensed trading houses, according to the reports of Spanish officers on the frontier. Independent traders bought Indian livestock to resell to rural settlers. Indians drove "gangs" of cattle to settlers in the northern part of the colony for subsequent export into Georgia. Although barter was no doubt one mode of exchange, the Indians demanded cash as well as goods, or perhaps a mixture of the two.[15] Deals that went sour for the Indians reveal that they expected to receive cash rather than credit which must be exchanged for trade items. When Buckra Woman (sister of the Alachua chief, Payne) sold cattle worth 6,807 chalks ($1,700) to Philip Yonge's company in 1804, she received about one-third in cash at the time. Four years later she secured a promissory note from Yonge for the unpaid remainder, and in 1827 was still trying to collect the money through the East Florida courts—now in the United States. On another occasion, the Spanish government itself delayed in paying a free black man, Juan Bautista Collins, whom it had commissioned to buy cattle, thus rendering him unable to pay the Alachua Indians. Chief Bowlegs's sister, Simency, journeyed to St. Augustine to testify on behalf of plaintiff-debtor Collins when he sued for the money.[16]

Despite their essential role in the Spanish economy, the Indians were the farthest removed, geographically as well as socially, from participation in the society of the province. They remained in the hinterland, except for brief trips to town or to raid. Spanish officials and the highest members of society did not deal directly with the Indian tribes to purchase cattle. The governor might invite a chief to parlay with him over boundaries, but neither he nor his immediate administrators rode to Indian country to negotiate more-mundane matters. Free blacks and mulattoes filled the intermediary role. Philip Edinborough (commonly known as Felipe Edimboro), a manumitted slave formerly the property of rancher F. X. Sánchez, and Juan Bautista Collins, a particularly enterprising free black, made trips to purchase cattle to feed the garrison and bureaucrats. Free mulatto John Gray traveled to Indian country to buy cattle for his plantation-owning employers living on the east bank of St. Johns River; these included the government meat contractor, Francis Philip Fatio, and Fatio's neighbor, the widow Hannah Moore.[17]

Free blacks also participated in the Spanish cattle economy as stock owners. For example, Edimboro, the Indian-language interpreter Tony Proctor, and Benjamin Wiggins, all free blacks, received government land grants a few miles west of St. Augustine. Wiggins realized $500–$600 per year as a pilot and stockkeeper. He owned thirty to forty head in 1812. Because "it was not always necessary to be with his cattle," he could absent himself to earn two dollars per day with his navigational skills and an additional dollar a day if he used his horse. He occasionally took cattle in payment of wages. "He always had money," stated a prominent white citizen, "but was private about his finances."[18]

However, money did not necessarily purchase respect for the free blacks. Interim government treasurer José Antonio de Yguíñiz displayed his low estimation of them in his official capacity. When Edimboro displeased Yguíñiz in connection with cattle purchases from the Indians, the treasurer convinced the governor to arrest Edimboro en route from Indian country at one of the river crossings. Emboldened by their skill in dealing with the Indians, Edimboro and Collins refused to be accomplices in, or victims of, what appears to have been Yguíñiz's machinations to profit personally from administering the beef purchases. Collins sued Yguíñiz for payment for cattle purchased and supplies expended on behalf of the government. When Collins refused to be bullied into settlement during an argument in Yguíñiz's office, the frustrated treasurer theatrically attacked Collins with a cowhorn in a tragicomic display of vexation.[19]

White cattle traders held peripheral social positions essentially the same as their black counterparts. James Allen was an Indian trader who lived on the "upperest" settlement on the St. Marys River. Although officially restricted to working for Panton, Leslie and Company, his isolated location allowed him to trade at will for his own benefit. Part of his merchandise was cattle. Allen reported ownership of 100 head in the 1789 population report of St. Marys settlers. Allen's herd was twice as large as that of any other St. Marys settler, except the 130 animals of Joseph Rain, a British holdover with twenty-years' residence in Florida. Allen probably intended to sell, rather than raise, the cattle, which most likely had been purchased from the Indians.[20]

Among the "respectable" whites who made the trip to the Alachua prairie to buy Indian cattle were government contractors Francisco Pellicer and Manuel Solana. Only after hard negotiations in which they had to cut their profit were they able to best the wealthier bidders, such as F. X. Sánchez or the agents of Panton, Leslie and Company. Pellicer had been the spokesman for the band of indentured Mediterranean laborers who fled maltreatment at Andrew Turnbull's indigo plantation at New Smyrna (discussed by Patricia C. Griffin in chapter 2). Disdained by the Spanish officials for their servile origins, the Minorcans' cohesiveness allowed them to challenge Spanish officials when the periodic auctions for the meat contracts resulted in awards that were not the most favorable for the public. The Minorcans protested in writing to the governor, and in some instances the auction was held anew.[21]

Pellicer and Solana might have traveled to Indian country with their slaves or black interpreters to oversee negotiations, but the wealthy Francis Fatio and Francisco Xávier Sánchez would never have condescended to do so when they held the contracts. Such activities were incompatible with their lofty social station in provincial society. In addition to any animals their agents might have purchased from the Indians, Fatio and Sánchez offered a convenient market for small ranchers wishing to sell their stock, and thereby extended their personal influence.

The social and economic relations of the cattle trade among the rural residents were not nearly so well documented when the transactions did not involve the government. While cattle-raising was a goal for many settlers in the South, for the more ambitious, livestock served as a means to acquire wealth beyond what a life of cattle-herding could provide. In South Carolina, cattle had financed the development of rice-growing establishments, and in the contemporary Mississippi region (also under Spanish dominion), cattle provided the capital to acquire slaves necessary for the transition to cotton.[22]

The increasing herd size implied by narrative reports and verified in censuses illustrates a determination among rural residents to accumulate livestock holdings beyond what an individual household could use. Unfortunately, the counting of livestock was limited to the very first years of Florida's second Spanish regime. Officials made counts in the rural area in 1784–85, 1787, and 1789. Not until 1814 was another census taken in the areas outside of St. Augustine, but it included only the human, not the animal, population. The censuses from the 1780s demonstrated that cattle-holding was increasing—both the number per household and the number of households. For example, the number of cattle-owning families in the St. Marys district tripled from eleven in 1784 to thirty-two in 1789. But the overall picture suffers because the largest holders, such as Sánchez and Fatio, tended to give evasive answers or were omitted altogether from the censuses.[23]

Some settlers immigrated from the United States with the idea that they could sell meat to "other residents not engaged in farm work" to acquire the money to "buy clothing and food for themselves and their slaves."[24]

Immigrants might well have seen new commercial opportunities available to them by virtue of Spain's possession of East Florida. Before the Revolution, merchants in the mainland British colonies had supplied food—including meat—to West Indian planters, who dedicated their own lands to lucrative tropical products. But the Spanish Indies were closed to foreign trade, and residence in East Florida offered an entree into the food trade with other Spanish colonies, especially Cuba and Mexico. Florida's harbors offered the advantage of proximity to the Caribbean (at least two days closer than Charleston), thus lowering shipping costs and the risk of food spoilage. Although East Florida's governor Vicente Manuel de Zéspedes complained with regularity about the problems of feeding his troops, his dilemma did not result from a lack of local foods within his jurisdiction.[25] East Floridians sent salted and smoked fish, potatoes, onions, and lard to Havana. No beef, however, appeared in the manifests of Cuba-bound ships, but cargoes of butter and cheese produced in East Florida far exceeded other foods. A large rancher, such as F. X. Sánchez, could send several thousand pounds of milk products at a time, but smaller farmers and ranchers also could participate through shippers who made the rounds purchasing the output of the smaller producers. At least for a while, the small farmers and ranchers of East Florida, along with the rest of the Atlantic seaboard, benefited from the "export" trade from the mainland to the Caribbean.[26]

The rural cattle economy was no peaceable kingdom. In many instances, only by ignoring the provincial laws could cattlemen make a living—a situation that bred violence, crime, and profiteering. Residents along the northern Florida rivers participated in a clandestine export trade of cattle into Georgia. To save time and avoid duties of 6 percent, settlers failed to acquire appropriate export permits from the governor's office in St. Augustine. At other times, the trade was forbidden altogether. In June 1790 William Cain, for example, supervised the delivery of cattle raised by the Indians to a U.S. shipper at Cumberland Island, Georgia, who had purchased the animals from James Allen. Thus Allen engaged in personal trade to the detriment of his employers (Panton, Leslie and Company) and against the governor's orders, and Cain removed goods without permission.[27]

The cattle trade often could be cutthroat, and there were settlers who did not hesitate to take advantage of their neighbors. John Peter Wagnon fueled rumors (with some basis) among his neighbors of a coming invasion by Georgians in 1793. Manipulating their alarm, Wagnon offered to buy up their cattle at a very low price before they lost them to the U.S.

expeditionaries. The next year, when the invasion threat from Georgia seemed imminent, Spaniards from St. Augustine did the war-profiteering. They bought cattle from the desperate settlers with the intention of selling the meat back to the very same sellers at "city prices" should an invasion result in a meat shortage. The price of meat in the countryside was traditionally about half of the price in town. F. X. Sánchez and Miguel Ysnardy each bought more than 200 cattle, while the size of purchases by Lorenzo Llanes and Fernando Arredondo went unreported. One of the rural settlers sold Sánchez 110 head at seven pesos. Another resident of the countryside owning 60 head and a neighbor with 40 head received only six and a half pesos per animal. The Spanish frontier commander reported that he was "scandalized" by the "extraordinary profit" to be made should the profiteers receive their asking price of twenty-five pesos per head. In 1795, when invasion threatened yet again, Wagnon once more amassed cattle. The frontier commander concluded that it was Wagnon's intention to take control of the cattle market in the region by "incapacitat[ing]" the government contractor's ability to provide meat at a time of high demand.[28]

Other residents entertained more-complex designs, in which cattle offered a means of insinuating themselves into profitable commerce in addition to the beef trade. The Indian trade and the cattle trade were inextricably tied. Panton, Leslie and Company, with access to British goods, could offer the cloth and tools upon which the Indians had come to depend, in exchange for Indian cattle and furs. Francis Fatio and others wanted to break the company's virtual monopoly of the Indian trade. Fatio, Cosifacio, and Ysnardy, with their special import licenses, were in a position to challenge the trading company's status, but the governors refused to allow anyone besides Panton, Leslie and Company to trade with the Indians. Control of a large number of cattle from another source (in this case, the rural residents) by Fatio, Ysnardy, or Cosifacio could have changed the balance. Perhaps Ysnardy's motive in buying up cattle when invasion threatened was as much to gain leverage with the governor through the meat supply for the troops as it was for the immediate profit. Even traders living outside the colony attempted to tap Florida's cattle trade. Samuel Hammond of Georgia worked through family operatives living in East Florida in an attempt to control the cattle trade, for he hoped ultimately to replace Panton, Leslie and Company in the Indian trade.[29]

Theoretically, the provisioning of meat to the government was open to all. Residents bid for the government meat contract in formal public proceedings. First, official notices were posted; then on the day of the auction, a drummer and a black-slave crier announced "in a loud and intelligible

Table 8.1. Meat contracts, 1788–1813

Year	Ounces per *real*	Contractor
1788	24	Fatio
1789	—	—
1790	—	Panton, Leslie & Co., Sánchez
1791	—	Panton, Leslie & Co.
1792	—	Panton, Leslie & Co., Solano, Fatio
1793	—	Panton, Leslie & Co., Sánchez, Hambly
1794	24	Fatio, Saavedra, Solana, Sánchez
1795	28.4	Sánchez
1796	32	Sánchez
1797	—	—
1798	36	Pellicer
1799	34	Huertas
1800	—	—
1801	28	Panton, Leslie & Co.
1802	—	—
1803	—	—
1804	—	—
1805	—	—
1806	24	Sánchez
1807	40	Montero
1808	—	—
1809	40	Reyes
1810	—	—
1811	—	—
1812	—	—
1813	35	Rovira

Source: Meat Contracts, Bundle 297O12; Communiqué from Governor Juan Nepomuceno de Quesada to Luis de Las Casas, January 2, 1794, bundle 24, East Florida Papers, P. K. Yonge Library of Florida History, University of Florida.

voice" the start of the bidding from the steps of Government House.[30] In the early years of the Second Spanish Period, the meat contract passed quickly, sometimes quarterly, from one citizen to another. As Spanish funds dwindled across the tottering empire, the meat contracts for East Florida became less lucrative. The royal governors ordered increasingly restrictive measures on any commerce in cattle within the colony in order to protect the government's ability to feed its dependents at a price that it could afford.

Spanish government regulations provided a ration of 12 ounces of fresh meat per day to its soldiers and administrators. East Florida's regime required 408 pounds of fresh meat, or about one and two-thirds beeves, per day in 1787.[31] These were not the massive beef cattle of today. The four quarters when butchered would yield about 250 pounds of beef. The "fifth part"—head, tongue, tripe, etc.—equaled one of the quarters in value. The meat contracts documented the prices that the government paid for beef (see table 8.1). The contractor's profit was theoretically fifteen pesos per day. In 1788 Francis Fatio won the bid at a price of 24 ounces per *real*. (One peso contained eight *reales*.) At that price, the contractor probably sold an animal for 250 percent more than he paid. Eight years later, the contractor had to provide one-third more meat for the same price, and by 1798 a *real* bought 50 percent more than ten years earlier. Prices bottomed out at 40 ounces to the *real* in 1807 and 1809, two-thirds more meat for the same price, and the "mark-up," therefore, was only 100 percent.[32] Sometimes the contract to supply the government also included preference in selling at the public market in St. Augustine. In 1807, when prices were lowest, the contractor received a monopoly on all sales in town.[33]

The lower prices did not satisfy the residents, for there was more than the cost of meat involved. In accomplishing the lowest prices, the legal market for fresh meat vanished by governmental decree, excepting the government contractor. Not only did the contractor hold the monopoly on sales, but only he was authorized to purchase cattle from the Indians. It was the ultimate monopoly—control at both ends.

In the first years after the Spanish returned, a somewhat fluid provisioning had taken place. When Francis Fatio was short on meat to deliver to the troops in 1788, another citizen received permission to make up the shortfall. In 1794 four simultaneous contractors were told by the governor "to work out the arrival of the deliveries among yourselves." But in 1796, F. X. Sánchez secured the contract to supply both the government and the public market in the St. Augustine town square (*plaza*), despite a price that offered two ounces less beef per *real* than his competitor, Manuel Solana. Sánchez had "sweetened" his offer with the promise of preferential delivery to government personnel. Feeling victimized, the residents, especially the Minorcans, reacted with formal complaints. They accused the government of imposing a 12.5 percent "tribute" upon the public by virtue of the higher price. They suggested that Sánchez continue his contract to supply the government while Solana would sell meat at his original offer and, in the process, purchase cattle from other residents. They opposed a single contractor for both the government and the public and asserted that only Sánchez and Panton, Leslie and Company had sufficient stock to supply both sectors as well as the financial means to sell to the government on credit.[34]

The governor found himself squeezed between his superiors and the subsidy, on one hand, and the citizenry, on the other. To enable continued provisioning of fresh meat to the troops, he forbade the purchase of cattle from the Indians (except by the meat contractor) and the trafficking in meat among the residents as well. Cattle could be imported but not removed from the province. His restrictions came at a time when there was a market in Georgia for Florida cattle.[35]

When the Indians found themselves caught in the monopoly, they quickly turned to other outlets. They initiated negotiations to sell their herds to the U.S. quartermasters. The Indians delivered livestock, including horses, to St. Marys River residents who sold the cattle illegally in Georgia. While the governor created his own legal monopoly in the cattle trade, residents on the St. Marys River attempted to create their own monopoly on the illegal exportation of cattle into Georgia. Georgia drovers complained to their own magistrates that East Florida resident Ludovic Ashley "selfishly" interfered with their illegal extraction of illegally purchased cattle destined for a Georgia official. Ashley had refused to ferry their bovine purchases, claiming it was "contrary to the laws of Spain," although he crossed animals that he wished himself to sell in Georgia. A Georgia resident stated that it was a "well known fact that the market of St. Marys had been chiefly supplied with beef by said Ashley and his brother" with cattle from Florida. The Georgians also reported that Chief Bowlegs of the Alachua tribe had delivered 200–300 head of cattle to Ashley, and also accused the Indians of stealing some of the animals from other Florida residents.[36]

Behind the profit in disobeying the Spanish decrees was the trend of farmers in the Southeast to dedicate a decreasing portion of their land to edible products, whether animal or vegetable. Every year more acres that had at one time supported food crops or grazing became cotton fields. Cotton growers had to look to sources ever farther from their farms for food. The labor requirements of cotton exacerbated the problem with a growing population to be fed in the face of decreased food production. East Florida planters also shifted to planting long-staple (sea-island) cotton. Florida's long growing season offered the environment for the lucrative, long-staple cotton, as did the nearby islands of the Georgia coast. Because of its length and luster, sea-island cotton was used to manufacture delicate laces and cloth of remarkable silkiness. Its price functioned largely independent of the vagaries of the short-staple variety, which was cultivated throughout the rest of South. Profitability encouraged monoculture. John Fraser claimed that there was the potential for $111,000 in cotton at

Greenfields Plantation near the mouth of the St. Johns River, where he kept 200 slaves. Cattle and corn crops appeared with less frequency on the inventories of the larger cotton planters. Why would they plant corn when one acre of cotton would purchase ten acres of the grain?[37] East Florida, like other parts of the South, exhibited the signs of moving toward dependence upon nonlocal foods in order to profit from cotton production. Reacting to this trend, Governor Enrique White prohibited the planting of the "more monetarily advantageous" cotton and ordered the immediate planting of corn, because planters "ha[d] not picked enough corn to take care of their slaves." The governor deplored the departure of money from the province to purchase foreign grain, but he was ill-provided with manpower to control it. He could neither regulate planting within his colony nor prevent the removal of cattle.[38]

The microcosm of the cattle trade offers a view of the intertwining of the economic and social lives of the colony's residents. Through this lens, East Florida appears as a society pulling in opposite directions at once. The best interests of the citizens and those of the government were usually not the same. The chief administrator, the governor, answered to superiors elsewhere, not to the residents, and his financial decisions often placed economic strains upon the public. Provincial fiscal policy might at times reflect events taking place within the colony, but, for the governor, the economic interests of the Spanish empire always superseded those of the colony's citizenry.

The meat contracts offered one opportunity for the citizens to profit from the government, yet the ability of the Indians to supply meat at low prices usurped profitable participation for most of the settlers. Foreclosed from commerce with the government and with a nearby alternative market for cattle in Georgia, the settlers turned to their Indian competitors to become their suppliers for the clandestine cattle trade. Part of the populace, the Minorcans, responded with cohesion and interdependence, as seen in the petitions protesting the price of meat and the support of their fellow citizens. But in other sectors, where social relations were more atomized, citizens acted in their own interest and at the expense of their neighbors in times of stress.

East Florida's cattlemen often functioned more as middlemen than as herders. They bought cattle from sources in Georgia or from Indians in Florida to convey to the Spanish government, or they reversed the direction and acquired Indian cattle to sell to purchasers in Georgia. Contemporaries in the Northeast region of the United States focused their energies on increased dairy production and animal weight amid a constricted land situation. Christopher Clark has demonstrated how cattle-raising was an important aspect of the household economy that dominated rural Massachusetts in the years following the American Revolution. Richard K. MacMaster found that the cattlemen in western Virginia's narrow valleys also worked toward intensive development of the industry through improving the animal itself.[39] In contrast, the government and cattlemen of East Florida "mined" the Indians' cattle with little accompanying development of the province's commercial or physical infrastructure.

Clark and MacMaster found kinship to be an important element of business dealings in the cattle trade in Massachusetts and Virginia. Family networks were active across the Spanish Florida–U.S. border also, but in endeavors that competed with other families and at times precipitated events that were destructive to the province overall. Anglo settlers of East Florida appear to have been every bit as "deeply materialistic" and "highly exploitive" as historian Jack P. Greene found the Virginians and Carolinians of the previous century. Spanish entrepreneurs were just as venal.[40]

Mere participation in the economy did not seem to suffice; control became the goal. Perhaps the example set by the government encouraged an every-man-for-himself attitude, and one monopoly begat others as rural residents attempted to establish control over the markets that were actually, if not legally, open to them. The cattle trade to Georgia functioned through a series of petty crimes which brought little retribution from the government in St. Augustine, while the Georgia authorities overlooked and often abetted the infractions of Spanish law.

In East Florida, the ease of entering the cattle trade offered opportunities to all members of society. The Indians played an essential role in the cattle trade, for they were frequently the source. Détente between the residents and the Indians was good business when cattle were in demand, but the dynamics would change as settlers came to desire the Indians' land for lucrative staple crops. In Spanish East Florida, lawlessness was not the legacy of brigands but rather the product of economic factors.

Notes

1. Lois Green Carr and Lorena S. Walsh, "The Standard of Living in the Colonial Chesapeake," *William and Mary Quarterly*, 3d ser., 45 (1988): 142; John Bartram, *A Description of East Florida*, 3d ed. (London, 1769), 3.

2. Jimmy M. Skaggs, *Prime Cut: Livestock Raising and Meatpacking in the United States, 1607–1983* (College Station: Texas A&M University Press, 1986), 3.

3. Frank L. Owsley, *Plain Folk of the Old South* (Baton Rouge: Louisiana State

University Press, 1949), viii; Forrest McDonald and Grady McWhiney blame Frederick Jackson Turner for relegating herders to a minor role ("The Antebellum Southern Herdsman: A Reinterpretation," *Journal of Southern History* 49 [1975]: 147–66).

4. Lewis C. Gray, *History of Agriculture in the Southern United States to 1860,* 2 vols. (Clifton, N.J.: A. M. Kelley, 1973; reprint of 1933 ed.), 1:107–10; George H. Dacy, *Four Centuries of Florida Cattle Ranching* (St. Louis, Mo.: privately printed, 1940), 22, 35; Joe A. Akerman, Jr., *Florida Cowman: A History of Florida Cattle Raising* (Kissimmee, Fla.: Florida Cattlemen's Association, 1976); Charles W. Arnade, "Cattle Raising in Spanish Florida, 1513–1763," *Agricultural History* 35 (July 1961): 116–24; Amy Bushnell, "The Menéndez Márquez Cattle Barony of La Chua and the Determinants of Economic Expansion in Seventeenth-Century Florida," *Florida Historical Quarterly* 56 (1978): 407–31; Bernard Bailyn, *Voyagers to the West: A Passage in the Peopling of America on the Eve of the Revolution* (New York: Alfred A. Knopf, 1986), 430–74.

5. Remaining British settlers would provide the core for Spanish Florida's rural society. See Susan R. Parker, "Men without God or King: Rural Planters of East Florida, 1784–1790," *Florida Historical Quarterly* 69 (October 1990): 135–55.

6. Helen Hornbeck Tanner's attribution of the illegal activities to the "cultural products of frontier society and wartime dislocation" omits the economic dimension; see her "The Second Spanish Period Begins," in *Clash between Cultures: The Second Spanish Period,* ed. Jacqueline K. Fretwell and Susan Parker, *El Escribano* 25 (1988): 26–29.

7. Allan J. Kuethe applied this phrase to Cuba's economic role, but it fits Florida just as well; see his *Cuba, 1753–1815: Crown, Military and Society* (Knoxville: University of Tennessee Press, 1986), ix.

8. Ligia María Bermúdez's research traced the Florida treasury's performance in the Second Spanish Period. Through quantitative analysis, she concluded that, contrary to previous assessments based on literary sources, the money to support the defense edifice *did* arrive in the colony and in the budgeted amounts. It was the governor's distribution system that kept the coffers perennially empty; see her "The Situado: A Study in the Dynamics of East Florida's Economy during the Second Spanish Period, 1785–1820," Master's thesis, University of Florida, 1989.

9. Elena Sánchez-Fabrés Mirat, *Situación histórica de las Floridas en la segunda mitad del siglo XVIII (1783–1819)* (Madrid: Ministerios de Asuntos Exteriores, 1977), 9, 111.

10. Vicente Martínez to Governor, December 8, 1785, bnd. 118A10, no. 139; Governor to Diego de Gardoqui, March 19, 1787, bnd. 101S8, no. 167; Richard Lang to Governor, August 23, 1788, bnd. 119B10, no. 195; José Tasso to Governor, March 11, 1790, bnd. 121D10, no. 19 [?]; Estate of Francisco Xavier Sánchez, bnd. 308, East Florida Papers, Library of Congress, microfilm copies (hereafter cited as EFP); Gray, *Agriculture in the Southern United States,* 2:841.

11. Artemis Elliott Ferguson to Governor, January 25, 1793, bnd. 123F10, no. 11, EFP.

12. Petition of William Pengree, November 30, 1786, bnd. 41B4, no. 89; Richard Lang to Governor of Florida, bnd. 119B10; Oaths of Allegiance, bnd. 350U4, EFP. Some immigrants used the hostilities as an excuse for otherwise prohibited immigration. I describe the problems of the Georgia-Indian war in "Men without God or King: Rural Settlers of East Florida, 1784–1790," Master's thesis, University of Florida, 1990, 31–37. The Indian war along the Florida-Georgia border is not discussed, however, in Kenneth Coleman, *A History of Georgia* (Athens: University of Georgia Press, 1977).

13. Richard Lang to Governor of Florida, June 19, 1790, bnd. 120C10, no. 71, EFP. In 1804 the chalk equaled twenty-five cents, and in 1820 it still bought twenty-five cents' worth of merchandise at the Indian store at Volusia on the St. Johns River (Buckra Woman vs. Philip R. Yonge, Box 176, folder 28, St. Johns County [Florida] Court Papers [conserved at St. Augustine Historical Society]; Bill of Sale by McKenzie, a Seminole, to Horatio S. Dexter and Francis P. Sánchez, December 6, 1821, Deed Book A, page 99, St. Johns County public records).

14. J. Leitch Wright, Jr., in *Creeks and Seminoles: The Destruction and Regeneration of Muscogulge People* (Lincoln: University of Nebraska Press, 1986), 59–60, states that "as much as anything these chalks entered on the factors' ledgers symbolized the extent to which the Muscogulges had become part of the capitalistic market economy of the western world." For a discussion of Panton, Leslie and Company, see William S. Coker and Thomas D. Watson, *Indian Traders of the Southeastern Spanish Borderlands: Panton, Leslie and Company and John Forbes Company, 1783–1847* (Pensacola: University of West Florida Press, 1986).

15. Depositions of Joseph McCullough, Charles Magill, Zacariah Magirt, October 1809–January 1810, bnd. 145B12, EFP.

16. Buckra Woman vs. Yonge; Juan Bautista Collins vs. José Antonio de Yguíñiz, January 20, 1810, bnd. 345T3, EFP. Collins's statement lists manufactured goods, in addition to the money, with which Collins "cajoled" the Seminoles to sell the cattle to him. Jane Landers relates the case in *Black Society in Spanish Florida, 1784–1821* (Urbana: University of Illinois Press, 1999), 91–93.

17. Richard Lang to Governor, June 19, 1790, bnd. 120C10, no. 71, EFP.

18. Deposition of Charles W. Clarke, September 30, 1834, File MC 31–75, Patriot War Claims, St. Augustine Historical Society; 1835 Township map of Range 28 East, Township 7 South, Florida Department of Environmental Protection.

19. José Antonio de Yguíñiz to Governor, August 23, 1808, bnd. 78; Governor to Damaso Yglesia, August 24, 1808, [?], bnd. 144A12, no. 185; Collins vs. Yguíñiz, bnd. 345T3, EFP.

20. "Report Affirming the Number of Families . . . of St. Marys and Nassau Rivers, Amelia and Talbot Islands," December 10, 1789, bnd. 120C10, no. 211, EFP. A translation of this report may be found in Parker, "Men without God or King," appendix; James A. Lewis, "*Cracker*—Spanish Style," *Florida Historical Quarterly* 63 (1984): 184–204.

21. Meat contracts, bnd. 297O12, EFP.

22. John Solomon Otto, *The Southern Frontiers, 1607–1860: The Agricultural Evolution of the Colonial and Antebellum South* (New York: Greenwood Press, 1989), 42; Christopher Charles Morris, "Town and Country in the Old South: Vicksburg and Warren County, Mississippi, 1770–1860," Ph.D. diss., University of Florida, 1991, 52.

23. Census Returns, bnd. 323A; "Report Affirming the Number of Families," December 10, 1789, bnd. 120C10, no. 211, EFP.

24. "Petition of the Captains of the Urban Militias" in Meat Contract for 1796, bnd. 297O12, EFP.

25. "[B]arrels of flour and salt meat, and the money to pay for them, constituted Governor Zéspedes's most fundamental problem throughout his administration"; see Helen Hornbeck Tanner, *Zéspedes in East Florida, 1784–1790* (Jacksonville: University of North Florida Press, 1963), 105.

26. For example, in January 1790, the *Nuestra Señora del Carmen* set sail laden with more than 13,000 pounds of butter and 2,400 pounds of cheese. Another ship departed that month with almost 12,000 pounds of butter and 5,000 of cheese, and the small *Santa Rosa* carried 5,600 pounds of butter and 4,500 of cheese. These dairy products were certified to be "fruits of the country," not reexports. Only a few of the slips of paper that served as "bills of sale" from the small farmers to the shippers still remain as proof of origin in the ships' registers. Their presence, along with marginal notes, indicates the gathering up by the shippers but is insufficient to construct even a tentative group of small producers (Ship Registers, January 1790, bnd. 243I19, EFP). "Export" in this sense is used in a descriptive sense; the goods shipped to Cuba from East Florida crossed no international boundaries.

27. Richard Lang to Governor, June 19, 1790, bnd. 120C10, no. 71, EFP.

28. Carlos Howard to Governor, October 8, 1793, bnd. 124G10, no. 264; Howard to Governor, November 6, 1794, bnd. 127J10, no. 246; Howard to Bartolomé Morales, June 16, 1795, bnd. 127J10, no. 322, EFP. The earliest of these letters is badly faded and difficult to read.

29. Wright, *Creeks and Seminoles*, 50–60; Charles E. Bennett, *Florida's "French" Revolution, 1793–1795* (Gainesville: University of Florida Press, 1981), 149; Governor Juan Nepomuceno de Quesada to Luis de Las Casas, January 2, 1794, enclosing Fatio's request of December 24, 1793, bnd. 24; Carlos Howard to Governor, November 6, 1794, bnd. 127J10, no. 246, EFP.

30. Meat Contracts, bnd. 297O12, EFP. Description of the auctions are in the reports on bidding that precede each contract.

31. A regular ration was twelve ounces of fresh meat per day. Higher-ranking officials and officers were entitled to two rations per day, while a standard ration for a hospital patient was sixteen ounces per day. Rations of tinned or salted meat or chicken were in different amounts (Gonzalo Zamorano, "Report of the Pounds of Daily Fresh Meat," January 2, 1787, bnd. 67B6, EFP). This report does not include the figures for meat needed to feed the convict laborers assigned to East Florida.

32. Carlos Howard to Governor, November 6, 1794, bnd. 127J10, no. 246; Collins vs. Yguíñiz, bnd. 345T3, EFP. This is a crude estimate. These computations are based on the purchase price of 6 pesos for one animal weighing an average of 250 pounds. In 1788 such an animal brought 166 *reales,* or 15 pesos, to the contractor. This is based on the price for cattle brought in from Georgia. There is little information on the price paid to the Indians, nor was information incorporated from those who raised their own beef.

33. Meat Contracts, bnd. 297O12, EFP.

34. Petition of Rafael Ximénez, January 8, 1788; "Terms of the contract," December 9, 1794; Proceedings of contract for 1797, bnd. 297O12, EFP.

35. Governor's decrees, June 1, 1807, December 24, 1807, bnd. 278O14; Fernando de la Puente to Governor, June 19, 1803, and August 8, 1808; Governor to de la Puente, August 13, 1808, bnd. 152I12, EFP.

36. Collins vs. Yguíñiz, bnd. 345T3; Depositions of Charles Magill, Joseph McCullough, Zacariah Magirt, November 1809–January 1810, bnd. 145B12, EFP. Ludovic Ashley's accomplice, his brother William, became a justice of the Camden County Inferior Court; see Marguerite Reddick, comp., *Camden's Challenge: a History of Camden County, Georgia* (Jacksonville, Fla.: Camden County Historical Commission), 1976, 21.

37. Claim of John Fraser, File MC 31–41, Patriot War Claims, St. Augustine Historical Society; Report of the Family of Don Francisco Phelipe Fatio, February 27, 1801; Fatio to John McQueen, March 12[?], 1801, bnd. 136E11, nos. 63, 77, EFP; Otto, *Southern Frontiers,* 106–12; Gray, *Agriculture in the Southern United States,* 2:731–39.

38. Decree of Governor White, January 2, 1800, bnd. 278O14, EFP.

39. Christopher Clark, *The Roots of Rural Capitalism: Western Massachusetts, 1780–1860* (Ithaca, N.Y.: Cornell University Press, 1990), 71–100; Richard K. MacMaster, "The Cattle Trade in Western Virginia, 1760–1830," in *Appalachian Frontiers: Settlement, Society and Development in the Preindustrial Era,* ed. Robert D. Mitchell (Lexington: University Press of Kentucky, 1990), 127–49.

40. Jack P. Greene, *Pursuits of Happiness: The Social Development of Early Modern British Colonies and the Formation of American Culture* (Chapel Hill: University of North Carolina Press, 1988), 12; Jack P. Greene, "Colonial South Carolina and the Caribbean Connection," *South Carolina Historical Magazine* 88 (1987): 198.

9

Spanish East Florida in the Atlantic Economy of the Late Eighteenth Century

James Gregory Cusick

On March 20, 1789, the following extract from a letter written in St. Augustine, Florida, appeared in the *Herald of Freedom and Federal Advertizer* (Boston):

> Our vessels are received with the greatest cordiality by the Spaniards. Governour Zelpadez [*sic*], pays the greatest attention to every American who comes properly recommended, and the friendly treatment our countrymen receive from the officers of the Irish brigade stationed in this town, must lay every American under the greatest obligations to these hospitable sons of Hibernia. Flour and all kinds of provisions from the United States find a good market here, the commerce in the above articles being entirely free. This indulgence we owe to the uncultivated state of this province.[1]

This anonymous testament to the role of trade in St. Augustine underscores one of the major political and economic changes taking place in Spanish East Florida during the late eighteenth century. The reception of U.S. trade in East, or peninsular, Florida owed as much to the colony's articulation with the Atlantic economy as to its "uncultivated state." By 1789, residents of East Florida found themselves straddling the border between two major regions in the world marketplace—the American South and the Caribbean. This border status created many repercussions in provincial economy. Governors wrangled with settlers and superiors over the question of free trade.[2] Merchants sailed weekly for U.S. and Spanish American ports.[3] In large and small aspects of life, the cultural and legal precepts of Spanish rule struggled with the idiosyncratic and self-centered ambitions of a largely immigrant population. Over a period of years from the 1780s through the first decade of the nineteenth century, merchants, planters, and administrators in Florida slowly developed a flexible system of commerce loosely based on official Spanish regulations but always open to local manipulation.

One means of understanding commerce in Spanish Florida is by fitting it into the larger regional picture of trade between the United States and the Caribbean. In particular, the mercantile classes of Florida can be seen as anchoring themselves to the broader economies of Havana and Charleston. These cities certainly were not the only ports visited by Florida merchants, but they were, by their proximity and size, the most important as outlets for exports and sources of imports. To maintain access to these ports, the traders of Florida and their government sympathizers faced a variety of impediments posed by trade restrictions. Spanish mercantile regulations of the Bourbon era, embodied in the principles of *comercio libre,* were not designed for the sort of free-trade environment coveted by many colonial Floridians. This chapter reviews the impediments to trade and their local solutions. In doing so, the presentation demonstrates a paradox of the borderland environment: that in their attempts to free themselves of obnoxious Spanish restrictions on trade, the colonials of Florida tended to adopt solutions that originated in Cuba and Spanish Louisiana. In their very dissent from Spanish regulations, the citizens of St. Augustine, Fernandina, and the hinterlands evinced an ironic fidelity to the Spanish colonial way of doing things. This fidelity is apparent in the struggle for free trade, the collection of import and export duties, the establishment of credit, and the patterns of commodity flow that characterized the provincial economy.

The Atlantic Trade

From New York to Buenos Aires, the late eighteenth century saw the rise of what has come to be known as the "Atlantic economy," a regional trade network that was gradually effacing the political and social boundaries of the Americas.[4] The development of the Atlantic trade with respect to the circum-Caribbean has been the subject of an extensive literature focusing on commercial networks between Spanish America and North America. After 1760, cities such as Havana and Caracas became increasingly integrated into regional systems of trade. Indeed, Havana, important as a harbor and supply station for Spanish fleets and now a major exporter of sugar, was Spanish America's third-largest city and second-largest port, surpassed only by Vera Cruz, Mexico.[5] Spain's efforts to fortify the Carib-

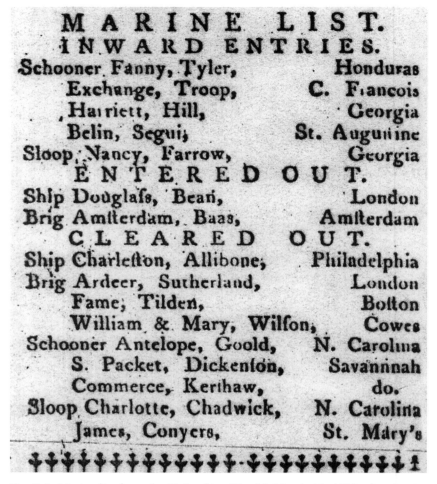

Fig. 9.1. Marine list from the *Columbian Herald,* March 13, 1788, showing inward- and outward-bound vessels, including the St. Augustine ships *St. Peter* [*San Pedro*], under Capt. Machoqui, entering, and the *Bellin* [*Nuestra Señora de Belem*], under Capt. Seguí, cleared out.

bean and promote more commerce with the colonies unintentionally abetted a trend toward regional trade. When Spanish sea power ultimately failed in the early 1800s, planters and merchants in the Spanish Caribbean turned readily to the United States as a source of imports and as a market for exports. Research on this topic has matured very quickly and includes such major publications as Liss's *Atlantic Empires,* Barbier and Kuethe's

The North American Role in the Spanish Imperial Economy, and Knight and Liss's *Atlantic Port Cities*.[6]

Life in Spanish East Florida was influenced by Spanish attempts to adapt to the Atlantic economy and retain strong commercial ties with the colonies. Under Charles III (1759–88), the most powerful Spanish monarch of the eighteenth century, Spain reorganized its colonial bureaucracy, tightened Crown control over officials, altered the defense strategy for Atlantic shipping, and introduced a liberalized trading policy—*comercio libre*—which allowed most Spanish and Spanish American ports to trade directly with one another.[7] During the 1780s and 1790s, colonials saw both the initial success and ultimate failure of these attempts at reform.

In the end, it was not reform but the collapse of Spanish naval and military power that ensured changes in colonial life. The crushing defeats Spain suffered at the hands of both England and France during the Napoleonic era permanently broke trans-Atlantic communications with the Americas and left the Spanish colonies adrift in a sea of their own volitions. For Floridians, much of the late colonial period was dominated, politically and economically, by regional events. Critical among them was the rise of Cuba as an economic power.

The fall of Havana to British forces in 1762 had shocked Madrid and forced Charles III and his ministers into a program of reforms. Cuba was the key strategic point in Spain's defense of its mainland colonial possessions. In order to ensure the island's future safety, Spain poured millions of pesos into the Cuban economy to strengthen harbor defenses and maintain a larger garrison.[8] The Crown intended to reforge Havana as the impregnable gate to the Gulf of Mexico.

Some of the island's shrewd entrepreneurs held a more expansive view of their future. In the 1760s Havana already had a diversified economy, based in sugar production, trade, and ship-building, as well as defense.[9] The influx of silver from Mexico now provided liquid capital for further expansion, especially of the sugar industry. These expenditures funded the renovation of docks and wharf facilities, increased public employment, and provided an economic spur to the consumer economy. Between 1760 and 1790, sugar production in Cuba trebled and Havana became a leading port in the trans-Atlantic trade with Spain.[10]

The wealthy planters and merchants of Cuba deluged the Crown with requests for economic concessions; first, for a lessening of restrictions on trade (1765), then for expansion of the slave trade (1792), and subsequently for enactment of land reforms that would open protected timberlands and create a surge in land speculation (1795–1830).[11] As Kuethe characterizes the situation, "Cubans repeatedly extracted the right to engage in neutral trade, a commerce directed largely to the United States which absorbed Cuban sugar while providing grain food supplies and lumber for sugar crates. While the Spanish government, under the stress of war, frequently granted similar concessions to its other colonies, the Cubans, wailing and moaning about their unique situation, specialized in anticipating these arrangements. . . . With few exceptions, Cubans traded freely with the United States from 1793 to 1808 and beyond."[12]

An essential feature in Havana's rise as an economic power was its increasing integration into the regional Atlantic economy, especially in trade partnership with the United States.[13] This partnership originated in Cuba's need to import flour and export sugar. Bread was essential to feed the garrison and provide a basic staple, but the flour for it had to be imported.[14] Prior to the eighteenth century, Havana had secured flour from Mexico or Spain. However, by the mid-1700s, merchants in the British colonies were outstripping these suppliers as cheap, reliable sources of flour.[15] Exports of flour from the thirteen colonies jumped during the American Revolution when Spain opened the port of Havana to trade with allied and neutral powers.[16] U.S. ships, primarily from Baltimore and Philadelphia, represented 20–30 percent of arrivals and departures in Havana's harbor between 1781 and 1783 and carried almost 90 percent of the flour trade.[17] Flour was off-loaded to Cuban factors in return for shipments of sugar.[18] Although this trade lasted openly for only a few years (1780–85), it was, as Barbier noted, merely "a rehearsal for the vaster operations destined to follow."[19] Throughout the turbulent 1790s and early nineteenth century, U.S.-Cuban trade persisted—openly when Spanish law allowed, undercover when it did not. Cuba remained an important destination for U.S. merchants, as evident from a steady 4 percent increase in traffic between Philadelphia and Havana between 1794 and 1822.[20]

Florida and the Cuban Model

It is within this framework that the late colonial period in Spanish East Florida must be understood. In the 1780s Governor Vicente Manuel de Zéspedes y Velasco characterized Florida as "a province that has just died for England and is in the process of being reborn for Spain."[21] Zéspedes had the difficult task of coruling Florida with the outgoing British governor Patrick Tonyn and of overseeing the removal of British evacuees who for twenty years had called Florida their home. The incoming Spanish, *Cubano*, and *Floridano* colonists were left to reestablish a hold over the colony at a time when Spain was weakened by war in Europe and when Cuba enjoyed prosperity through its ability to win concessions for its sugar industry. The Caribbean orientation of the Spanish colonists is essential to understanding the history of the colony. Early historians of the period frequently interpreted late colonial society as predestined to failure, a vain Spanish attempt to prevent Florida from becoming part of the United States. In fact, it is important to recognize that Spaniards returned to Florida with the determination and the knowledge to make it a paying and prosperous settlement.

Local attempts to develop Florida's economy in the late colonial period closely resembled strategies employed in contemporaneous Cuba. The contingent of colonists who arrived with Zéspedes came from the very center of the Spanish American possession that extolled open trade, entrepreneurial spirit, and commercial ties to the United States. They could not help but be aware of the economic revolution that was transforming the island of Cuba. Some of them were *Floridanos* who had arrived in Havana only a year after its fall to the British. Others were native *Cubanos* or, like Governor Zéspedes, Old World Spaniards who had held important royal offices in Cuba during the early years of the sugar boom.[22]

One important way in which the community at St. Augustine followed patterns of behavior prevalent throughout the Spanish Caribbean was in the use of *situado* moneys, the annual military and administrative subsidy to the local treasury. Numerous eighteenth-century accounts call attention to the military cast of the provincial capital of St. Augustine. Especially in the 1780s, St. Augustine was portrayed as a military garrison town: "All are either in the service of the garrison, or live on a small liquor trade or other mercantile business of little consequence."[23] Such comments were not entirely accurate. The Minorcan settlers of Florida (discussed by Patricia C. Griffin in chapter 2) invested much of their time in farming, fishing, and commerce; more-prosperous settlers, such as Francisco Xavier Sánchez (discussed by Jane G. Landers in chapter 4), managed large herds of cattle or, like Francis Philip Fatio (discussed in chapter 3 by Susan R. Parker) and Zephaniah Kingsley (discussed in chapter 5 by Daniel L. Schafer), managed diverse agricultural plantations. It was true, however, that in its overall social structure, St. Augustine resembled Spanish American presidio-ports more than North American ports. Depending on how one calculates occupational sectors for St. Augustine, the administrative and military sector of the town accounted for between 12 and 22 percent of the adult male population.[24] In this respect, St. Augustine was more similar to other, albeit larger, Spanish American presidio-ports, such as

Cartagena, than to typical ports of the United States. The differing occupation structures between the presidio-ports and the ports reflected the heavy investment Spain made in fortifying key posts in its strategic system.

The existence of a significant bureaucratic and military contingent in St. Augustine had a direct impact on trade. Just as Cubans were diverting Crown moneys away from fortification and toward internal improvement, governors in Florida, on a much smaller scale, habitually used their annual allotments of *situado* moneys as pledges against credit to purchase materials from the United States. Pablo Tornero Tinajero and Ramón Romero Cabót, in their studies of ship arrivals and departures in Spanish Florida, have established that exports of oranges, woods, and cotton were countered by enormous influxes of foodstuffs from U.S. ports. According to Tornero, this process slowly converted Spanish Florida from a peripheral colony of Spanish American into an economic satellite of the United States. A study of the *situado* by Ligia María Bermúdez supports Tornero's assertion. Bermúdez concludes that much of the money provided by the *situado* was pledged in advance to the coffers of U.S. factors in Charleston and Savannah in order to maintain credit for Florida. In essence, St. Augustine suffered from the same imbalance of trade that characterized commerce between the United States and Cuba (an imbalance that funneled Spanish silver to the north for settlement of debts).[25]

It is also with the Cuban model in mind that one must understand the willingness of Florida's governors to circumvent official Spanish policies in order to promote growth in Florida. Zéspedes, who governed from 1784 to 1790, endeavored to resolve the colonies' three major problems: defense, settlement, and finance. To achieve his ends, he frequently opted to waive or ignore official Spanish policies, establishing a pattern that would be followed by governors Quesada (1790–95) and White (1796–1811). Scholars have devoted much attention to policies related to the Indian trade and to immigration.[26] However, it was in the struggle over free trade that the perplexities of life in Florida can be shown most clearly.

As noted in the extract from the *Herald of Freedom* which opened this chapter, Zéspedes had a reputation for being an official who favored the growth of trade in Florida. Shortly after arriving, he wrote to a superior about conditions in Florida: "That a poor immigrant at the end of one year, when he has made his first crop, or a Minorcan with a wife and four or five children who does not earn half a *peso fuerte* a day, should have to provide his family with goods bought from that place [Havana] and feed them with food from New Spain—I must honestly say that I consider such a thing impossible even with the most industrious effort on their parts, at least until this country has developed several years with some measure of free trade."[27]

This demand, initiated by Zéspedes, was later taken up and pressed by Governor Quesada. Indeed, both officials seemed to possess a knack for rhetoric: While Zéspedes spoke of Florida being "reborn for Spain," Quesada criticized Spanish restrictions on trade, arguing that, in treating Florida like New Spain or Cuba, the intendant at Havana "does not take into account the wide difference between an embryo and an adult."[28]

The case for allowing Florida some period of free trade—which essentially meant the right to trade with the United States, although direct trade with Britain and France was also contemplated—rested on several points of argument. These arguments appeared not only in the correspondence of the governors but also in petitions sent by merchants of St. Augustine to Madrid. The first argument was that Spain already had liberalized trade regulations for Cuba by allowing it to have open commerce with the United States during the American Revolution. The second was that the Crown had granted a dispensation to Spanish Louisiana in 1782, giving that province the right to trade with its former mother country, France, for a period of ten years. The third argument was that Spanish Florida simply could not survive if Havana was to be its sole link to the outside world.[29]

Authorities in Spain were not immediately receptive to any of these arguments, but under pressure they promulgated a new royal *cédula* in 1793, which granted Spanish Florida the right to trade with ports of "friendly nations having treaties of commerce with this Crown."[30] Although ostensibly resolving the problem of trade, the *cédula* in fact precipitated a crisis because Governor Quesada, unsure of how to interpret the "treaties of commerce" clause, refused to implement the *cédula*. Local anger at this unexpected setback was partially responsible for the wave of rebellion that rippled through the colony two years later. Only with the issuance of an additional *cédula* in 1797, specifically allowing colonies to trade with neutral powers, did trade between Florida and the American South receive official sanction.

In retrospect, however, it can be seen that the *cédulas* simply legalized practices that already were being carried out more surreptitiously. Throughout the 1780s, merchants in St. Augustine were making regular trips to the United States, exploiting a loophole in Spanish regulations that permitted Florida to import "emergency" provisions from nearby ports.[31] This practice continued through most of Quesada's term as governor. Between 1797 and 1802, Governor White closed the port of St. Augustine to ships from the United States. However, this ban seems to have been di-

Table 9.1. Ships off-loading cargo at St. Augustine

Port of departure	1787	1794	1803
Charleston	41	13	19
Other U.S. ports	22	5	16
Havana	10	9	15
Other Spanish ports	7	1	11

Source: James G. Cusick, "Across the Border: Commodity Flow and Merchants in Spanish St. Augustine," *Florida Historical Quarterly* 69, no. 3 (1991): 277–99.

rected at U.S. traders rather than at U.S. trade; it did not curtail the flow of U.S. imports. Local St. Augustine ships, traveling under Spanish registry, remained at liberty to visit U.S. ports and return with cargoes. By 1803, thirty-five of the fifty-three ships recorded as entering St. Augustine harbor were discharging goods from ports in the United States (see table 9.1).[32]

Hence, with or without the blessing of royal *cédulas,* trade between Spanish Florida and the United States was a fact of life throughout the late colonial period. While merchants thus succeeded in overcoming restrictions on trade, they were less successful in evading that other bane of Spanish commerce, the import and export tax. In contrast to their loose regulation of trade with non-Spanish ports, officials in St. Augustine seem to have been meticulous and scrupulous in the collection of customs duties. Under the 1793 *cédula,* "merchants handling commerce between the colonists and foreign nations had to pay an import duty of fifteen per cent and an export tax of six per cent."[33] Assessment of this tax was a process that both captivated and annoyed those who were unaccustomed to it. A few citations will illustrate how the system worked.

In 1805, John F. Watson, a young American in his twenties, sailed to Havana from New Orleans and recorded his experiences in a diary. Watson spoke English and French but only rudimentary Spanish, and, limited in his ability to converse with *Habaneros,* he seems to have spent much of his time in an examination of the city's physical layout and its habits. Describing the passage through customs, he wrote: "The Custom House is so formal in their examination of goods not intended to be passed under bribery, that they open goods even to . . . counting the pieces on nankeen in each bundel tho [*sic*] the bundle should forever be the same and then they brand twice each piece. This slow process makes dry goods longer getting through examination when nankeen or other goods have been smuggled."[34]

Fig. 9.2. The counting house and royal treasury of St. Augustine, 1764. Original watercolor sketch, British Library, London. By permission of the St. Augustine Historical Society, St. Augustine, Florida.

James Pitot, a merchant from Normandy and later a naturalized citizen of the United States, observed a similar customs operation during his years in New Orleans in Spanish Louisiana between 1796 and 1802. Pitot advocated a lowering of the customs duties and an end to the unpacking of merchandise, explaining, "A ship's cargo or pacotille [should be] admitted without forcing a complete unpacking, which, by deteriorating the merchandise, would annoy both the foreigner and the colonist."[35]

William Walton, in his work advising British merchants on the types of wares that would find a market in the Spanish Caribbean, also drew attention to the practice of unpacking goods. "All piece-goods in whatever kinds or descriptions of package, ought to be accompanied with bale cards, in order to avoid opening the same, and ought to correspond perfectly." He added that, once through customs, "it is advisable also to sell by the package, as the shop-keepers would cull your goods and leave many of little or no value, or at least choose the most saleable."[36]

After 1793, this same laborious process of unpacking cargoes was carried out rigorously in St. Augustine. Manifests of cargoes issued at U.S.

ports were rarely accepted at face value, especially as they listed dry goods under the nondescriptive term of "sundries." Near the town wharf, customs officials opened barrels and crates one by one and itemized the contents in exacting detail, down to the last half-set of dishes and the last bolt of cloth. The time-consuming unpacking and repacking of cargoes must have elicited the same feelings of aggravation and delay among Florida merchants as it did elsewhere, and yet, unlike the case with free trade, there were no petitions or appeals to terminate the process. Everyone, it would seem, was resigned to living with customs duties.

Administrative attentiveness to customs duties was also apparent at Fernandina—Spanish East Florida's increasingly prosperous port town located on the St. Marys River bordering Georgia. In an analysis of Fernandina and Amelia Island, Ward has demonstrated that this deep-water port was a major thoroughfare for exports of cotton and lumber from Florida's northeastern plantations and forests. Total cotton exports amounted to 77,620 pounds in 1805 and 65,915 pounds in 1806. War and international trade embargoes soon were to change this picture, however. When the Jefferson administration implemented the Non-Intercourse Act in 1806 and followed it with the Embargo Act in 1807, Fernandina and Amelia became, in Ward's words "an important link in a chain that enterprising merchants forged to bypass American trade restrictions." The U.S. embargo did not apply to Spanish territories, and therefore Fernandina was exempt. During the years of the embargo, exports of cotton from Amelia increased from tens of thousands of pounds to hundreds of thousands of pounds, and exports of lumber rose into the millions of feet. This increase represented the combined impact of higher demand for Florida exports and the enormous quantity of material that was being transshipped through the port by U.S., French, and British merchants. With the passage of the U.S. ban on the African slave trade, slave traders also moved into Fernandina, where they could continue to practice their human trafficking legally under Spanish law. Governor White responded to the trade boom by imposing new import and export taxes in addition to those already in force at the harbor. In 1809 the Spanish government garnered more than 46,000 pesos from duties levied at Amelia, and in 1810 more than 33,000 pesos. According to Bermúdez, these funds were comparable to the colony's normal *situado*.[37]

A review of vessel arrivals in St. Augustine for the years 1787, 1794, and 1803 also illustrates Florida's articulation within the region. In particular, vessel arrivals show St. Augustine's relations with the commercial centers of Charleston and Havana. Havana was St. Augustine's anchor, the source of its soldiers, equipment, and funds, as well as its regular port of call for many commodities. However, trade in St. Augustine was also firmly integrated with ports of the Anglo-American sphere. On average, for the years surveyed, there were twice as many ships off-loading cargoes from U.S. ports as there were from Spanish ports. Merchants would travel as far as Philadelphia and New York in search of goods.

The organization of local merchants in St. Augustine is not well understood. As would be expected in a borderland, merchants formed a diverse group. The *Floridano* planter Francisco Xavier Sánchez and the Swiss planter Francis Philip Fatio also engaged in commerce. Prior to 1800, those who can be identified reliably as ship owners or ship captains included Spanish Americans, Canary Islanders, Minorcans, Greeks, Italians, Anglo-Americans, and at least one free black. After 1800, due to immigration, the merchant community was augmented by French, Irish, Scottish, and U.S. traders.[38]

Previous research has outlined the general nature of St. Augustine's commercial linkages to Havana, Charleston, and other ports during the 1790s. These linkages reflect a regional pattern of commodity flow. St. Augustine's place in the Atlantic economy was conditioned by the workings of regional trade as outlined by Peggy K. Liss. "From 1789 to 1793," she explains, "United States commercial emphasis shifted from Spain to Latin America, and, with war in Europe, much carrying trade fell to United States ships. . . . With the general decree of 1797 opening ports to neutrals, massive shipments of United States flour went to Havana [and] Anglo-Americas legally supplied most Caribbean food imports."[39] Indeed, beginning with the American Revolution, a pattern of trade between North America and Havana was clearly established. Flour and foodstuffs went south; sugar and silver went north.[40]

The importation records of St. Augustine suggest that a somewhat similar pattern prevailed in Florida. Generally speaking, Caribbean products such as sugar, coffee, and rum, as well as Spanish wines and brandies, and some leather products of New Spain and Cuba, all came through the port of Havana. Cloth, crockery, furniture, manufactures, and virtually all imported grains, vegetables, lard, butters, salted meats, and salted fish came from the United States, most often through Charleston. For example, the flow of foodstuffs into St. Augustine indicates that here, as elsewhere in the Caribbean, the United States was the principal granary. With the exception of sugar, most perishable foods that could not be provided adequately by local farming came from the ports of New York, Philadelphia, or Charleston (see table 9.2).[41]

Table 9.2. Foodstuffs off-loaded in St. Augustine

	Fish	Grain	Butters/oils	Meats	Produce	Spices	Sugar
1787							
Charleston	21,408	33,500	165,765	8,746	7,164	324	40
Havana	128	—	8,282	340	1,706	52	40,532
New York	11,820	30,468	80,137	21,293	7,485	820	180
Philadelphia	4,864	17,132	23,600	5,037	6,372	250	—
Savannah	—	11,456	500	—	588	—	
1794							
Charleston	1,728	57,462	39,429	22,648	3,836	6,156	576
Havana	144	—	6,230	324	2,588	1,175	48,545
New York	—	—	—	—	—	—	—
Philadelphia	—	—	—	—	—	—	—
Savannah	—	26,000	—	1,359	—	—	—
1803							
Charleston	17,248	81,632	35,530	7,616	19,904	1,080	—
Havana	—	—	2,406	—	227	—	116,576
New York	2,048	1,776	11,500	3,072	8,790	—	—
Philadelphia	—	—	—	—	—	—	—
Savannah	344	12,010	14,266	1,482	100	272	—

Note: Foodstuffs expressed by cargo value in Spanish *reales*.
Source: Ship Arrivals, microfilm reels 91–93, 96, East Florida Papers, P. K. Yonge Library of Florida History, University of Florida.

Other commodities reflected regional availability. For example, while the United States was the principal source of tea, circum-Caribbean products such as coffee and chocolate came almost exclusively through Havana (see table 9.3). Imports of alcohol followed a similar pattern (see table 9.4). Wine imports consisted primarily of wines from Catalonia and Málaga, purchased in Havana and other Caribbean ports, augmented by smaller amounts of French vintages obtained in Charleston, a leading transshipment center for French products. Rum and brandy came almost exclusively from Havana, while beer and gin, usually in small quantities, were imported from North American ports.

The flow of manufactures exhibited a less predictable pattern. Basic supplies, such as candles and soap, came principally from North American ports, but were also common parts of cargoes from Havana (see table 9.5). However, earthenwares, pots, and pans came principally from Charleston. The same is true for importations of textiles. Most cloth was obtained in

Table 9.3. Coffee, chocolate, and tea off-loaded in St. Augustine

	Coffee	Chocolate	Tea
1787			
Charleston	—	—	1,680
Havana	400	370	—
New York	—	5	1,960
1794			
Charleston	120	40	1,680
Havana	7,604	304	—
New York	—	—	—
1803			
Charleston	—	—	840
Havana	3,920	420	—
New York	—	—	1,120

Note: Coffee, chocolate, and tea expressed by cargo value in Spanish *reales.*
Source: Ship Arrivals, microfilm reels 91–93, 96, East Florida Papers, P. K. Yonge Library of Florida History, University of Florida.

Table 9.4. Alcoholic beverages off-loaded in St. Augustine

	Rum	Brandy	Wine	Beer	Gin
1787					
Charleston	160	800	33,170	7,776	—
Havana	52,140	26,940	5,716	—	—
New York	—	—	800	1,548	224
Philadelphia	—	600	1,010	11,592	—
Savannah	—	—	1,000	—	—
1794					
Charleston	2,620	—	20,460	2,118	1,760
Havana	68,198	1	6,640	44,636	—
Savannah	—	—	—	—	1,120
1803					
Charleston	1,600	—	3,400	864	80
Havana	29,280	5,000	18,700	—	—
New York	—	—	2,200	—	—
Savannah	480	400	2,600	1,872	184

Note: Wine, beer, and alcohol expressed by cargo value in Spanish *reales.*
Source: Ship Arrivals, microfilm reels 91–93, 96, East Florida Papers, P. K. Yonge Library of Florida History.

Table 9.5. Household wares off-loaded in St. Augustine

	Pottery	Pots/pans	Glassware	Candles	Soap
1787					
Charleston	1,760	304	36	4,383	3,054
Havana	350	8	—	12	185
New York	160	128	—	2,551	857
1794					
Charleston	4,640	2,384	—	6,928	7,075
Havana	208	84	156	476	833
New York	—	—	—	—	—
Savannah	320	—	—	301	1,453
1803					
Charleston	2,400	1,000	—	6,231	2,115
Havana	—	—	—	—	—
New York	—	—	—	2,222	855
Savannah	160	234	—	1,763	1,140

Note: All items expressed by cargo value in Spanish *reales*.
Source: Ship Arrivals, microfilm reels 91–93, 96, East Florida Papers, P. K. Yonge Library of Florida History, University of Florida.

Table 9.6. Clothing and textiles off-loaded in St. Augustine

	Blankets	Garments	Piecework	Cloth
1787				
Charleston	—	2,120	44	15,148
Havana	—	15,192	394	5,580
New York	120	324	116	3,616
1794				
Charleston	28	78	—	13,889
Havana	NA	807	244	2,030
1803				
Charleston	300	1,842	—	2,332

Note: All items expressed by cargo value in Spanish *reales*.
Source: Ship Arrivals, microfilm reels 91–93, 96, East Florida Papers, P. K. Yonge Library of Florida History, University of Florida.

Charleston (see table 9.6). Havana, in the first years after the Florida colony was reestablished, was an important source of hats, shoes, and other finished apparel, usually the products of New Spain. However, after 1790, importation of these goods dropped sharply.

These patterns are consistent with what is generally known about regional trade for the late eighteenth century. St. Augustine's heavy reliance on food staples from the United States is not surprising. During and after the American war for independence, U.S. factors were the principal suppliers of flour and other basic foodstuffs to most of the Spanish Caribbean, including Havana. Charleston's main function was as a transshipment center.[42] Hence, it was a practical destination for Floridians, having the threefold advantage of being nearby, being a source of foodstuffs, and being a market for European products. The influx of goods from Charleston to St. Augustine bear out, in quantitative terms, the observation made by André Michaux, the French botanist, in his account of Charleston in 1802:

> The commercial intercourse of the Upper Carolines and Georgia is carried on, in a great measure, with Charleston, which is not much farther than Wilmington and Savannah. The inhabitants go there in preference, because the commerce is more active, and the sales more easy. The articles they carry there consists chiefly in short cotton, tobacco, hams, salt butter, wax, stag, and bear skins, and cattle. They take, in return, coarse iron ware, tea, coffee, powder sugar, coarse cloths, and fine linen. . . . The oranges they gather in Carolina are not good to eat. Those consumed here come from the island of St. Anastasia, situate opposite St. Augustine, the capital of East Florida; they are sweet, very large, fine skinned, and more esteemed than those brought from the Carribbees.[43]

This brief overview of Spanish Florida's commerce should demonstrate the need for more-extensive analysis of records relating to the exchange of population and goods between Florida and the United States. As David J. Weber has noted recently, "It is the power of frontiers to transform cultures that gives them special interest." Analysis of St. Augustine's commercial life helps demonstrate how this statement applies to Florida. Its transformation stemmed in part from efforts by Spanish colonials to accommodate themselves to the new economic conditions of the Atlantic world and in part from external, regional trends that integrated Florida into a larger network of trade. For Florida, the result seems to have been a commercial system that was both flexible and transitory. By tying Flor-

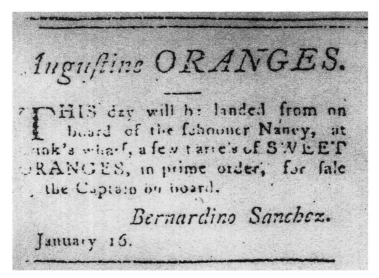

Fig. 9.3. Advertisement for St. Augustine oranges, placed by Bernardino Sánchez in the *Columbian Herald,* January 19, 1796.

ida economically to the United States, governors succeeded in bringing some degree of economic and political stability to an inherently unstable borderland. Their apparently illogical strategy succeeded until 1812. However, unlike more dynamic Spanish territories, Florida had no economic leverage. Cuba sent Spain revenues from its commerce with the United States. Florida sent only bills. Under these circumstances, Spanish interest in the province waned, and Florida's commercial integration with U.S. ports foreshadowed its ultimate political and social absorption into the United States.

Author's note

I am indebted to several institutions and granting agencies for their support of this research. Work at the John Carter Brown Library, accomplished through one of the library's six-month NEH fellowships in 1997, provided much of the comparative information on Florida and other Spanish colonies. A research fellowship at the Winterthur Museum and Library in 1994 and support for dissertation research provided by the St. Augustine Historical Society in 1993 greatly assisted in interpreting the material culture and trade of St. Augustine.

Notes

1. Extract of a letter from a gentleman in St. Augustine, East Florida, to his friend in Alexandria, January 12, 1789, (Boston) *Herald of Freedom and the Federal Advertizer* 2, no. 2 (Friday, March 20, 1789), 7.

2. Janice Borton Miller, "The Struggle for Free Trade in East Florida and the Cédula of 1793," *Florida Historical Quarterly* 50, no. 1 (1976): 48–59; Janice Borton Miller, *Juan Nepomuceno de Quesada, Governor of Spanish East Florida, 1790–1795* (Washington, D.C.: University Press of America, 1981).

3. James G. Cusick, "Across the Border: Commodity Flow and Merchants in Spanish St. Augustine," *Florida Historical Quarterly* 69, no. 3 (1991): 277–99.

4. Franklin W. Knight and Peggy K. Liss, *Atlantic Port Cities: Economy, Culture, and Society in the Atlantic World, 1650–1850* (Knoxville: University of Tennessee Press, 1991).

5. Mark A. Burkholder and Lyman L. Johnson, *Colonial Latin America* (New York: Oxford University Press, 1990), 278–80; Allan J. Kuethe, "Havana in the Eighteenth Century," in *Atlantic Port Cities*, ed. Knight and Liss, 13–39.

6. The rise of cities in the Spanish American periphery is reviewed in Peggy K. Liss, *Atlantic Empires: The Network of Trade and Revolution, 1713–1826* (Baltimore: Johns Hopkins University Press, 1984), in John Robert McNeill, *Atlantic Empires of France and Spain: Louisbourg and Havana, 1700–1763* (Chapel Hill: University of North Carolina Press, 1985), and, more briefly, in Burkholder and Johnson, *Colonial Latin America*, 273, 278–83. Two edited volumes include case studies by region: Jacques Barbier and Allan J. Kuethe, *The North American Role in the Spanish Imperial Economy, 1760–1819* (Dover, N.H.: Manchester University Press, 1984), and Knight and Liss, *Atlantic Port Cities*. Contributors to these volumes have also written more comprehensive studies of the port cities on which they focus. Kuethe deals with the impact of military spending and U.S. trade on development of Havana in *Cuba, 1753–1815: Crown, Military, and Society* (Knoxville: University of Tennessee Press, 1986). Susan M. Socolow examines kinship relations and commerce and the impact of the Atlantic trade on Buenos Aires in *The Merchants of Buenos Aires, 1778–1810: Family and Commerce* (New York: Cambridge University Press, 1978).

7. See David A. Brading, "Bourbon Spain and Its American Empire," in *Colonial Spanish America*, ed. Leslie Bethell (New York: Cambridge University Press, 1987), 112–62; Burkholder and Johnson, *Colonial Latin America*, 257–87; James Lockhart and Stuart B. Schwartz, *Early Latin America: A History of Colonial Spanish America and Brazil* (Cambridge: Cambridge University Press, 1983), 346–68; John Lynch, "The Origins of Spanish American Independence," in *The Independence of Latin America*, ed. Leslie Bethell (New York: Cambridge University Press, 1987), 13–16.

8. Burkholder and Johnson, *Colonial Latin America*; Kuethe, *Cuba, 1753–1815*; and Kuethe, "Havana in the Eighteenth Century."

9. Kuethe, "Havana in the Eighteenth Century."

10. Ibid., 27.

11. Franklin W. Knight, *Slave Society in Cuba in the Nineteenth Century* (Madison: University of Wisconsin Press, 1970); Kuethe, "Havana in the Eighteenth Century."

12. Allan J. Kuethe, "Los Llorones Cubanos: The Socio-military Basis of Commercial Privilege in the American Trade under Charles IV," in *North American Role,* ed. Barbier and Kuethe, 141–57.

13. Knight, *Slave Society,* 6–7.

14. James A. Lewis, "Anglo-American Entrepreneurs in Havana: The Background and Significance of the Expulsion of 1784–1785," in *North American Role,* ed. Barbier and Kuethe, 112–26.

15. Lewis, "Anglo-American Entrepreneurs," 114; Lynch, *Origins.*

16. Lewis, "Anglo-American Entrepreneurs," 115.

17. Ibid., 117; Pablo Tornero Tinajero, "La participación de Cádiz en el comercio exterior de La Habana (1776–1786)," *La Rábida: Primeras Jornadas de Andalucia y América* 88 (1981): 89–92.

18. Lewis, "Anglo-American Entrepreneurs," 116.

19. Barbier and Kuethe, *North American Role,* 3.

20. Linda K. Salvucci, "Anglo-American Merchants and Stratagems for Success in Spanish Imperial Markets, 1783–1807," in *North American Role,* ed. Barbier and Kuethe, 112–33; Linda K. Salvucci, "Supply, Demand, and the Making of a Market: Philadelphia and Havana at the Beginning of the Nineteenth Century," in *Atlantic Port Cities,* ed. Knight and Liss, 40–57; Knight, *Slave Society;* Kuethe, *Cuba, 1753–1815,* and "Havana in the Eighteenth Century"; Lewis, "Anglo-American Entrepreneurs"; Liss, *Atlantic Empires.*

21. Vicente Manuel de Zéspedes to Juan Ignacio de Urriza, St. Augustine, September 30, 1785, in Joseph Byrne Lockey, *East Florida 1783–1785, A File of Documents Assembled, and Many of Them Translated,* ed. and with a foreword by John Walton Caughey (Berkeley and Los Angeles: University of California Press, 1949), 728.

22. Sherry Johnson, "The Spanish St. Augustine Community, 1784–1795: A Reevaluation," *Florida Historical Quarterly* 67, no. 1 (1989): 27–54; Helen Hornbeck Tanner, *Zéspedes in East Florida, 1784–1790* (Jacksonville: University of North Florida Press, 1989).

23. Description of East Florida, St. Augustine, March 18, 1785, in Lockey, *East Florida,* 481; *Herald of Freedom,* March 20, 1789, 7.

24. For a discussion of occupational sectors of U.S. port towns, see Jacob M. Price, "Economic Function and the Growth of American Port Towns in the Eighteenth Century," in *Perspectives in American History,* ed. Donald Fleming and Bernard Bailyn, vol. 8, (1974): 123–86. For St. Augustine, a database on occupations was constructed from the following sources: "Description of the Private Plan of the City of Saint Augustine of East Florida, Year of 1788" (English transcription), and "Florida, Year of 1790, Inventories, assessments, and sale at public auction of the house and lots of the King" (English transcription), both in "De-

scriptions of the City of St. Augustine, East Florida, 1788, 1790," (Jacksonville: WPA Historical Records Survey, 1939), copy on file at the St. Augustine Historical Society; Philip D. Rasico, *The Minorcans of Florida: Their History, Language and Culture* (New Smyrna Beach, Fla.: Luthers, 1990), 158–70; Philip D. Rasico, "The Minorcan Population of St. Augustine in the Spanish Census of 1786," *Florida Historical Quarterly* 67, no. 2 (1987): 160–84; Patricia Griffin, *Mullet on the Beach: The Minorcans of Florida, 1768–1788* (St. Augustine: St. Augustine Historical Society, 1990), 152; Lockey, *East Florida*, 198–99, 202–4; Landers, "Black Society in Spanish St. Augustine 1784–1821," Ph.D. diss., University of Florida, Gainesville, 1988, 70.

25. Pablo Tornero Tinajero, *Relaciones de Dependencia entre Florida y Los Estados Unidos, 1783–1820* (Madrid: Ministerio de Asuntos Exteriores, 1979); Ramón Romero Cabót, "Los Ultimos Años de la Soberania Española en la Florida, 1783–1821," Master's thesis, Universidad de Sevilla, Sevilla, 1983; Ligia María Bermúdez, "The Situado: A Study in the Dynamics of East Florida's Economy during the Second Spanish Period, 1785–1820," Master's thesis, University of Florida, 1989, while not specifically concerned with shipping, provides data on the source of credit that underwrote trade.

26. Cusick, "Across the Border"; Griffin, *Mullet on the Beach;* Johnson, "St. Augustine Community"; Landers, *Black Society;* Susan R. Parker, "Men without God or King, Rural Settlers of East Florida," Master's thesis, University of Florida, Gainesville, 1990; Tanner, *Zéspedes;* David J. Weber, *The Spanish American Frontier in North America* (New Haven, Conn.: Yale University Press, 1992); Arthur Preston Whitaker, ed. and trans., *Documents Relating to the Commercial Policy of Spain in the Floridas, with Incidental Reference to Louisiana* (DeLand: Florida State Historical Society, 1931).

27. Whitaker, *Commercial Policy,* 57.

28. Miller, *Quesada,* 80–81.

29. Miller, *Struggle for Free Trade,* 48.

30. Ibid., 55.

31. Cusick, "Across the Border," 304.

32. Ibid.

33. Miller, *Struggle for Free Trade,* 55–56.

34. John F. Watson, "Journal of a Voyage from Orleans to Havanah, 1805," Col. 189, Watson Family Papers Box, Location 16/c, Manuscript Division, Winterthur Museum and Library, Winterthur, Delaware, 22–23.

35. James Pitot, *Observations on the Colony of Louisiana from 1796 to 1802,* trans. with an introduction by Henry C. Pitot (Baton Rouge: Louisiana State University Press, 1979), 47.

36. William Walton, *Present State of the Spanish Colonies, Including a Particular Report of Hispaniola of the Parish of Santo Domingo, With a General Survey of the Settlements on the South of Continent America as Relates to History, Trade, Population, Custom, Manners, &c.* (London,: Longman, Hurst, Rees, Orme & Brown, 1810), 1:349.

37. Christopher Ward, "The Commerce of East Florida during the Embargo, 1806–1812: The Role of Amelia Island," *Florida Historical Quarterly* 68, no. 2 (1990): 160–79.

38. Johnson, "St. Augustine Community," 27–54; Griffin, *Mullet on the Beach,* 135–49, 162–83; Landers, *Black Society,* 47–51.

39. Liss, *Atlantic Empires,* 113.

40. Ibid., 147–71; Lewis, "Anglo-American Entrepreneurs," 112–26; Salvucci, "Anglo-American Merchants," 127–33; Salvucci, "Supply, Demand, and the Making of a Market," 40–57; and Tornero Tinajero, "La participación de Cádiz."

41. All information on imports represents breakdowns of data originally accumulated from shipping manifests for vessel arrivals in St. Augustine during 1787, 1794, and 1803, as recorded in East Florida Papers, "Imports," Bundles 215G17 and 216H17, reels 92–93, 1787; Bundle 219K17, 1794; and Bundle 22H18, reel 96, 1803. Some of these data have been previously reported in tabular form. For a description of how data were quantified, see Cusick, "Across the Border," 282–86.

42. Price, "American Port Towns," 162.

43. F. A. Michaux, *Travels to the West of the Alleghany Mountains in the States of Ohio, Kentucky, and Tennessee, and Back to Charleston, by the Upper Carolinas; Comprising the Most Interesting Details on the Present State of Agriculture, and the Natural Produce of Those Countries; Together with Particulars Relative to the Commerce That Exists between the Above Mentioned States, and Those Situated East of the Mountains and Low Louisiana, Undertaken, in the Year 1802,* 2d ed. (London: D. N. Shury, Berwick Street, 1805), 282–92.

Appendix

Richard Oswald to James Grant, May 20, 1767, London

Delivered by Captain Richard Savery of ship St. Augustine carrying cargo of merchandise to our settlement of Bance Island in Africa and from thence to proceed to St. Augustine with about seventy Negroes . . . for the use of my plantation on Timoka River. . . .

I have sent complete sutes of cloathing for them all which I have desired, the Captain to deliver out to them when he draws nigh the Coast of America. This I apprehend may be necessary as they will arrive in ye beginning of winter. I have likewise sent cloathing for the Negros now on the plantation which are to be delivered unopened, together with sundry tools and such. . . .

I had no intention of risking any more Negros on the Florida Scheme, until I had farther advice to the purpose from your Excellency but having so good an opportunity on a ship going to our African settlement, and the Captain being well acquainted with your Road and Bar, I thought it a pity to miss it, especially as I apprehend it might be of bad consequence if the men slaves now on the Plantation remained longer unprovided with wives. For their supply I have ordered thirty young women to be shipped and thirty more lads and large girls of such age as they may be fit for field labor in about two years. Besides these I have directed the agents in Africa to send a few full grown men, not exceeding ten in number . . . of such as have been used to the Trades of the country believing they will become soon useful and handy in a new plantation. As our contract with the French merchants is not yet out and though we cannot ship of any Prime Slaves but to them, I have ordered the agents to buy them with Bills of Exchange, and in order to have them of the best quality, I have allowed them to give as high as twenty guineas or twenty-two Sterling per head, which with freight and risk of mortality shall make them dear before they arrive.

I send also by the Ship, a House carpenter for the service of the plantation. His name is Herries, a good, sober man who had been a sergeant in the army. I hope he will be useful. He will go down along with the slaves. *Source:* Bundle 295, Ballindalloch Castle Muniments, Scotland.

Governor James Grant to the Earl of Hillsborough, September 1, 1770

St. Augustine
1st September 1770
My Lord/

In my letter No. 30 I had the honor to lay before your Lordship, an account of the helpless and distressed State of the Greek Settlement at Smyrnea, and took the Liberty to observe to your Lordship the necessity there was of continuing His Majesty's most gracious Bounty for the support of those Adventures.

Last Years Bounty has been laid out entirely for their subsistence and has actually saved them from starving for without that well timed help from Government, there must have been an end of that numerous promising Settlement.

Dr. Turnbull [is] diligent and Assiduous, he resides constantly with his Greek Colonist[s] and does as much as Man can do, to repair the first fault of exceeding the number of people to be imported, and of course the funds which his Constituents had agreed to advance in place of six thousand which was the stipulated Sum, they have actually My Lord paid L34000 and are determined to go no further.

The Greek Settlers having been well fed last Year have got into Health and Spirits, they work well, and have cleared a great deal of Ground which the Doctor has put in very good Order—the Greeks this year have raised a considerable quantity of provisions, such as Indian corn, pease, potatoes and Greens of all kinds, and if supported, they will soon get into a comfortable State, and be able to supply themselves with every necessity of Life-Produce and 'tis to be hoped usefull Produce to Great Britain will of Course follow.

But at present they are destitute of every convenience they are ill clothed many of them almost naked—and are obliged to live in small Hutts put up in a hurry to shelter them from the Weather upon their first arrival. Doctor Turnbull has neither money nor credit to supply them with Cloths and has not the necessary Tools and Materials to build Houses for them, in that distressed condition he can only look up to His Majesty for his most gracious support by ordering the Royal Bounty to be continued to enable him to carry on extensive and usefull undetaking into Execution with Success—he presses me to lay his case before Your Lordship and to transmit to Your Lordships consideration an Indent of such things as are absolutely necessary for the existence of the Settlement.

The Indent amounts to £1000—if the Bounty is continued and Your Lordship is pleased to order Mr. Nixon the Doctors Agent to receive that Money at the Treasury, he will be very carefull in the Purchase and Package of the Assortment, which may be sent to Charles Town if no Vessel offers for this Port—the remaining thousand if your Lordship approves of this method, I shall continue to draw for upon the Treasury for the support of the Settlement, in the same manner as I drew for the Bounty last year.

I have etc.
James Grant
(The Earl of Hillsborough)

Indent of Clothing, Tools &c wanted for the Distressed Greek Settlement at Smyrnea—Under the direction of Andrew Turnbull Esquire

Best blue Plains	3000 yards at 1/4 d per Yard	£200
Best whit Plains	5000 yards at 1/4 d per Yard	33.6.8
Check't Linnens	3000 yards at 1/-per Yard	150.-.-
Strip't Cottons	5000 yards at 1/3 d per Yard	31.5.-
Strip't Linnens	2000 yards at 1/-per Yard	100
Scots Canabraggs	4000 yards at 6 d per Yard	100.-.-
Neger Blankets	600 at 5 sh each	150.-.-
Mens shoes of different sizes	600 pr at 2/3 d per pair	
Indigo Sickles	60 Doz. at 6/6 d per Dozen	25.10
Broad Hoes, Crowley's, of a Middling size,	60 Dozen at 20/ per Dozen	60.-.-
Building Nails the greatest part Sixpenny		100.-.
		£ 1050.1.8

Source: Governor James Grant to the Earl of Hillsborough, September 1, 1770, C.O. 5/545, 33–34, 37.

Francis Fatio to Don Josef del Rio, July 26, 1787

My Dear Sir:

I have replied prior to this letter which you have taken the trouble to write me on the 21st of this month. You have found fault with me with such *indelicate* expressions, and which are so little *deserved,* especially for a man such as myself. I am in no way your subject or *subordinate.* That said, I wait for your apology.

After several attempts (which did not satisfy me) to answer you in Spanish, which I confess I don't understand, I found it necessary to use French, which is the most familiar and the Captain General has allowed me to do so.

My inclination, rather than any obligation, has made me anticipate the orders of His Excellency, the Governor, which have been presented to me on several occasions. I am flattered and have completely fulfilled them with the honor of passing on to you, respecting your letter of last April, and which has been communicated to you.

My son Louis has fulfilled with vigor and in my stead, the task requiring such distances and time as you wished during your *rapid excursion* made to reconnoiter the forests, and rivers of this province. I had orders to receive you with all urbanity and attentions possible. You were taken to my plantation, with my house, my boats and my horses at your disposal. To my way of thinking you ought not have assumed the right to insult me *with impunity* and to write to me so harshly. It is one thing that I would not expect from a man of your profession. You expected too many advantages. I am in fact only a simple man, an old man, who wants to live in peace and harmony with the whole world. It seems overly bold for you to insult me.

My son don Louis and I have already assisted you verbally in advancing the objectives which were your responsibility. You ought to have been more attentive and observant. You lightly traversed a small portion of the province and you want me to work at my own expense to fulfil the obligations of your mission and to improve upon it.

The questions that you put to me to resolve are within everyone's capacity [to answer]. It is easy to avoid being wordy in the answers.

First Question: The number of barrels of naval stores that can be extracted yearly given the state of the population.

Since the re-establishment of the Spanish government, no barrels or naval stores of any sort have been made until this past spring. Some of what was made during the British dominion yet remains. There was no reason to make more until His Excellency, the Governor, decided to assure me that no naval stores will be admitted coming from outside the province.

The old residents of the St. Johns and St. Marys rivers, who refuged themselves here by virtue of the war, live here under a time extension and on a temporary basis, awaiting the decisions of His Catholic Majesty. When the establishments become permanent, then it will be possible to calculate how much will be made, but we will not be able to calculate the annual production. This will depend on the incentives that will be given. Never will the materials be lacking.

Second Question: The value of each class bought in the ports of the province.

Because none is made, there is no price. One can compute that pitch will be three pesos a barrel. Tar three and a half, and turpentine four. The distillation of the last named naval store produces yellow resin, and the hard which is called fine, after having extracted all the spirits possible. Resin is worth at this time five pesos per barrel, and spirits of turpentine, four *reales* [half a peso] for a bottle the size of a Paris pint.

Third Question: Ports in Havana or Cadiz for the same inhabitants.

We do not have vessels employed in this branch. Commerce is not open with Spanish ports because the Court has not given orders to that effect. Or at least such orders have not been communicated to us.

Fourth Question: The weight of each barrel.

In the prices put forth above, I have computed the net weight of each barrel at eight *arrobas.*

Fifth Question: To deliver a barrel of each class to be taken to Havana on the boat under [the lieutenant's] command.

You could have and should have received them from my son when you were on the St. Johns River. They were cheerfully offered by him and by me. Since you arrived at my plantation, you could have taken them in the small schooner that accompanied you. You have at your command sailors and boats that could go to bring them from the St. Johns. Why should I have to suffer? Because I have to run the risk of losing the labor of six or seven slaves, and I have no sailors. Why should I *suffer the results of this poorly executed commission of yours?* I have here some samples of pitch, tar, resin and spirits of turpentine that are at your service. We have not made any turpentine this year. One of our neighbors, Mr. Pengree, has gathered a portion.

I will give orders to the end that a supply of each class be put on board my bilander, the Countess of Galvez, which should be carrying wood, tar and other articles of the products of this province to Havana. My captain will have my orders to deliver them to you upon his arrival. I do not expect either *payment or any compensation* for them, neither for anything else which I have done for the good of the country; and having received no reward of [your] gratitude, rather it is causing me all sort of insults and disgusts, which will not be ignored at Court.

Sixth Question: That you explain to me with complete clarity the value of each cubic cubit, yard (*vara*) and foot of wood as well as boards, staves and oars.

I am ignorant of the different knees; I form some idea of the figures when I actually see them but it is hardly more than a very confused theory of boat construction. In order to answer with *that great precision and clarity* that you require of me, you should have had your master builder or draftsman pass on to me a detailed list of the knees that they most need with a plan of the figure and dimensions and the amount of each species used in the construction of a boat. Such details would have facilitated my ability to relay to you what might be the value of each around the globe. The price of each species taken separate just will not work. The price of a knee in a single piece to be used for a stern-post for a boat of seventy-four cannon, a knee of *brusarda* and others difficult to find would be worth considerable sums, when taken all together, however, one finds moderate pricing. I have never cut just a single knee for construction purposes for sale to the Spanish government since its restoration here. I have news that our neighbors in Georgia have begun cutting green oak for France and also for the merchant marine of Holland. Their prices are a *real* and a half to two *reales* and a quarter per cubic foot of rough timber.

Here we send out nothing but pine boards. I am almost the only planter who is working within the prices as regulated by the Engineer Commander of this post at 18 pesos 6 *reales* per thousand running feet taken at my plantation on the St. Johns River or thirty pesos of the same amount delivered to the sites. The same amount of thin beams and squared pieces at 12 pesos delivered on the St. Johns and at 20 pesos in town. Few staves are produced. Until now it is prohibited for the temporary river residents to cut wood, and in giving the order, the following prices apply: for uncut white oak for liquids and barrels for twenty-five to thirty pesos per thousand. Those for [?] from 20 to 25 pesos and for a quarter cask or barrel from 16 to 20 also per thousand. Those of red live-oak, *alguacil* live-oak, cypress or cedar are worth less because of the quality of the wood. By the thousand, staves without bottoms [for barrels] are paid for differently:

250 pieces of bottoms equal a thousand staves, and are worth more less half the price[?].

Oars of *arerno* or of pine are worth a half or three-quarters *real* per foot on the St. Johns River.

Seventh Question: If during British rule, these were worth more than now.

Until the beginning of the last war Florida was little known and poorly populated. Not a single Spanish family remained on the river in 1764 who could show, instruct or direct new owners. *If one had been found, they would have been selected and treated differently than I was.* Outside of St. Augustine, there seemed to be no vestige of cultivation. The English dedicated themselves from the beginning to cultivation of indigo of superior quality. The war with the Americans obliged English ships to frequent our ports to carry to the islands the wood and naval stores they lacked. This contributed to the path that the province took. Until the end of the war the shipment of the foregoing materials was considerable and all the naval stores as well as wood rose to excessive prices. Pitch was the first, from 18 *reales* to five or seven pesos [40 to 56 *reales*]. Tar rose from 20 to 22 *reales* to seven or eight pesos and turpentine from three pesos to eight or ten. [The price of] resin and spirits of turpentine, for which my son established the first and only still, rose proportionately. The consumption of pure resin is very short; it is mixed with pitch in order to make a superior tar; Spirits commonly were worth a peso per bottle. Pine boards, stern-posts and squared wood doubled in price and remained so until the evacuation of the province. At that time huge amounts were still being extracted and sent to the islands and British colonies. Since then, the present government has not found anyone other than my son and me who has been able to supply wood for public works.

Take that, sir, a compendium of the information that you demanded of me. You have not given me a venue nor any gain so that what is extended to you might be even more instructive. You wrote me on the 21st of this month. The night of the 23rd Reverend Father Don Miguel O'Reilly came to inform me of your impatience. You insulting letter disgusted me, but I didn't waste even a quarter of an hour of effort. Not considering that this was an inferior mission, I wished to serve the province and laid aside your insults. This morning you have renewed with a complaint containing little basis or exactitude in its recitation of the facts. You say that you disdain me, thus I repay you in the kind. I hope for means to justify myself in front of *our superiors* and at least prevent these bad communiques that I have come to expect from you. It is not *easy*, but it will not be *impossible* to compensate me. I do not care to have another occasion to pass on to the minister such well detailed information about the products of this province. His Excellency, the Lord Governor and Captain General, will not command so, especially after I have convinced him, which will be easy for me, that *you have not sufficiently fulfilled your commission.* If you allege that I placed obstacles in your way, it will only serve to demonstrate that you were not capable of doing it alone. I am given to understand that I am a lost man but I will sacrifice my *honor* and *resentments* toward you for the public good. If I were dead, Florida would neither be lost nor forgotten. The king will always find a loyal vassal to replace me and you as well.

Be aware that a copy of this letter will reside in the same place as yours.

I have the honor to be, my dear sir, your most humble servant,

Francisco Phelipe Fatio=26 July 1787=To Don Josef del Rio, Lt. Of the Navy of His Catholic Majesty.

Source: East Florida Papers, Library of Congress Manuscript Collection, bnd. 98G8, no. 44. (Underlined words and passages were underlined by Fatio in the original.)

Inventory of the Estate of Francisco Xavier Sánchez

Inventory and appraisal of the lands, plantations, slaves, livestock, and various other properties that were left on the death of Don Francisco Xavier Sánchez, with distinction of the various locations of said lands and their boundaries, which we, the undersigned, Don Bartolome de Castro y Ferrer and Don Fernando de la Maza Arredondo, experts appointed for the purpose by the widow and other interested [parties] in the writs of inventory which are taking place, and it is as follows—

Plantation named San José, located on the east bank of the St. John [River] of this province, bounding on the north with lands of Don Gerado Forrester, on the south with another plantation belonging to this estate, named Ashley, on the west with said river, and on the east with the royal road to San Nicolás—

Lands
For thirty-eight *caballerías*[1] and eight acres of land, included therein four *caballerías* and eleven acres of the site named Santo Domingo, located north of this plantation, about one third of them being land useful for planting and under cultivation, and the rest pine groves
valued altogether at   4220
For the fences of split pales   200

A frame dwelling house with its chimney at		50
A house for the overseer at		30
Three houses for storing the harvest		100
A kitchen		15
A hut for the mill		10
Another id. for shelling maize		10
		4635
Sum brought forward		4635
A stable		15
Three huts for Negroes		25

Livestock

Ninety-eight head of bovine cattle *de progresso* [coming along] at eight pesos	784
A black horse	130
Two chestnut horses at	60
A dark mare with its colt at	15
A sorrel id	80
Fifteen pigs of various sizes at 5 pesos	75

Utensils

Twenty half-worn hoes at 4 *reales*[2]	10
Eight half-worn hatchets at 6 *reales*	6
A plow at	6
Two grind stones at	12
A whetstone	3

Harvest

Eight hundred bushels of maize at 8 *reales*	800

Slaves

Names	Ages	
Peter	70 years	200
Elsy	40	300
Ben	21	400
James	19	350
Sam	45	350
José, son of Villy	7	200
		8556
Sum brought forward		8556
Sampson	45 years	350

Munday	44	350
Hector	50	330
Prince	40	330
Isaac	23	400
Billy	45	330
Rose	30	400
Isabel	8	200
Domingo	2	100
Billy	4	120
Dick	36	300
Becky	30	300
Toney	13	300
Charlote	40	300
Juan	13	300
Rumias	24	330
Beary	11	200
Rafael	8	175
Lucia	2	100
Cesar	30	400
Rosa	25	350
Teresa	7	150
Flora	1	75
Benito	6 months	50
		14,796[3]

Source: East Florida Papers, Testamentary Proceedings, microfilm reel 141, folios, 42–46, P. K. Yonge Library of Florida History. Translation by Luis R. Arana.

Petition of Zephaniah Kingsley, Jr. to Honorable Raymond Reid, Judge of the Superior Court

July 25, 1812.
Destroyed and Plundered at Laurel Grove:

Andrew, son of Polly, a boy	7 to 8 yrs
Jacob, a prime Eabo Negro	30
Camilla, his wife, Rio Pongo, prime	25
Jim, boy, child of Jacob & Camilla	7 to 8
Bob, a New Calabar, prime	28
Molly, his wife, do	26
Boy Sammy, to do	7 or 8

Prince, a New Calabar, prime	32
Woman M Badie, his wife, do	26
girl Charlotte, to do	8 or 9
Barbara, same	6 to 7
Peggy, to do	4 to 5
boy Toby, to do	2 to 3
Man Jack, Zinquibari, Carpenter, very prime	30
Woman Tamassa, his wife, very prime	28
Boy Ben, son to do	8 to 9
Boy M toto, to do	6 to 7
girl Molly, to do	4 to 5
Rose, to do	2 to 3
Man Philip, Calabari, prime	35
Titi, his wife, to do	28
boy Badja, to do	8 to 9
Man Martin, M Guinda	26
Woman Jenny, Zinguibara, prime	28
boy Billy, to do	4 to 5
Girl Hannah to Old Rose	8 Man to 9
Breechy, Eabo nation, prime	36
Woman Adda, his wife do	30
boy July, to do	8 to 9
boy Dick, to do	6 to 7
girl Hannah, to do	4 to 5
Man Aibo, Calabari	40
Man M Sooma, Carpenter, Zinguebari, very prime	28
Woman Eliza	26
boy March, to do	7 to 8
Boy Mike, to Old Jenny (or Ginny)	8 to 9
Man Jun, Calabari, driver, very prime	34
Woman Anobia, his wife, very prime	28
Charles, Soo Soo, very prime	24
Man Old Paul, Eabo nation	48
Man Cabo Mouse, sailor, very prime	26

Say 41 Negroes carried off by the Indians, value at that time was 500
dollars each, making: $20,500

300	To one new barn 25 by 40 ft burned 25 July 1812
1,000	which contained 800 bu corn worth then $1.25
200	one fodder house $100 & 910,000 lbs. fodder $1.00
375	300 bu. peas $ 1.25

150 one cart house and 3 carts

 75 chains, harness and 3 ploughs

500 12 good Negro houses burned same day

120 furniture, clothing, etc. in Negro houses

100 working tools of do in use

 50 2 pan mill stones, frames, houses, etc.

 15 one large steel mill

600 frame cotton house, 30' x 40' burned same time with 30,000 (300,000?) lbs seed cotton of 1810 crop still in 4,500 store and burned same time—15 cents pound.

10,500 60 bags of crop of 1811, ginned & packed. each bag was 350 lbs. each or 21,000 lbs at 50 cents a pound.

750 3 double cotton machine gins, $250 each

100 one outside wheel, 40' diameter & 2 bands

400 frame carpentry shop, 30'x40' burnt

192 11 whip saws ($12 each) & 6 cross cuts ($10 each)

 60 12 hand saws ($5 each)

128 64 long-shanked pod augers, assorted, ($2)

 ?? 68 68 short-shanked pod augers, assorted, ($1) [absent]

 82 72 large hatchets ($1) 10 common small axes ($1)

 60 18 warranted axes ($2); 6 broad axes ($2)

184 carpentry adzes and variety of adzes, axes, compress tools

 30 Blacksmith shop burnt same time

 80 contained 2 pair belows 30 ea, 1 large anvil 20, 1 small anvil 10, 2 mauls 10, 2 froes 6.

 91 28 hoes $1, 2 mill puks, 2 pair grind stones with poys, spindley and etc. 60

1,000 Montarro, the black smith, a very prime young man killed the same day. [aka Morton]

The Ship Yard at Doctors Lake burned same day.

 50 one work shop 20 by 30 with posts in the ground

160 one store house

100 one dwelling house

100 one large steaming stove burnt, kettle broke

 60 one black smith shop 20 by 30

300 Ornamental live oak trees round the house, burnt

315 9 Negro houses at 25 each; 3 grind stones standing 30

600 Dwelling house at Laurel Grove, being a good, frame building with double piazzas & brick chimneys, incldg kitchen, 30' x 35'

350 household miscellaneous & large stock of poultry

    62 spring shuttle loom; com. shuttle loom

  500 salt store house, 26 by 30 frame,

1,500 including 1,500 bu. salt, at $1 each bushel

  180 120 gallons Jamaica spirits at $1.50 each

  350 5 hogsheads taffa, 70 gals ea. (350 gals at $1 each)

  270 6 boxes Crown Havannah Sugar at 45 cents

  400 4 barrels gunpowder, 100 lbs each

69.50—100 lbs lead in bars, 12 & 1/2—37.50 and 2 boats sailg masts and 2 sprutts

9.24—33. cut: wrought nails assorted 25 cents

The plantation near Laurel Grove called Spring field, burned up & destroyed same day.

  100 Driver Peter's home, a large board house

  100 corn house do

1,375 700 bu. corn & 400 peas (1.25)

   60 4 stacks fodder $15

  450 15 new Negro houses at 30 each

  150 furniture, cloth, etc. for above houses $10 each

  250 sundry tools for 50 or 40 working hands ($5 each)

   75 mill house, 3 mill frogs or froes, spindles $25

1,000 driver Peter, mechanic & valuable manager killed same day

  300 150 stock hogs, at 2 each

   90 poultry, 15 dozen at 6 each

4,000 To the store & another dwelling house at Laurel Grove, new frame bldg, 35' x 40' two-stories high with brick chimney, and covered with cedar shingles. Burnt and destroyed in year 1813.

  571 dwelling house furniture, beds, valuable books and charts, crockery

  111 muskets & bayonets

   18 cartouche boxes at $3

  100 2 four-pounders, with carriages at 50 each

   30 30 cartridges for same

37.50—300 lbs. iron balls & grape shot 12 1/2

2,684.50—Store contained large supply of every article for plantation & family use & was kept for the supply of the surrounding country, all of which were burnt with the house in 1813.

   50 one deep well, lined with cypress, burned to bottom

   90 cypress posts & clapboard fence round yard, 7' high and 100 x 200 entirely consumed by fire.

3,750 orange grove of 9 acres & 750 choice Mandarine orange trees.

Some old & bearing, others just beginning to bear. $5

 1,000 2000 feet of bearing orange hedges to shelter & surround the whole grove

236.25 2520 feet of 12' high cypress picketing to surround & protect grove: 6300 picket at 37 & 1/2 cents each.

 120 60 days work of 2 prime men on pickets to fix and ram 3' deep or 120 days work at $1

 300 2 & 1/2 miles of new 1B (13)?? rail fence staked & ___? with 2 cross fences in & all 30 mi rails at $10 per mi, and setting up & 900 cart loads of rails, 1 man & 1 300 horse & cart, 150 days of work with fence road at $2

20,000 entire loss of 1812 crop—200 acres cotton, say 200 lbs clean to acre or 40,000 at 50 cents

 1,375 800 bu. corn & 300 bu. peas of 1812 at $1.25

 300 potatoes, fodder, etc. provisions of 1812

21,675 Loss of entire crop for 1813

 250 expenses fitting & furnishing US troops under Colonel Newnan—versus Indians into Alachua

 250 transporting troops to Picolata

 100 one horse branded ZK on mounting shoulder. 4–5 yr. old horse was taken by Indians

  90 one bay horse, same brand (ZK) about 10 years old

  90 one gray horse, Old Peter, 11 years, strut & junky

 200 one high bred white charger

 532 stock cattle (76 at $7 each)

 400 hogs (200 at $2)

Drayton Island Plantation; April 1812 losses

 200 board dwelling house 16'x24' burned

 500 Negro Pablo, 45 years, carried off

 500 Juan, a Soo Soo, 30 years

  50 one large steel mill & household furniture

 320 16 old bearing orange trees cut down, $20 each

 400 m. each year at $10

 500 crop of corn for 1812, and for 1813 at $250 each

187.50—potatoes for two years 500 bushel at 37 & 1/2

$113,410.25 total losses

Source: East Florida Claims; Zephaniah Kingsley, Jr., B131 F16, Claims, 1843; St. Augustine Historical Society, The Patriot War Papers and Patriot War Claims, 1812–1846; MC 31, on loan from the Clerk of Circuit Court, St. Johns County. (Kingsley used "do" and "to do" to mean same as the above.)

The Claim of Susanna Sanchez

City of St. Augustine
East Florida
Susannah Sanchez being sworn says that the matters & things set forth in the foregoing memorial are true to the best of her knowledge, information and belief.
Susan (her mark) Sanchez
Sworn & subsented before me by making her mark this 10th Sept. 1834
John Lee Williams
Justice of the Peace
The Claim of Susanna Sanchez
Col. Jos. S. Sanchez Witness

Knew Lewis Sanchez and Diana his wife—they are now dead, but were living in 1812–1813. Witness also knows the claimant who is the only child of Lewis Sanchez & Diana, his wife and their heir.

Lewis Sanchez and his wife owned a plantation about 4 miles north of the city—which plantation they hastily abandoned, as witness is informed upon the approach of the troops to St. Auustine. They were obliged to fly for safety to St. Augustine. Sánchez was a very industrious man—he was very comfortably situated upon his plantation. His cornfields contained about 8 or 10 acres—he planted pease and potatoes, ground nuts, pumpkins, mellons etc. He owned a small stock of cattle & a few hogs and a considerable number of poultry & three or four horses. He was an excellent farmer and his farm was well supplied with farming utensils and being a job carpenter, he must have owned carpenters tools. He possessed household & kitchen furniture and bedding—There were buildings upon the place, two small dwelling houses, worth about 150, the other houses about 20 or 30 each, they consisted of corn house, kitchen & fowl house. The plantation was under good fence—Witness was on the plantation in 1810 when it was in a flourishing state. Witness saw it again in 1815—The place was broken up and the owner living in town. Witness left St. Augustine for St. Marys in 1810 and did not return until 1815.

These persons were of color; they were free and Spanish subjects.

Witness has heard & has no doubt that when Lewis Sanchez came to town in 1812 he was placed under arms—When witness returned in 1815 he was still in service. The claimant and her father and mother were never remunerated for the losses sustained and now claimed.

Witness has examined the account contained in the petition and he thinks it highly probable that it furnishes a correct statement of the losses of Lewis Sanchez. He was an honest, hardworking man, and a good farmer, and was living in a very comfortable way. There is no doubt that he was broken up, and ruined by the revolution and witness supposes his losses were occasioned by the presence of the United States troops in the province.

Witness has no interest direct or indirect in this claim.

The enemy's camp was about a mile from Sanchez's plantation, and between the plantation and St. Augustine.

To the Honorable

Robt. Raymond Reid Judge of the Superior Court for East Florida, and specially authorized by act of Congress to receive, examine and adjudge all cases of claims for losses occassioned by the troops of the United States in East Florida in the years 1812 & 1813.

The memorial of Susanna Sanchez, the daughter and only legal heir and representative of Lewis Sanchez and his wife Diana decd—an inhabitant of East Florida, respectfully sheweth that the said Lewis Sanchez and his wife in their lifetime, to wit, in the years 1812 & 13, were subjected to, and sustained in East Florida on their plantation near Augustine the damages, injuries, and losses herein set forth, to wit—

Stock of the preceding years provisions on hand consisting of to wit (abandoned by them on their plantation, on the appearance of the troops)

40	Bushels corn $2.50 per bushl	
20	Do[ditto] pease . . . $2.50 " " (Prices in planting season)	
20	Do potatoes . . . $1.50 " "	$180
60	Hd of stock cattle taken away & destroyed @ $10.00	$600
90	Fowls & ducks @ 37 1/2 c 32.75. 20 turkies @ 1.50. $30	
		$63.75
1	Corn mill $10. 2 ploughs $9. 2 spinning wheels $7. 1 castnet $1	
		$32.00
1	Canoe 30$. hoes & axes 6$. 1 cart $20. 1 wagon $70. 1 grindstone $3	$129
6	Work-horses $30 each average value—1 Pr oxen $40.	$220
2	Timber chains $12. Carpenters tools $10. 1 cross cut saw $5.	
		$27

Household. kitchen & dairy furniture & utensils $30

	Bedding & clothing $20	$50
1	Log dwelling house with Piazza 20 Ft by 15	$50
1	Do do do without piazza $40. 1 log barn $30	$70

1	Poultry house $10. Potatoe cellar $6	$16

$1447.75

Amount brought over $1447.75

320 pannels fencing used by troops for fuel at 50 ¢ per pannel $160.00

26 Head of stock hogs @ 3$ $78.00

The entire crops of 1812 consisting of 13 acres land worked by 4 hands. viz 9 acres of corn say 180 bushls at $1 & 60 do pease $1 (prices at harvest time)

2 do Sweet potatoes say 300 bushls 50

2 do Irish—do pumpkins & ground nuts $470.00

The crop of 1813 valued at $470

Total $2625.75

All which losses, damages, and injuries to the said Lewis Sanchez & wife were occasioned by the Troops of the United States in East Florida in the years 1812 & 1813 and no part thereof was sustained previous to the entrance into East Florida aforesaid of the troops of the United States or their agents. That at the time of suffering said losses, damages, and injuries, the said Lewis Sanchez & wife were actual Spanish subjects and residing on their plantation about 4 miles from St. Augustine—That neither did the said Lewis Sanchez or his wife in their lifetime, nor has your memorialist since their death received any compensation for said losses, injuries & damages—or any part thereof. Nor has a claim for the same been heretofore presented to the Judge of the Supr Court—Wherefore your memorialist humbly prays that her claim may be received, examined, and adjudged to her to the extent of said losses, injuries, and damages as by act of Congress—An act for the relief of certain inhabitants of E. Florida approved 26 June 1834. She is rightfully entitled—All which is respectfully submitted by your memorialist—Dated at St. Augustine this ___ day of Sept 1834

Susanna (her mark) Sanchez

Witness, B. A. Putman

Source: Patriot War Papers and Patriot War Claims 1812–1846, MC 31–69, Claim of Susanna Sanchez, St. Augustine Historical Society.

William Bartram's description of the Seminole town of Cuscowilla, 1774

The town stands on the most pleasant situation that could be well imagined or desired, in an inland country; upon a high swelling ridge of sand hills, within three or four hundred yards of a large and beautiful lake, the circular shore of which continually washes a sandy beach, under a moderately high sloping bank, terminated on one side by extensive forests, consisting of Orange groves, overtopped with grand Magnolias, Palms, Poplar, Tilia, Live Oaks, and others already noticed; and the opposite point of the crescent, gradually retires with hommocky projecting points, indenting the grassy marshes, and lastly terminates in infinite green plains and meadows, united with skies and waters of the lake. Such a natural landscape, such a rural scene, is not to be imitated by the united ingenuity and labour of man. At present the ground betwixt the town and the lake is adorned by an open grove of very tall Pine trees, which standing at a considerable distance from each other, admit a delightful prospect of the sparkling waters. The lake abounds with various excellent fish and wild fowl; there are incredible numbers of the latter, especially in the winter season, when they arrive here from the north to winter.

The Indians abdicated the ancient Alachua town on the borders of the savanna, and built here, calling the new town Cuscowilla: their reasons for removing their habitation were on account of its unhealthiness, occasioned, as they say, by the stench of the putrid fish and reptiles in the summer and autumn, driven on the shore by the alligators, and the exhalations from marshes of the savanna, together with the persecutions of the musquitoes.

They plant but little here about the town; only a small garden plot at each habitation, consisting of a little Corn, Beans, Tobacco, Citruls, &c. Their plantation, which supplies them with the chief of their vegetable provisions, such as Zea, Convolvulus batata, Cucurbita citrulus, Cuc. lagenaria, Cuc. pepo, Cuc. melopepo, Cuc. verrucosa, Dolichos varieties, &c. lies on the rich prolific lands bordering on the great Alachua savanna, about two miles distance. This plantation is one common enclosure, and is worked and tended by the whole community; yet every family has its particular part, according to its own appointment, marked off when planted; and this portion receives the common labour and assistance until ripe, when each family gathers and deposits in its granary its own proper share, setting apart a small gift or contribution for the public granary, which stands in the centre of the plantation.

The youth, under the supervisal of some of their ancient people, are daily stationed in the fields, and are continually whooping and hallooing, to chase away crows, jackdaws, black-birds, and such predatory animals; and the lads are armed with bows and arrows, and being trained up to it from their early youth, are sure at a mark, and in the course of the day load themselves with squirrels, birds, &c. The men in turn patrole the corn fields at night, to protect their provisions from the depredations of night rovers, as bears, raccoons, and deer; the two former being immoderately fond of young corn, when the grain is filled with rich milk, as sweet and nourishing as cream; and the deer are as fond of the Potatoe vines.

Source: *Travels of William Bartram*, ed. Mark Van Doren (New York: Dover Publications, 1955), 169–70.

Letter of Carlos Howard to Governor Juan Nepomuceno de Quesada

November 6, 1794

Governor Sir,

Ever since the militiamen along this river began eating fresh beef, and even last year they were given 20 pounds [of meat] for a peso. Capt. Andrew Atkinson has informed me that at this very time the enemy is considering hostilities along this coast, and I have, with Your Lordship's approval, ordered patrols along the length of the beach as necessary, and that the troops engaged in this service be provisioned in the area of San Diego Plains as usual. I added, without my either getting involved in nor knowing who is to provide the meat, that it would seem to me to be fair and just to pay for said meat in that area at the rate of one-half *real*[4] per pound. (Yes, it later came at my attention that the supplier was to be Don Francisco Xavier Sánchez without his having set a price.) It turns out that Capt. Atkinson spoke with Don Francisco regarding the price and told him what I had said about the price of one-half *real* per pound being sufficient. Sánchez replied that I was not to involve myself in establishing prices and that the militiamen had to pay for the meat they consumed at the same price for which it is sold in the city [St. Augustine]. That price is 12 pounds per peso, and if this price were not given, then any seller was a man who indeed wished to give away the meat to the crown.

Without putting myself in the position to interpret the spirit of this proposition, I will say that I have never believed myself to have the ability whatsoever to determine the price; but I also ought to say that as an individual, I do form an opinion on the justice or injustice of prices of basic necessities, particularly those, such as meat, which affect the sustenance of the militiamen whom you have put under my immediate command. Although as an individual I say in confidence, not wishing to be rude, that it seems beyond reason to me that Don Francisco Sánchez is demanding that he be paid the same price for the beef at San Diego as that in St. Augustine.

I base this on the fact that generally meat sells for less for as far as 7 or 8 leagues[5] outside the capital [city]. I understand that San Diego is only half that distance.

Also contradicting his asking price are the circumstances of Don Francisco's purchasing 105 head of cattle himself from Capt. Hollingsworth at 7 pesos each on this side of the [St. Johns] river after the disturbances in the countryside;[6] 60 from Lt. Hogan and 40 from Sgt. Hogan at 6½ pesos. Likewise, Don Miguel Iznardy bought 120 head from Joseph Rain and his sons at 6 pesos and 100 from William Ashley at 6½ pesos. Also Don Fernando Arredondo and Lorenzo Llanes made similar purchases, but I do not know the details of number nor prices.

Such purchases have resulted in a scarcity of cattle for now in these parts and I understand that by yesterday that the last beef destined for the militia had been killed at the slaughterhouse.

Yet they were so abundant on the other side of the St. Johns River and on the Florida side of the St. Marys River during the recent months of February, March, April and early part of May. But their owners hurried to sell them at any price in light of the rumors that were spread (whether out of malice or misunderstanding) that the militia would not be paid nor would the residents be compensated for losses suffered because of abandoning their homes. Those who believed the rumors and those who were in doubt now regret their actions, after the arrival of assurances of payment to the militia and seeing, in fact, the price of 20 pounds per peso. If we suppose that the four parts of a beef, weighing only 250 pounds, would produce 12½ pesos, excluding what is called the fifth part, which is worth along this river at least 3 pesos, then that an entire beef would be worth 15½. The four quarters at 250 pounds [if] sold at the city price would cost 20 pesos and 7 *reales,* and adding 4 pesos for the fifth part, a head of beef would cost one *real* less than 25 pesos—an exorbitant profit for anyone who had purchased an animal at 6, 6½ or 7 pesos.

It is not my intention to inject myself into the trafficking or into anyone's profits. My only goal in all that I have expressed herein is to assist Your Lordship in determining if it is just that the inhabitants of the countryside and particularly the militiamen under my command should be obliged to pay the same price for meat as that in the city.

May God safekeep Your Lordship for many years.

San Vicente Ferrer, 6 November 1794.

Carlos Howard

[To] Señor Don Juan Nepomuceno de Quesada

Source: East Florida Papers, bnd. 127J10, no. 246 (microfilm reel 51), Library of Congress Manuscript Collection.

Extract of a letter from a gentleman in St. Augustine, East-Florida, to his friend in Alexandria, dated January 12, 1789

Our vessels are received with the greatest cordiality by the Spaniards. Governour Zelpadez [Zéspedez], pays the greatest attention to every American who comes properly reccomended; and the friendly treatment our countrymen receive from the officers of the Irish brigade stationed in this town, must lay every American under the greatest obligations to these hospitable sons of Hibernia. Flour and all kind [*sic*] of provisions from the United States find a good market here, the commerce in the above articles being entirely free. This indulgence we owe to the uncultivated state of this province; for St. Augustine, the garrisons on St. John's and St. Mary's, are the only inhabited parts of East-Florida, and these are occupied by men of the military professions, who raise nothing except money, the whole of which is laid out in American produce. Since my arrival here I had the satisfaction of conversing with the famous Alexander McGillivray, whose name you have to[*sic*] often seen in our publick prints—this interview has fully convinced me that he really is the man our papers sometimes represent him to be, and that his neighbours the Georgians have much to fear from his penetrating genius and great address. The attention paid him by the Spaniards, seems to have something more than common politeness in view—they tell me he holds a General's commission under the crown of Spain; this I have reason to believe, as I have seen him in Spanish uniform at the Governor's table, and receive the military honors of the garrison. This is a policy for which they are not to blame, as McGillivray's connections, from his infancy up to this day, with the different Indian tribes in the southern part of America, has established him the Supreme Legislator over their countries. The Spaniards, but indifferently established in this quarter, and sensible of his power, dread his consequences. A new treaty has lately been established between them and McGillivray, as King of the Creek nations, by which it is stipulated that the navigation of that part of the Gulph of Mexico, on which St. Mark (an old abandoned fort) is situated, shall be free for the vessels belonging to the said nations.—Agreeable to this article, McGillivray, in connection with some of the most respectable merchants on the island of Providence, has actually established warehouses, at St. Mark, in West Florida; from whence he carries on an extensive and most profitable trade with the Indians and even our white settlements on the Western waters. Thus you see! An individual, with no other than savage connections, has concluded a treaty of navigation, which the exertion and wisdom of Congress never yet could obtain.

Source: The Herald of Freedom, and the Federal Advertiser 2, no. 2 (Friday, March 20, 1789), p. 7, col. 1.

Notes

1. A *caballería* in Florida consisted of a lot one hundred by two hundred feet and sufficient arable land to produce five hundred *fanegas* (one *fanega* was 1.6 bushels) of wheat and barley and fifty of Indian corn; ten *huebras* (as much land as a yoke of oxen could plow in a day) for a garden and forty *huebras* of woodland; pasture land for fifty breeding sows, one hundred cows, twenty-five breeding mares, five hundred ewes, and one hundred goats.

2. Four *reales* equaled a half *peso*. A *peso* was equivalent to a U.S. dollar of the day.

3. The inventory goes on to detail the lands, plantations, slaves, livestock, and other property on the Ashley, San Diego, Capuaca, Torope, and Santa Barbara plantations, as well as town properties that Sánchez owned in St. Augustine. The total value of Sánchez's estate was estimated at 32,589 pesos and 6 *reales*.

4. A *peso* equaled eight *reales*. Thus at the price of one-half a *real* for a pound, a *peso* would buy sixteen pounds.

5. The length of a league varied from about two and a half to four miles. Based on subsequent mileage correlation, a league in Spanish Florida at this time was about two and a half miles.

6. The disturbances to which Howard refers were the evacuation of the northern part of the colony and the destruction of buildings and crops as part of a "scorched-earth policy" ordered by the Spanish government in January 1794 to deprive filibustering expeditions from Georgia of assistance and supplies. See Richard K. Murdoch, *The Georgia-Florida Frontier, 1793–1796: Spanish Reaction to French Intrigue and American Designs.* (Berkeley and Los Angeles: University of California Press, 1951), 44–45; and Charles E. Bennet, *Florida's "French" Revolution, 1793–1795* (Gainesville: University Press of Florida, 1981).

Contributors

James Gregory Cusick is curator of the P. K. Yonge Library of Florida History, Department of Special Collections, George A. Smathers Libraries, University of Florida.

Patricia C. Griffin is a research associate at the St. Augustine Historical Society and an independent scholar.

Jane G. Landers is associate professor of history at Vanderbilt University.

Susan R. Parker is an independent scholar.

Daniel L. Schafer is professor of history at the University of North Florida.

Brent R. Weisman is associate professor of anthropology at the University of South Florida.

Index